JOURNAL FOR THE STUDY OF THE NEW TESTAMENT
SUPPLEMENT SERIES
70

Executive Editor
Stanley E. Porter

JSOT Press
Sheffield

AFTER THE THOUSAND YEARS

Resurrection and Judgment in Revelation 20

J. Webb Mealy

Journal for the Study of the New Testament
Supplement Series 70

For the Reverend Father Chris Brain
In Honour of your Ordination

Copyright © 1992 Sheffield Academic Press

Published by JSOT Press
JSOT Press is an imprint of
Sheffield Academic Press Ltd
The University of Sheffield
343 Fulwood Road
Sheffield S10 3BP
England

Typeset by Sheffield Academic Press
and
Printed on acid-free paper in Great Britain
by Billing & Sons Ltd
Worcester

British Library Cataloguing in Publication Data

Mealy, J.W.
    After the Thousand Years: Resurrection and Judgment in
    Revelation 20
    —(JSNT Supplement Series, ISSN 0143-5108; No. 70)
    I. Title II. Series
    228.066

    ISBN 1-85075-363-6

CONTENTS

ACKNOWLEDGMENTS

I would like first to thank my wife and children, who have constantly loved and cared for me while I have been working on this project, and to thank my father and mother, who have lent very generous financial and moral support over the years.

I would also like to honour the memory of my late uncle, James McClellan, whose bequest to me was providential for my family's support during my postgraduate studies.

For my training in biblical exegesis, I owe a great deal to my former teachers, among whom I would especially like to acknowledge Robert Gundry (under whose guidance I first studied the book of Revelation), Moisés Silva and William Lane.

For crucial guidance and encouragement on this study while it was being developed as a PhD thesis at the University of Sheffield, and for constructive criticism of my work that was always both timely and meticulous, I owe Andrew Lincoln very many thanks.

Dr Stanley E. Porter has my appreciation for the careful attention he devoted to the proofs of this book, as do my reader, Emma Fleetwood, and my indexer, Steve Birkinshaw. I also wish to thank David Hill for his acceptance of this manuscript into the JSNT Supplement Series.

For the vital personal and pastoral care that has supported me and my family for the years I have been working on this study, affectionate thanks to the leaders of the Nine O'Clock Trust, Sheffield.

Lastly I would like to offer my deepest thanks to God, who is the ultimate source of every good thing. To the extent that anything good or true is to be seen in this study, the credit belongs exclusively to him.

ABBREVIATIONS

AB	Anchor Bible
ANCL	Anti-Nicene Christian Library
ATANT	Abhandlungen zur Theologie des Alten und Neuen Testaments
AUSS	*Andrews University Seminary Studies*
BAGD	W. Bauer, W.F. Arndt, F.W. Gingrich and F.W. Danker, *Greek–English Lexicon of the New Testament*
BeO	*Bibbia e oiriente*
BETL	Bibliotheca ephemeridum theologicarum lovaniensium
BEvT	Beiträge zur evangelischen Theologie
BFCT	Beiträge zur Förderung christlicher Theologie
Bib	*Biblica*
BibLeb	*Bibel und Leben*
BK	*Bibel und Kirche*
BSac	*Bibliotheca Sacra*
BZNW	Beihefte zur *ZNW*
CBQ	*Catholic Biblical Quarterly*
CNT	Commentaire du Nouveau Testament
ConBNT	Coniectanea biblica, New Testament
CSEL	Corpus scriptorum ecclesiasticorum latinorum
EBib	Etudes bibliques
ETL	*Ephemerides theologicae lovanienses*
ETR	*Etudes théologiques et religieuses*
EvQ	*Evangelical Quarterly*
ExpTim	*Expository Times*
HDR	Harvard Dissertations in Religion
HNT	Handbuch zum Neuen Testament
HNTC	Harper's NT Commentaries
ICC	International Critical Commentary
Int	*Interpretation*
ITQ	*Irish Theological Quarterly*
JBL	*Journal of Biblical Literature*
JETS	*Journal of the Evangelical Theological Society*
JSJ	*Journal for the Study of Judaism in the Persian, Hellenistic and Roman Period*
JSNT	*Journal for the Study of the New Testament*
JSNTSup	*Journal for the Study of the New Testament*, Supplement Series
LAB	*Liber Antiquitatum Biblicarum* (*The Biblical Antiquities of Pseudo-Philo*)

LCL	Loeb Classical Library
MeyerK	H.A.W. Meyer (ed.), Kritisch-exegetischer Kommentar über das Neue Testament
MNTC	Moffatt NT Commentary
NASB	*New American Standard Bible*
NCB	New Century Bible
NEB	*New English Bible*
NICNT	New International Commentary on the New Testament
NIV	New International Version
NovT	*Novum Testamentum*
NovTSup	*Novum Testamentum* Supplements
NRT	*La nouvelle revue théologique*
NTAbh	Neutestamentliche Abhandlungen
NTD	Das Neue Testament Deutsch
NTS	*New Testament Studies*
OTL	Old Testament Library
RAC	*Reallexikon für Antike und Christentum*
RelS	*Religious Studies*
ResQ	*Restoration Quarterly*
RevExp	*Review and Expositor*
RevistB	*Revista biblica*
RevScRel	*Revue des sciences religieuses*
RevThom	*Revue thomiste*
RNT	Regensburger Neues Testament
RQ	*Römische Quartalschrift*
RSV	Revised Standard Version
RTP	*Revue de théologie et de philosophie*
SANT	Studien zum Alten und Neuen Testament
SBL	Society of Biblical Literature
SBLTT	SBL Texts and Translations
SJT	*Scottish Journal of Theology*
SNT	Studien zum Neuen Testament
TDNT	G. Kittel and G. Friedrich (eds.), *Theological Dictionary of the New Testament*
THKNT	Theologischer Handkommentar zum Neuen Testament
TS	*Theological Studies*
TTZ	*Trierer theologische Zeitschrift*
TU	Texte und Untersuchungen
VC	*Vigiliae christianae*
VF	*Verkündigung und Forschung*
WTJ	*Westminster Theological Journal*
WUNT	Wissenschaftliche Untersuchungen zum Neuen Testament
ZNW	*Zeitschrift für die neutestamentliche Wissenschaft*

Chapter 1

GENERAL CHARACTERIZATION OF THE ESSAY

This study is essentially exegetical. It undertakes to develop both a
new approach and new solutions to the exegetical 'problems' of the
twentieth chapter of Revelation. It goes without saying that this chapter belongs among Revelation's most difficult exegetical territories.
Ancient sources reveal that the meaning of the 'millennium' (Rev.
20.1-10) has been disputed virtually from the time Revelation was
written.[1] Moreover, judging from the number and variety of interpretative proposals published by scholars in this century, the subject
remains just as much at issue as ever.

On the one hand, most readers—scholars included—have always
been willing to interpret the millennium more or less at face value: as
teaching that Christ's parousia ushers in a mixed age during which
resurrected and non-resurrected people populate the earth side by
side.[2] On the other hand, however, a very significant number find reason to hesitate, not only over the fact that no other NT text supports
this conception, but also that it seems to sit uncomfortably within the
overall picture of the future presented in Revelation itself.[3]

Speaking generally, one or more of the following kinds of solution
have most typically been employed by exegetes who find difficulties in
interpreting the millennium as a future 'mixed' age. (1) Develop an
allegorical or spiritual interpretation of the thousand year reign.[4]
(2) Suggest that the author of Revelation may not have been overly

1.   E.g. Justin, *Dial. Tryph.* 80.
2.   The classic monograph that argues for this mainstream position is
H. Bietenhard, *Das tausendjährige Reich: Eine biblisch-theologische Studie* (Zürich:
Zwingli-Verlag, 1955).
3.   E.g. R. Schnackenburg, *God's Rule and Kingdom* (London: Nelson, 1963),
pp. 343-46.
4.   E.g. Allo, Bonsirven, Morris.

concerned with creating a fully consistent eschatological scheme. In the case of apparent inconsistencies, appeal to the notion that he was consciously drawing together disparate (and sometimes not altogether reconcilable) materials into a mosaic of traditional eschatological themes.[1] (3) Propose that the author used the traditional picture of a future messianic age in order to communicate an essentially theological (non-temporal) point.[2]

It is probably fair comment on these solutions that view (1) claimed the allegiance of the most influential exegetes from the fourth to the eighteenth centuries, (2) gained a majority in the present century, and (3) has begun to exert growing influence during the past two decades.

The present study will be seen to be most closely related to the last of these approaches. Although it does not find positive evidence within the book of Revelation that its author meant to *undermine* the temporal character of the millennium, it nonetheless holds much in common with such an approach, especially: (1) the persuasion that ch. 20 of Revelation makes sense as the creation of a single author who was well in control of his raw materials,[3] and (2) an interest in trying to interpret the millennium (and the related subjects of resurrection and judgment) as far as possible in a way that harmonizes with the larger eschatological themes and teachings of the book. As will be seen, this means above all that the idea of a mixed kingdom, in which resurrected and non-resurrected peoples find themselves equally at home, must be resisted, and another approach must be sought. Is it possible to interpret Revelation 20 both consistently and meaningfully on the assumption that only the resurrected enjoy the blessings of the millennium?[4] The title of this essay, 'After the Thousand Years: Resur-

---

1. E.g. Bousset, Court, Kraft.

2. E.g. Fiorenza, Mounce (ambivalently), Pohl, Schnackenburg, Wikenhauser.

3. E.g. E.S. Fiorenza, 'Revelation', in *The New Testament and its Modern Interpreters* (ed. E.J. Epp and G.W. MacRae; Philadelphia: Fortress Press, 1989), pp. 412-13. For a helpful critical discussion of source- and redaction-historical studies of Revelation, cf. F.D. Mazzaferri, *The Genre of the Book of Revelation from a Source-Critical Perspective* (BZNW, 54; Berlin: de Gruyter, 1989), pp. 8-32. The present study will assume the unity and coherence of the text in the absence of compelling evidence of disunity.

4. So claim, e.g., M. Rissi, *The Future of the World: An Exegetical Study of Revelation 19.11–22.5* (London: SCM Press, 1972), and W. Metzger, 'Das Zwischenreich', in *Auf dem Grunde der Apostel und Propheten* (Festschrift Bischof T. Wurm; ed. M. Loeser; Stuttgart: Quell-Verlag der Evangelische Gesellschaft,

rection and Judgment in Revelation 20', has been chosen in order to highlight my opinion as to the central subject at issue in the answering of this question.

The exegetical *method* to be employed here has as its most salient characteristic the attempt to make fuller use of the highly self-referential and contextual character of Revelation than has been done in previous studies. In the past, commentators have most often tended to approach the idea of 'context' in a textually localized way,[1] in spite of the fact that attention has been drawn to the extensive network of cross-references and allusions that affects the interpretation of virtually every passage in Revelation.[2] That is, context in Revelation consists of a system of references that progressively build up hermeneutical precedents in the text, precedents that precondition the meaning of each new passage in highly significant ways. It is thus only by placing passages and their elements correctly in the network of such precedents that they can be effectively interpreted.[3] The present essay will attempt to make progress in this direction by developing an exegesis of Revelation 20 and the surrounding materials (19.11–21.8) that traces the context of each key element in the text under discussion. To

1948), pp. 110-18. As will be seen, the present study takes up and confirms a crucial but more or less unnoticed interpretative suggestion made by Metzger.

1.   A conspicuous exception to this rule is E.S. Fiorenza's monograph *Priester für Gott: Studien zum Herrschafts- und Priestermotiv in der Apokalypse* (NTAbh, 7; Münster: Aschendorf, 1972).

2.   On this point, cf. E.S. Fiorenza, 'Composition and Structure of the Book of Revelation', *CBQ* 39 (1977), pp. 344-66. It is interesting that Fiorenza has thought it suitable to publish the following statement recently (1989): 'All scholarly attempts to arrive at a definite interpretation of certain passages or of the whole book seem to have failed. This failure suggests that the historical-critical paradigm has to be complemented by a different approach that can do justice to the multivalent character of Revelation' ('Revelation', p. 416; originally written in 1980).

3.   Expanding on the last sentence in the previous note, Fiorenza sets an agenda similar to that proposed here in 'Visionary Rhetoric and Social-Political Situation', in *The Book of Revelation: Justice and Judgement* (Philadelphia: Fortress Press, 1985), pp. 181-203, esp. 188: 'Only a "proportional" analysis of its [Revelation's] images can determine what they are about within the structure of the work by determining the phase of action in which they are invoked. Such an analysis of symbolic relations must highlight the hortatory or persuasive functions of the multivalent images and symbols in producing cooperative or non-cooperative attitudes and actions.' As Fiorenza recommends, the present study will constantly take the *pastoral* significance of key images and symbols into account.

my knowledge, this will be the first time such a systematic account has been offered of the way in which Revelation's contextual network functions to help the reader interpret an extended passage.

In terms of overall shape, the study will fall into three parts. The first part will comprise two chapters. The first (Chapter 2) will be devoted to a brief characterization and discussion of the most common modern approaches to the millennium, such as the 'historical pre-millennial', the 'a-millennial' and the 'post-millennial' models. The second (Chapter 3) will move on to a discussion of certain approaches that have been dubbed 'alternative', because they do not fit into any one of these three categories. Among the alternative models considered will be those of L. Gry, E.S. Fiorenza and W. Metzger. Looking at such attempts to understand Revelation 20 will provide both a way of assessing the current 'state of the question', and a forum for raising the key interpretative questions regarding the millennium.

The second part will comprise the main exegetical section of the book. Although in a sense the section as a whole constitutes a running exegesis of Rev. 19.11–21.8, it will be divided for the sake of convenience into chapters at the divisions between key sections. Individual chapters will cover Rev. 19.11-21, 20.1-3, 20.4-6, 20.7-10, 20.11-15 and 21.1-8. In the first of these, the method to be employed will be introduced, and remarks will be made on the place of the entire section 19.11–21.8 and its subsections in the literary structure of Revelation.

The third part will comprise a single chapter (Chapter 10) summarizing results and offering concluding remarks.

Chapter 2

MODERN APPROACHES TO THE MILLENNIUM

1. *The Majority View*

In this review of modern[1] approaches to the millennium, the first
agenda item will be a brief characterization and discussion of the view
that has been held, with minor variations, by the large majority of
commentators in this century.[2] This majority interpretation shows
itself to be closely related to that of such early church interpreters as
Lactantius.[3]

The model in question has the following characteristics. (1) It
regards the millennium as beginning with the parousia of Christ, and
as ending before the last judgment of Rev. 20.11-15. (2) It also sees

---

1. Matters of space unfortunately preclude the discussion of views from the sec-
ond to the twentieth centuries. For a good introductory survey in English of Revelation interpretation in the first centuries of the Christian era, cf. H. Bietenhard, 'The
Millennial Hope in the Early Church', *SJT* 6 (1953), pp. 12-30. For the period after
Augustine, cf. B. McGinn, 'Revelation', in *The Literary Guide to the Bible* (ed. R.
Alter and F. Kermode; London: Collins, 1987), pp. 523-41, esp. 531-38. Cf. also
G. Maier, *Die Johannesoffenbarung und die Kirche* (WUNT, 25; Tübingen: Mohr,
1981), pp. 108-447; G. Kretschmar, *Die Offenbarung des Johannes: Die Geschichte
ihrer Auslegung im 1. Jahrtausend* (CTM, Reihe B, 9; Stuttgart: Calwer Verlag,
1985), pp. 107ff. For a detailed bibliographical and methodological overview from
the mid-seventeenth century onwards, cf. O. Böcher, *Die Johannesapokalypse*
(Erträge der Forschung, 41; Darmstadt: Wissenschaftliche Buchgesellschaft, 1976),
pp. 1-13. On the millennium in particular, F. Düsterdieck presents a good survey of
views in *Kritisch-exegetisches Handbuch über die Offenbarung des Johannes*
(MeyerK, 16; Göttingen: Vandenhoeck & Ruprecht, 4th edn, 1877), pp. 564-66.
2. The classic monograph that argues for this mainstream perspective is Bietenhard, *Das tausendjährige Reich*.
3. Cf. *Divine Institutes* 7.24-26, cited from *The Works of Lactantius*, I (trans.
W. Fletcher; ANCL, 21; Edinburgh: T. & T. Clark, 1886). Cf. also Lactantius,
Epitome of the Divine Institutes 72.

the new creation spoken of in Rev. 21.1 as chronologically following the last judgment, so that the millennial kingdom is pictured as taking place in the context of the present creation, rather than in the context of the new creation described in Rev. 21.1–22.5. (3) It assumes that John's intention was that his readers should picture considerable numbers of people who had not followed Christ during the career of the 'beast' (ch. 13) being spared at the parousia. (4) It interprets these people as the 'subjects' who live under the millennial kingship of Christ and the saints. They are thus pictured as sharing the earth with Christ and the resurrected saints, yet living 'natural' (i.e. mortal) lives, and presumably multiplying during the millennial period. Thus the attack of Gog and Magog, which John says will happen at the end of the millennium (20.7-10), is interpreted on this view as a last rebellion by these non-resurrected peoples and/or their offspring.[1]

There are one or two important points to be put forward in favour of this way of interpreting the millennium. First of all, it can boast of maximum accessibility and simplicity. That is, it takes events described at face value, and does not require any particular appeal to supposed literary complications such as chronological recapitulation,

---

1.   The one salient point on which this model of the millennium differs from that of Lactantius is the question of marriage and procreation on the part of certain saints in the millennium. In this century, it would be generally agreed that no hint of this element is to be found in the description that John gives of the millennium (however, cf. the view of J.S. Deere, below). It might plausibly be conjectured that this line of interpretation had its origin in the idea of saints living up to the parousia (taken from other NT passages such as 1 Thess. 4) being conjoined with OT prophecies such as Isa. 6.12 (LXX), which speak of the surviving remnant of humanity multiplying in the earth. Cf. Irenaeus, *Adv. Haer.* 5.34.2; 5.35.1. One can see how the overall way in which early interpreters such as Irenaeus and his 'elders' (e.g. Papias) handle the Scriptures could lead them to this kind of view: they take a harmonistic approach to all prophetic texts, they work from a relatively literal view of OT prophecies and their fulfilment, and they exclude all but the saints from the millennial kingdom. *Therefore*, the OT prophecies that refer to procreation in the messianic kingdom must somehow refer to certain saints in the millennium. For a modern interpreter who explicitly follows this line of reasoning, cf. J.S. Deere, 'Premillennialism in Revelation 20.4-6', *BSac* 135 (1978), pp. 58-73. Lactantius himself will not have been forced into this way of construing things, because he pictured non-Christian people surviving into the millennial period, i.e., he could have chosen to see *them* as the ones to fulfil prophecies such as Isa. 6.12. Thus conceivably Lactantius will have embraced the notion of saints procreating in the millennium because of its place in the models of respected earlier theologians.

subtle hints and allusions, and double meanings. It is to be admitted, in other words, that, when taken by themselves, the events of Rev. 19.11–21.8 fall into place as narrated without undue difficulty. (1) Christ returns and slays the beast and his armies (19.11-21). (2) Satan is bound and imprisoned in the abyss so that he cannot deceive the nations any longer (20.1-3). (3) Christ and the martyred saints rule for a thousand years (20.4-6).[1] (4) Satan, now released, deceives the nations again, leads them into attack against the city of the saints, and is destroyed along with them (20.7-10). (5) The dead are raised and brought to final judgment (20.11-15). (6) The whole creation is renewed, the New Jerusalem is set on the new earth, and complete communion between God and the saints is announced (21.1-8). This is a reasonably plausible chain of events, given what can be known about the range of ideas about the end of the world that would have been available to first-century Jews and Christians.[2]

2. *Shouldering the Burden of Proof*

To say these things is to admit that the 'burden of proof' rests on the shoulders of the person who proposes a more complicated alternative interpretation of the millennium and its related topics in Revelation, rather than with the person who finds the majority or 'received'[3] view adequate. But the recognition of this is not in itself an endorsement of

---

1. Many exponents of this view do not interpret Rev. 20.4 as restricting participation in the millennial age to those whose witness costs them their lives (i.e. martyrs in the strict sense). For example, G.R. Beasley-Murray (*The Book of Revelation* [NCB; London: Oliphants, 1974], pp. 292-95) offers a careful argument for the idea that Rev. 20.4a ('I saw thrones and they sat on them, and judgment was given to them') refers to the saints generally, or, in other words, the church at large (cf. Dan. 7.22). This question will be discussed fully in Chapter 6, below.

2. Cf., for example, J.W. Bailey, 'The Temporary Messianic Reign in the Literature of Early Judaism', *JBL* 53 (1934), pp. 170-87, for a survey of apocalyptic literature, and O. Böcher, 'Das tausendjährige Reich', in *idem, Kirche in Zeit und Endzeit: Aufsätze zur Offenbarung des Johannes* (Neukirchen: Neukirchener Verlag, 1983), pp. 133-43, who adduces parallels to most aspects of the millennium from a wide variety of contemporary sources. A. Wikenhauser ('Das Problem des tausendjährigen Reiches in der Johannes-Apokalypse', *RQ* 40 [1932], pp. 13-25), takes into account rabbinic interpretations of Ezek. 37–39 in particular.

3. For convenience, this term will be used to refer to the general view characterized above; the value-free sense of 'usual' or 'typical' is intended.

the received view: rather, it is an acknowledgment that alternative views (including the one to be presented in this study) are under obligation to demonstrate the necessity of their main points, not just the possibility of them. In other words, given two views which both seem to be possible, no one can be faulted for preferring the one that is less complicated.

Thus, if a view is to claim full acceptance in place of the received view, its presentation might be expected to satisfy such criteria as the following. (1) It will be able to demonstrate that the literary function of the millennium (and its environs: Rev. 19.11–21.8) within the book of Revelation hinges on clear contextual ties with other parts of the book.[1] (2) It will be able to give an account of these ties and their workings that is reasonably compelling from a literary standpoint. (3) It will be able to demonstrate that the contextual ties it has identified combine to *rule out* the received interpretation and suggest its replacement with a different one. (4) It will be able to provide an exegesis of the main section under consideration (19.11–21.8) that not only interprets it plausibly in the context of the wider connections that have been demonstrated, but that also shows that a satisfactory (and ideally, *more* satisfactory) account can be given of the main section in and of itself.

In this century, many have attempted to argue for alternative understandings of the millennium, but few have done so in a way that could claim to address all the points of the foregoing agenda. The importance of such an agenda will nonetheless become progressively more evident in the following review of attempts to make sense of the millennium.

3. *The A-Millennial Approach*

Augustine of Hippo developed what historically became a highly influential alternative model for interpreting the millennium. Comparing Rev. 20.4-6 with other texts of the NT, he argued that the reign of the saints with Christ was the picture of the *present* position of Christians: 'raised with Christ' and 'enthroned with Christ in heavenly places' (Col. 3.1; Eph. 2.6).[2]

---

1.   The idea is that if the received view shows itself compatible with Rev. 19.11–21.8 as viewed in isolation, then, in order to be convincing, an alternative interpretation must show that this section is not intended to be taken in isolation.

2.   Cf. the stimulating discussion in Augustine, *de Civ. Dei* 20.6-20.

Augustine's 'a-millennial'[1] model is obviously attractive from the point of view of systematic theology, since it interprets Revelation in line with the general eschatological teachings of the rest of the NT.[2] But it has lost nearly all support by Revelation specialists in this century, on the valid grounds that it fails to do justice to the unique eschatological perspective of Revelation itself.[3]

For the present purposes, the Augustinian 'a-millennial' approach amounts to the attempt to see in Rev. 20.1-3 a chronological stepping back or recapitulation, such that the capture and imprisonment of Satan happens prior to the parousia (e.g. presumably at the cross or resurrection). In this case, the scene of Rev. 20.7-10 is interpretable as a symbolic perspective on the career of the beast, who comes up out of the abyss to deceive the nations into making war on the saints (13.1-7; cf. 11.7). But there is a simple and unavoidable problem with this idea: when Rev. 20.7-10 is then related to 20.4-6, it appears that the saints martyred by the beast are incongruously resurrected to reign with Christ in 20.4-6 before the beast ever gets a chance to kill them.[4]

In what is presumably a response to this problem with the Augustinian model, there has occasionally been the attempt to look at

---

1.   The term 'a-millennial' will be used here in its usual sense in spite of the misleading *a*-privative: paradoxically, a view will be characterized as a-millennial if it denies that the millennium is presented as an independent age that follows the present age *in the world view of Revelation*, but not if it objects to the teaching of the millennium *per se*. An aside of Bietenhard's sums up the latter position: 'As an exegete he supports chiliasm but his dogmatic-theological "no" is palpable' (*Das tausendjährige Reich*, p. 133).

2.   Cf. M. Wilcock, *I Saw Heaven Opened* (Leicester: Inter-Varsity Press, 2nd edn, 1979 [1975]), pp. 187-94; P.E. Hughes, 'The First Resurrection: Another Interpretation', *WJT* 39 (1977), pp. 315-18.

3.   E.g. a Roman Catholic interpreter such as J. Sickenberger ('Das tausendjährige Reich in der Apokalypse', in *Festschrift Sebastian Merkle gewidmet* [ed. J. Hehn, W. Schellberg and F. Tillmann; Düsseldorf: Schwann, 1922], p. 316) can straightforwardly admit that the Augustinian approach of E.-B. Allo (*L'Apocalypse* [EBib; Paris: Gabalda, 1921]) 'does violence to the text'.

4.   The fact that reign manifestly follows martyrdom is recognized as the decisive problem of the Augustinian model by J.-L. D'Aragon, 'The Apocalypse', in *The Jerome Biblical Commentary* (ed. R.E. Brown, J.A. Fitzmyer and R.E. Murphy; London: Geoffrey Chapman, 1968), p. 490.

Rev. 20.7-10 as a new viewpoint on the 'Battle of Har-Magedon', or, in other words, as the defeat of the beast and his armies at the parousia, which is described in ch. 19.[1]

But this approach unfortunately encounters just as many difficulties as did its predecessor. For since on this view Satan's release from prison and destruction (Rev. 20.7-10) is connected with the parousia, then the time of his imprisonment 'so that he should deceive the nations no longer' (20.3) seems to be coterminous with the career of the beast (which also ends at the parousia). But this is impossible, since the beast's career is portrayed in Revelation as the time of Satan's greatest success ever in deceiving the human race.[2]

Further, it does no good for this view to over-interpret the report of Satan's release from the abyss in Rev. 20.8 to mean that the only sense in which Satan had previously been bound was that he could not then deceive the nations in such a way as to 'gather them together for the war'.[3] For to do this is not only to ignore the explicit cosmological import of such passages as Rev. 12.9-17,[4] but it is also to forget the fact that 'Har-Magedon' is but the last episode in Satan's 'war' with the saints. In Rev. 13.7 it was the beast himself who was given authority throughout his career and who was, in concert with Satan, to 'make war with the saints and to overcome them'. The beast's career, in other words, far from being the time of Satan's binding in this regard, is undeniably the time of his power *par excellence* to deceive the nations into making war on the 'camp of the saints'.[5] It is thus only at

---

1.   Cf., for example, J.A. Hughes, 'Revelation 20.4-6 and the Question of the Millennium', *WTJ* 37 (1975), pp. 281-302; L. Morris, *Revelation* (Tyndale New Testament Commentaries; London: Tyndale House, 1973), pp. 233-35.

2.   In Rev. 12.9, Satan is characterized as the one who 'deceives the whole world'. In context, the events of ch. 13 graphically picture the full outworking of this deception, and by no means its limitation. Cf. W.H. Shea, 'The Parallel Literary Structure of Revelation 12 and 20', *AUSS* 23 (1985), pp. 45-47.

3.   As, e.g., Hughes, 'Rev. 20.4-6', pp. 281, 282 (cf. his n. 3), and Morris, *Revelation*, p. 236.

4.   In Revelation, the earth is definitely *not* the abyss: cf. J.M. Ford, *Revelation* (AB, 38; Garden City, NY: Doubleday, 1975), p. 330. The cosmology of Revelation will be examined in detail in Chapters 8 and 9, below.

5.   The expression 'the camp of the saints' is intentionally used here in the very sense that one would presumably be forced to give it, given the a-millennial interpretation under criticism. That is, if one takes 'the camp of the saints' in Rev. 20.9 as a reference to the church militant on earth prior to the parousia, as opposed to the

the parousia that the power to practise even this particular kind of deception is taken away from Satan.

What is taken away for the first time at the parousia is however *given back* a thousand years later, when Satan is released from the abyss, and is permitted once again to instigate an attack on the people of God (Rev. 20.7-10). Thus a completely lucid and coherent sequence is established between Rev. 19.11–20.3 on the one hand, and 20.7-10 on the other: the power to deceive is first removed from Satan, and then subsequently restored. This means that the battle described in 20.7-10 can in no way be identified with the battle of Har-Magedon, since in spite of any similarities between the two scenes, what happens to Satan in the one manifestly precedes what happens to him in the other.[1]

There is a separate (but interrelated) interpretative move which it is necessary to make if the a-millennial claim that Rev. 20.4-6 refers to a period prior to the parousia is to be reconciled with the fact that resurrection manifestly follows martyrdom in that passage. That interpretative move consists in the claim that the first resurrection of Rev. 20.4-6 represents the reception of the Christian's soul in heaven upon death.[2] But this idea fails to convince for each of two independent reasons. First, Rev. 6.9-11 already pictures the state of martyred souls in heaven, and there they are told to wait for their vindication until all the rest of the martyrs have given their lives:

> And when He broke the fifth seal, I saw underneath the altar the souls of those who had been slain because of the word of God, and because of the testimony which they had maintained. And they cried out with a loud voice, saying,
>
> 'How long, O Master, holy and true, wilt Thou refrain from judging and avenging our blood on those who dwell on the earth?'
>
> And there was given to each of them a white robe, and they were told that they should rest for a little while longer, until the number of their

---

eschatological community of the kingdom following the parousia (*sc.* the New Jerusalem), then it follows that the most salient feature of the beast's three and a half year career is that it is that time during which he prosecutes an all-out war on 'the camp of the saints' (cf. 12.6, 13-17; 13.5-7).

1. Cf. the similar argument of R.A. Ostella, 'The Significance of Deception in Revelation 20.3', *WTJ* 37 (1975), pp. 236-38.

2. So, e.g., M.G. Kline, 'The First Resurrection', *WTJ* 37 (1975), pp. 366-75.

fellow servants and their brethren who were to be killed even as they had
been, should be completed also (6.9-11).[1]

It becomes obvious in all that follows that the era of continued
martyrdom anticipated in Rev. 6.11 is being assumed to extend right
up to (and to be brought to an end by) the parousia.[2] Equally obvious
is the fact that the priestly reign of Rev. 20.4-6 does not parallel the
passive situation pictured in this vision. Rather, Rev. 20.4-6 presents
the parousia as the future time which the earlier vision anticipates, when
God will answer the prayer of the martyrs. The heavenly court of
20.4 fairly and appropriately vindicates them by decreeing resurrection from the dead in their case, while refusing resurrection to their
persecutors.[3] The first resurrection, in short, is firmly tied to the
parousia.

As was mentioned, there is a second and independently fatal difficulty with the 'soul's assumption into heaven' model, namely that the
resurrection spoken of in Rev. 20.4-6 must be bodily resurrection in
order for the passage to retain even a minimum level of coherence.
For to deny bodily resurrection in v. 4 is to assert that the same
expression 'they came to life'[4] signifies, in a single context, first bodiless communion with Christ in heaven, and then (in the very next
sentence) bodily resurrection. And in the absence of any obvious play
on words, this is untenable. For if (as seems obvious) bodily resurrection was the experience being denied to 'the *rest* of the dead' who
'*did not* come to life' for the duration of the millennium (cf. 20.5, 12,

1.   All quotations of the Bible are from the NASB (The New American Standard
Bible, © 1960, 1962, 1963, 1968, 1971, 1972, 1973, 1975, 1977 by the Lockman
Foundation; used by permission), unless otherwise indicated.

2.   For example, Rev. 6.12-17 (the sixth seal) encourages interpretation as an
immediate and graphic portrayal of the parousia as God's response to the prayer of
6.11. So also the martyrdom and assumption of the two witnesses in 11.12 occur (in
view of 11.2-3) only at the very end of the beast's career, which, as the reader will
later learn, is to continue up to the parousia. Thus, in 12.13-17 and all of ch. 13, the
assumption is that Satan, after trying abortively to persecute the 'woman', will use
his remaining time on earth (which extends up to the parousia) to persecute Christians. Earlier promises as well (esp. 2.25-28; cf. 22.16) look to the parousia as the
end of the battle of perseverance in suffering (2.19).

3.   So J.R. Michaels, 'The First Resurrection: A Response', *WTJ* 39 (1976),
pp. 107-108, and Fiorenza, *Priester für Gott*, pp. 307-309.

4.   Cf. G.E. Ladd, 'Revelation 20 and the Millennium', *RevExp* 57 (1960),
p. 169.

13), then it goes without saying that bodily resurrection was the experience of those who *did* 'come to life' (ἔζησαν) for that age. In addition, there is something exceedingly implausible about denying that resurrection is really meant in 20.6 ('the first resurrection'), when 20.6 is the only passage in Revelation in which the word 'resurrection' actually occurs.[1]

Given the insoluble difficulties connected with these a-millennial models, it is not surprising to find that the great majority of scholars feel constrained to build their views on the foundational assumption that the millennium is at least *pictured* as beginning at the parousia. There are partial exceptions however: so-called 'post-millennial' views raise an entirely different set of questions by suggesting that Rev. 19.11–20.3 is not to be taken as signaling the parousia of Christ in the fullest sense of those words.

4. *The Post-Millennial Approach*

As an example, I shall consider the approach to the millennium suggested by the Roman Catholic scholars J. Sickenberger and J.-L. D'Aragon. In an improvement on the above a-millennial models, their interpretation begins from the premise that the thousand year reign of the saints happens after the career of the beast. But noting that the New Jerusalem is only seen coming down after the millennium (Rev. 21.2), and Rev. 20.4-6 says nothing about the location of the saints' reign, they make the following proposal: Christ and the resurrected martyrs reign from heaven for the thousand years.[2] Sickenberger thus

---

1. So H. Kraft, *Die Offenbarung des Johannes* (HNT, 16a; Tübingen: Mohr [Paul Siebeck], 1974), p. 257. If anything, it is the resurrection of the 'rest of the dead' (which apparently results in damnation: cf. Rev. 20.6, 13-15) which cannot properly be called by that term. John is conspicuously unwilling to name that experience either 'resurrection' (ἀνάστασις) or 'coming to life' (the ingressive aorist ἔζησαν).

2. Cf. D'Aragon, 'The Apocalypse', pp. 490-91; J. Sickenberger, *Erklärung der Johannesapokalypse* (Bonn: Peter Hanstein, 2nd edn, 1942), pp. 173-83; *idem*, 'Das tausendjährige Reich', pp. 306-308. For a much earlier example, cf. C.A. Auberlen, *Der Prophet Daniel und die Offenbarung Johannis in ihrem gegenseitigen Verhältniss betrachtet und in ihrem Haupstellen erklärt* (Basel: Bahnmeier, 1854 [2nd edn, 1857; 3rd edn, 1874]), p. 378; and most recently cf. M. Gourges, 'The Thousand Year Reign (Rev. 20.1-6): Terrestrial or Celestial?', *CBQ* 47 (1985), pp. 676-81. Sickenberger makes the unnecessary mistake of denying that the physical resurrection of the martyrs is meant when all the evidence is against him (cf. above).

characterizes the millennium as a golden age of the earthly church:

> When Satan is bound in hell and the saints reign with Christ in heaven, on earth the church will experience a more successful period—but not perfect, since sin is possible without the Devil. . . It will have been a comfort to the Seer and his readers, that there would be a final period in the life of the church on earth in which trouble and demonic attack would no longer frighten Christians, but rather heavenly light would shine on them.[1]

On first appearances, this view would seem to solve two main problems of the standard model for the millennium. (1) Because the resurrected saints remain in heaven, the oddity of an age where resurrected and non-resurrected people share the earth is dissolved,[2] and (2) it makes sense of the fact that the marriage announcement can be made in Rev. 19.7-9 and the New Jerusalem can be seen coming down out of heaven only after the millennium in 21.2. But it nonetheless replaces these difficulties with others equally insuperable.

As Fiorenza and others have pointed out, the idea of resurrection in and of itself suggests an earthly setting. Further, Revelation has already encouraged such thinking in the previous promise that those redeemed by Christ would 'reign on the earth' (5.10).[3] The force of this point is not lessened by an appeal to a supposed shift of perspective from earth (in Rev. 20.1-3) to heaven (20.4-6),[4] since the immediate background of the passage is Daniel 7, whose perspective encompasses both heaven and earth. On the one hand, the Son of Man comes *on the clouds* to the Ancient of Days (Dan. 7.13), and on the other hand, the beast who ruled the earth is destroyed, and the saints inherit the kingdom *of the earth* (7.17-18). The context of the saints' rule is

1. *Erklärung*, pp. 181-82. H.B. Swete proposes a related idea, but looks for the symbolic fulfilment of the prophecy of Rev. 20.4-6 in the success of the earthly church following a historical period of intense persecution (*The Apocalypse of St John* [London: Macmillan, 1906] p. 263): 'That the age of the Martyrs, however long it might last, would be followed by a far longer period of Christian supremacy during which the faith for which the martyrs died would live and reign, is the essential teaching of the present passage'. R. Schnackenburg (who cites other references) fairly criticizes this view: 'this explanation in terms of world and church history becomes impossible if 19.11 seq. is a description of the parousia, and this can scarcely be called in question' (*God's Rule and Kingdom*, p. 340). Cf. similarly Kraft, *Offenbarung*, p. 247.

2. Cf. the remark of M. Rissi, *The Future of the World*, p. 33.

3. E.g. *Priester für Gott*, pp. 291-92 and n. 3.

4. So Sickenberger, 'Das tausendjährige Reich', p. 306.

assumed quite consciously by John from this chapter:

> And he will speak out against the Most High and wear down the saints of
> the Highest One. . . and they will be given into his hand for a time, times
> and half a time. But the court will sit for judgment, and his dominion will
> be taken away, annihilated and destroyed forever. Then the sovereignty,
> the dominion, and the greatness of all the kingdoms under the whole
> heaven will be given to the people of the saints of the Highest One; His
> kingdom will be an everlasting kingdom, and all the dominions will serve
> and obey Him (Dan. 7.25-27).[1]

As striking as the parallels here may be, it should be noted that the
present argument does not depend on the relationship between this
Danielic passage and Revelation. For even if one should ignore such
literary connections and draw one's interpretation from within the
exclusive boundaries of Revelation itself, the conclusion remains
inevitable that the saints' reign in Rev. 20.4-6 must be on the earth.
For, as will later be shown, there is no question of any non-Christian
surviving the judgment of the parousia as described in Rev. 19.11-21.
The 'earth-dwellers' are to be completely ousted (cf. 13.8; 14.9-11).

This, being so, there remains no reason for the saints to delay in
claiming the earth which has been promised them (Rev. 5.10). In
other words, it creates a pointless anticlimax to imagine the resurrected saints (= the New Jerusalem) hovering in the stratosphere for a
thousand years after the dramatic appearance of Christ and his heavenly armies in 19.11-14, and his equally dramatic victory over the
pretended possessors of the earth in 19.15-21.[2]

---

1.   Cf. the connections between this passage and Rev. 13.5-7 (persecution for
42 months, i.e., three and a half years, interprets the three and a half times: cf. Rev.
12.14); 19.20 (the final destruction of the beast: also cf. Dan. 7.11); 20.4 (the judgment and handing over of the kingdom to the saints). On this general subject, cf.
G.K. Beale, 'The Influence of Daniel upon the Structure and Theology of John's
Apocalypse', *JETS* 27 (1984), pp. 413-23.

2.   This line of criticism goes equally for an interesting but unnoticed suggestion
by the popular (and eccentric) late-nineteenth century American Seventh Day Adventist interpreter U. Smith (cf. *Daniel and the Revelation* [Nashville: Southern Publishing Association, rev. edn, 1944 (1888)]). His commentaries are still held in high
regard among Seventh Day Adventists, and his position on this issue is still considered viable, as is shown by the various hints of it which are to be found in the recent
article of Shea, 'Parallel Literary Structure', pp. 37-54. Smith pictures the New
Jerusalem as hovering above a formless and lifeless earth for the duration of the millennium. For Smith, the inchoate earth *is* the abyss where Satan is confined (cf.

It should perhaps be added that significant problems remain for Sickenberger's and D'Aragon's model even if one lays aside for the sake of argument this criticism of the non-survivability of the parousia. For, as Sickenberger himself admits, the millennium is impossible to interpret in isolation, but must be interpreted in the larger context of the ongoing war between Christ and Satan.[1] And looking to this larger context, one discovers that from the very beginning Revelation has kept offering its readers an identity that draws them into this war. Not only have they been told that they must participate in the conflict, but they have also been promised over and over that for them the personal result of resisting to the end will be resurrection to life and to the gift of reigning with Christ *at his coming*.[2]

Thus, it is completely at odds with the context steadily built up throughout Revelation to propose a model for the millennium in which Christians, who have remained faithful to Jesus without being killed, go on living normal (mortal) lives in that age. There can in other words be no doubt that Revelation has been composed in such a way as to put exactly two options before the Christian reader at this point: encountering Revelation 20 in the context of the rest of the book, each will intentionally feel forced to see him- or herself either as a participant in the resurrected reign of 20.4-6, or as one of the 'rest of the dead' who are vulnerable to the 'second death' (20.6).[3]

But D'Aragon's and Sickenberger's model immediately begins to collapse when these clear and indispensable contextual factors are

---

Gen. 1.2!), and the heading of his commentary on Rev. 20 (p. 739) is 'The World's Millennial Night'. This idea of an eschatological world-night prior to the new creation is fascinating (cf. e.g. *4 Ezra* 7.30), but it fails to find roots in the terminology and imagery of Revelation itself, and, in particular, of the key passage 20.1-10. (Rev. 8.1 refers to something else, *pace* M. Rissi, *Time and History: A Study on the Revelation* [trans. G.C. Windsor; Richmond, VA: John Knox, 1966], pp. 3-6, and J.P.M. Sweet, *Revelation* [SCM Pelican Commentaries; London: SCM Press, 1979], p. 159, and others.) For full discussion of this issue, see Chapter 9, §3b, below.

1. Cf. 'Das tausendjährige Reich', p. 309.

2. Cf. especially Rev. 2.8-11, 25-27; 3.5 (22.14), 11, 21; 5.10; 11.18; 17.14; 20.4-6; 21.6-7. Full discussion of these and related passages will be offered in Chapters 4 and 6, below.

3. This point is well stated by Fiorenza, *Priester für Gott*, pp. 306, 332, 342. Full literary and exegetical evidence for it will be offered in Chapter 6, below.

taken into account. At least two difficulties appear when one attempts to admit that Revelation presents the parousia as the only time for Christians to be raised and united with Christ, while proposing that Christ and his own are to be pictured as reigning in heaven for the millennium.

1. The anticlimax spoken of above is taken to its limit: on the one hand the beast and his cohorts are ousted (Rev. 19.11-21), yet on the other, the earth is subsequently inhabited only by non-Christians, and meanwhile the saints must wait their turn for a thousand years in heaven. Nothing in the book of Revelation speaks in favour of an age following the defeat of the 'beast' which could be characterized by a 'saintless' earth. Nor does there seem to be any reason why the author might have put forward such an idea. But assuming that there were some way to get over this difficulty, there is another.

2. Given the manifest absence of any *textual* information suggesting that the millennium might be a time of conversion and re-establishment of an earthly church, one will be justified in assuming (on this view) that the epithets 'Gog and Magog' (Rev. 20.7-10) are intended to encompass all the mortal inhabitants of the earth. One must further picture them gathering on earth to surround the heavenly New Jerusalem, which will presumably have been called the 'camp of the saints' (20.9) because it does not yet rest on the earth, its intended final location (21.2, 10). But in what way can earthly nations pose any threat to a heavenly Jerusalem?[1] The whole scenario has simply become pointless, and has effectively collapsed under the weight of its own implausibility.

5. *Summary of Analysis*

It may be wise at this point to pause and take stock of what has been discovered, before beginning to explore in a different direction. It was noted at the beginning of the present discussion that the majority of scholars in this century have held an interpretation of the millennium that ran along similar lines to that of Lactantius and certain other early church interpreters. This method of interpretation assumes that Rev. 20.1-10 anticipates a 'mixed' age beginning at the parousia,

---

1. For this criticism, cf. J. Wellhausen, *Analyse der Offenbarung Johannis* (Berlin: Weidmann, 1907), p. 168. Incidentally, Smith's view is vulnerable to this criticism as well (*Daniel and the Revelation*).

during which Christ and the resurrected saints rule on an earth inhabited largely by ordinary mortal people. It was then conceded that, at least from the evidence to be found within the confines of chs. 19–21, such an assumption can lay claim to a straightforward sort of coherence and plausibility. And it was suggested that the implication of this admission was that the burden of proof would have to rest with any view that sought to challenge the majority view. A four-point agenda for a successful alternative approach to the millennium was then proposed. The agenda could be abbreviated as follows:

1. It will show that the literary function of the millennium hinges on clear contextual ties with other parts of the book.
2. It will give a persuasive account of how these ties work.
3. It will show that such contextual ties combine to *rule out* the received interpretation and suggest its replacement with a different one.
4. By assuming the different interpretation, it will be able to provide a more satisfactory exegesis of the main text (Rev. 19.11–21.8) than that offered by the majority interpretation.

Attention was then turned towards various representative versions of the so-called 'a-millennial' and 'post-millennial' models. In retrospect, it should be apparent that neither model can really hope to succeed in addressing the first two points of the agenda proposed above.[1] For, in the foregoing discussion, the most devastating criticisms of these views came out of the literary connections that were clearly demonstrable between Revelation 20 and the previous chapters, and *not* directly from haggling about the meaning of particular words and phrases in Rev. 20.1-10.

---

1. The article by Hughes, 'Rev. 20.4-6', albeit far from convincing, is yet a dauntless *attempt* to frame the problem in its literary aspect.

Chapter 3

A-TEMPORAL AND OTHER ALTERNATIVE APPROACHES
TO THE MILLENNIUM

It is appropriate at this point to look at a number of approaches that take a different tack from those examined so far. The following scholars have in common an acknowledgment that the millennium invites one to *picture* it as an age of earthly reign intermediate between Christ's parousia and a subsequent last judgment, but most of them also hold in common a conviction that this chiliastic *picture* paradoxically invites one or the other non-literal *interpretation*.

1. *Düsterdieck*

Perhaps a good way to introduce this way of thinking is to look at a quotation from the commentary of F. Düsterdieck. Düsterdieck says that Rev. 20.1-10 invites interpretation as an ideal representation whose individual features make sense in terms of the rest of Scripture only when

> the ideal nature of the whole poetic picture is fully appreciated. That which falls on the single future day of the Lord according to the clear didactic teaching of Scripture (i.e. the resurrection of all the dead. . . and the world judgment) appears in the apocalyptic description to be divided into a long succession of distinct but connected episodes [*Akte*]. It is on this [method of John's] that the lively beauty of the apocalyptic drama depends. But this beauty will not only be destroyed, but will even be distorted into chiliastic irrationality, if one mistakes the ideal picture for a straight piece of theological information [*eine theologische Lehrmitteilung*].[1]

In terms of critical methodology, Düsterdieck's openness in assuming theological unity among all parts of the canon has long since gone out of fashion. Yet, in itself, the motivation to find harmony does

---

1. Düsterdieck, *Kritisch-exegetisches Handbuch*, p. 568.

nothing to disqualify his contention about the literary workings of Revelation. What is needed (and what Düsterdieck does not supply) is a case, built on evidence from within Revelation itself, proving that the picture of the millennium is not intended to be taken at face value.

2. *Gry*

The attempt to make such a case is perhaps made for the first time in L. Gry's monograph *Le millénarisme dans ses origines et son développement.*[1] In preparing the ground for his own view, Gry points out certain alleged oddities that arise if one assumes the received view. For example, he suggests that the reader of Revelation will be puzzled as to how the nations can still be capable of believing Satan after spending a thousand years with Christ.[2] He also asks where one is to imagine the 'last judgment' (Rev. 20.11-15) being held, if earth and heaven have fled in 20.11, and are not to be replaced until 21.1.[3] In the same vein he points to the apparent contradiction in the fact that 'the nations' are assumed to be in existence in 21.27 and 22.2 after seemingly having been destroyed by fire in 20.9.[4]

Gry's remarks here are not simply random shots taken at the received view in order to dismiss it: instead he is trying to argue for the presence of tensions in the text of chs. 20 and 21, which create dissatisfaction with a straightforward reading and push one to look afresh at the work as a whole in search of a different interpretative model.

Gry attempts to base such a model on his claim that the present reign of Christ (Rev. 5, etc.) has replaced the future messianic kingdom in the author's theology, without changing the usual expressions of apocalyptic expectation through which it is communicated. He asserts that John did not mind leaving some incoherences uncorrected, because his aim was to assure the readers of the substance of what he said, while using the language of apocalyptic to which his hearers were accustomed. In other words, incoherences can be seen to arise

---

1. Paris: Picard et Fils, 1904.
2. *Millénarisme*, pp. 53-54. Kraft cites an unnamed commentator's puzzlement at the idea of such ingratitude (*Offenbarung*, p. 258).
3. *Millénarisme*, pp. 53-54.
4. *Millénarisme*, pp. 53-54.

from the presentation of new ideas in old forms.[1]

Gry, having argued the need for such an approach, proceeds to reinterpret the details according to his own theory, which may be encapsulated by quoting the following statement about the martyrs of Rev. 20.4-6:

> The earthly joy of the thousand years is the image, very Jewish and very concrete, of the joy which they already now enjoy in a better world.[2]

According to Gry, the millennium is a picture that uses the materials of apocalyptic, because the author wished to communicate his message in a form familiar to his readers. But it is a picture actually intended to subvert the classical apocalyptic expectation of an interim earthly kingdom and replace it with the present blessing of the church in heaven. In other words, Gry sees in Revelation an attempt to correct the error of apocalyptic 'millenarianism' by taking up its terminology and imagery while implying the presence of a different content.[3]

Gry's thesis is thought-provoking, and to some extent it can be seen as programmatic for subsequent a-millennial studies of the millennium. The key to its methodology lies in its attempt to grapple with the fact that the millennium appears, at least on a surface reading, to present a future limited earthly messianic kingdom. But Gry's proposal as to how the millennium invites reinterpretation cannot be sustained for two fundamental reasons.

First and most decisively, he fails to prove that Revelation reapplies future apocalyptic expectations to the present at the point crucial for his thesis: namely, the question of the reign of the saints. For though it goes without saying that in Revelation *Christ* reigns now rather than exclusively in the future (e.g. Rev. 1.5-6; 3.21; 5.9-14), yet many of the very texts that place Christ's reign in the present also conspicuously place the reign of the saints in the eschatological future (e.g. 2.26-27; 3.21; 5.10).[4]

---

1. *Millénarisme*, pp. 55-56.
2. *Millénarisme*, p. 60.
3. *Millénarisme*, p. 61. Along these lines, Gry attempts to show that Rev. 7.9-17 pictures the present blessed state of the departed overcomers in heaven, and that Rev. 20.4-6 belongs to the same context (pp. 59-61). In the presentation of the present study, it will be demonstrated that the first of these suggestions is mistaken, but that the second (the common context between 7.9-17 and 20.4-6) is correct.
4. Although scholars may *assert* that Rev. 1.6 affirms the present reign of the

Secondly, Gry ends up virtually proving that, according to his own hypothesis about John's *aim* in presenting the millennium as he did, there was an effect completely opposite to the intent attributed to him. Gry claims that John meant to discredit the contemporary 'error' of expecting a temporary earthly messianic kingdom,[1] yet on his own admission it was nothing other than the interpretation of Revelation itself that served as the major impetus for such thinking in the post-apostolic church.[2]

3. *Wikenhauser*

A. Wikenhauser shows that he is thinking similarly to Düsterdieck and Gry when he says,

---

saints (e.g. Beasley-Murray, *Revelation*, pp. 57-58), the words themselves say nothing of the kind. For the 'leader of the kings of the earth' (1.5) to make his redeemed ones into *a kingdom* (βασιλεία, vv. 6, 9) is not yet to confer on *them* any kingly authority. What *is* conferred on them is an identity as priests to the King's God and Father (1.6; cf. 5.10). It may further be pointed out that the promises of *reign* in the letters function in parallel with other promises to the overcomer that are to be made good *at Christ's parousia*. Rev. 5.10 confirms this by explicitly placing the promised reign of the saints on earth. Schnackenburg holds a judicious discussion on the subject: *God's Rule and Kingdom*, pp. 330-31. Fuller argumentation of these points will be provided in the following chapter.

1. *Millénarisme*, p. 61.

2. E.g. *Millénarisme*, pp. 66-75. These two criticisms apply equally to the argument of P. Prigent, who claims that John's intent was to 'demythologize' the contemporary Jewish belief in a limited messianic reign by tying it to the church's present experience of Christ's presence and reign in worship (cf. 'Le millennium dans l'Apocalypse johannique', in *L'apocalyptique* [ed. F. Raphael *et al.*; Etudes d'histoire des religions, 3; Paris: Guenther, 1977], p. 156). Prigent suggests that the millennium is pictured as the return of paradise, and that paradise imagery is closely linked to the eucharist in Revelation. Cf. his 'Une trace de liturgie judéo-chrétienne dans le chapitre XXI de l'Apocalypse de Jean', *RevScRel* 60 (1972), pp. 165-72. Both of these observations may be valid, yet the inference Prigent draws from them cannot be sustained. The function of eucharistic symbolism in eschatological promises is certainly that of enriching future hope by analogy with present experience, as opposed to that of redirecting the main reference of those promises from the future to the present (*sc.* teaching realized eschatology). In other words, the readers will understand from such promises that the present experience of worship stands as a foretaste of the eschatological blessing being promised for the future.

In the Apocalypse, one must always distinguish between the vision (i.e. the figure pictured in the vision), and the meaning of the vision. In my opinion, it can not be denied that John really pictured the physical resurrection of the martyrs and their rule with Christ on earth in. . . Jerusalem. But the question is, 'What does this vision signify?' The two must be sharply distinguished from one another.[1]

Wikenhauser then offers the opinion that

the entire episode of the thousand year reign in Revelation is only a means of bringing to expression the concept that the martyrs are worthy of a special reward.[2]

In terms of clarity, Wikenhauser has here stepped beyond Gry, who sometimes fails to resist the pull of the traditional hidden agenda of a-millennialism, whereby one is required to find in Rev. 20.1-6 a picture of the present age. For instance, Gry's vestigial antipathy towards recognizing the future setting of the millennial scenario becomes more than evident when he tries to interpret the parousia vision of Rev. 19.11-16 as referring to the Incarnation.[3]

For his part, Wikenhauser looks upon this kind of thinking as a temptation to be resisted. In itself, he concedes, the picture of Rev. 19.11–20.15 is at least clear enough that an honest and impartial reader will find implausible any symbolic interpretation that seeks to apply the action of 20.1-10 to the present age. But this is not the same as saying that the author either expected, or wanted his readers to expect, events to happen simply as pictured.[4] After all, few visions in Revelation *could* be taken that way. Rather, given that the picture is of an earthly reign of the saints in Jerusalem commencing at the parousia, the interpreter has the responsibility of asking, in the context of Revelation as a whole, what reality this picture is intended to reveal. The question, in other words, is whether the reality of future *events* concerning the saints is being revealed, or perhaps only the reality of their future *condition*.[5] Sadly, Wikenhauser stops short of tackling the

1. 'Das Problem des tausendjährigen Reiches', p. 20.
2. 'Das Problem des tausendjährigen Reiches', p. 21.
3. *Millénarisme*, p. 57.
4. Cf. Düsterdieck's reasoning above.
5. Protestant scholars have also faced this question and made related suggestions: e.g. I.T. Beckwith, *The Apocalypse of John* (Twin Brooks; Grand Rapids: Baker, 1979 [1919]), pp. 736-38. Beckwith goes beyond Wikenhauser (and Gry) in focusing not on the *author's* intent to reveal the special reward of the martyrs under

next and essential question, that of the literary mechanics by which
Revelation might be seen training its readers to make this sort of
interpretative jump.

4. *Schnackenburg*

R. Schnackenburg offers a thoughtful and carefully presented variant
of this 'a-temporal' interpretation. He wisely establishes the context
for his discussion of the millennium with a survey of the many other
references to the rule of God and Christ in Revelation.[1] From this
survey he draws a number of points, of which the most trenchant are
the following. (1) In the previous hymns and proclamations there is
no hint of a special kingdom of Christ that appears prior to the 'real'
kingdom of God. God's kingdom and Christ's kingdom are not to be
split off from one another as though they were two distinct things.[2]
(2) Rev. 11.17-19 sees the eschatological battle, God's final assertion
of his reign, the reward of the saints and the judgment of the dead as a
single movement.[3] (3) The marriage of the Lamb (19.7) and the
appearance of the New Jerusalem as the bride (21.2) are not to be
separated:

the figure of a temporary messianic reign, but on the issue of divine inspiration and
historical relativity. For Beckwith, it is not necessarily by the conscious decision of
the human author that the reward of the martyrs is pictured in temporal form: instead,
he thinks in terms of the truth 'revealed' to the prophet being interpreted temporally
by him according to the natural restraints of his world-view. Cf. the introductory
section, 'Permanent and Transitory Elements in the Apocalypse Distinguished'.
R. Mounce endorses Beckwith's suggestion as one possible interpretative option,
and paraphrases the point as follows: 'In short, John taught a literal millennium, but
its essential meaning may be realized in something other than a temporal fulfillment'
(*The Book of Revelation* [NICNT; Grand Rapids: Eerdmans, 1977], p. 359). Less
conservative in approach are E. Lohse (*Die Offenbarung des Johannes* [NTD, 11;
Göttingen: Vandenhoeck & Ruprecht, 2nd edn, 1966], pp. 101-102) and T. Holtz
(*Die Christologie der Apokalypse des Johannes* [TU, 85; Berlin: Akademie Verlag,
2nd edn, 1971 (1962)], p. 183), who frankly criticize John's teaching of the millennium as coming out of a 'Jewish conception' incompatible with broader Christian
teaching on eschatology.

    1.   Schnackenburg, *God's Rule and Kingdom*, pp. 329-39.
    2.   *God's Rule and Kingdom*, pp. 343, 346.
    3.   *God's Rule and Kingdom*, pp. 343-44.

> The Church awaits her Lord until the Parousia, but then all her yearning is
> assuaged. No room is left for an interval of rule between the Parousia
> (19.11 seq.) and the marriage of the Lamb (19.7, 9; 21.2).[1]

As Schnackenburg looks at Rev. 19.11–20.10 in the light of these
observations, he feels constrained to suppose that he is seeing the
expansion of the judgment of the parousia into scenes that deal successively with its key topics, rather than the prediction of an actual
limited messianic interregnum.[2] The apparent temporal distinctions
between the key scenes are thus not to be pressed:

> The doubling of events in 19.11-21 and 20.7-10 may have taken place for
> descriptive reasons. The final destruction of all God's enemies, those on
> earth and the Satanic forces behind them, required a successive descrip-
> tion to create a strong impression.[3]

> According to the peak of the vision in [20.6, the Christian idea of the mil-
> lennial setting]. . . must be the rule of the previously humiliated martyrs
> (12.11; 13.7-10, 16 seq.) with Christ; their superiority to Satan (12.11
> seq.), their special closeness to Christ, their dignity and [their] worthiness
> to receive a special reward may have found significant expression in this
> intervening vision which represented no interval in actual fact.[4]

Referring to the agenda above for assessing arguments in favour of
a given reinterpretation of the millennium, it appears that Schnackenburg has done well at the level of demonstrating the literary connectedness of 20.1-15 with other parts of Revelation. He has also made

---

1. *God's Rule and Kingdom*, p. 346. Schnackenburg offers little more than a
statement of this important point. Later on in the present study, it will be shown that
a very strong case can be made in support of it.

2. Cf. *God's Rule and Kingdom*, p. 342: 'On closer examination, there would
seem to be no place even in the Apocalypse for an interregnum of Christ'. He
summarizes his point on p. 346: 'For John the seer the future fulfillment of the world
and the future aeon are one whole; there is only one kingdom of God and of Christ.
If he employs different pictures, succeeding and blending with one another, this is
merely to bring out different points of view.' Once again, comparing these remarks
with those of Düsterdieck above shows marked similarity of perspective.

3. *God's Rule and Kingdom*, p. 344. D'Aragon, whose post-millennial
interpretation was considered above, gives partial endorsement to Schnackenburg's
suggestion: cf. 'The Apocalypse', p. 490.

4. *God's Rule and Kingdom*, p. 345. Although he does not say so explicitly,
Schnackenburg is obviously agreeing here with the conclusion of Wikenhauser, 'Das
Problem des tausendjährigen Reiches', p. 21 (cf. the quotation in §3, above).
Schnackenburg cites this article in the immediate context.

fair points about the impossibility of the received view, given these connections. What is missing is an exegetical account of the main texts in question that supplies positive evidences that the author of Revelation meant to encourage this view in particular, and not some other alternative view. And Schnackenburg does not shrink from admitting that, though it lies well beyond the scope of his own study, such an excursion into the complications of exegesis is necessary. He therefore offers his view in terms of a suggestion, and leaves the following assertion as a challenge:

> the fundamental explanation of 20.1-6 must lie in the direction that the vision is a symbolical description of the martyrs' victory and their special, appropriate reward.[1]

5. *Fiorenza*

Schnackenburg's challenge was soon accepted by his pupil E.S. Fiorenza, who ably developed his view in her doctoral dissertation published under the title *Priester für Gott*.[2] Since Fiorenza presents the fullest argumentation for the a-temporal view she shares with Wikenhauser and Schnackenburg, it will be her version of that view to which a fuller appraisal will be given.[3]

The following questions serve to introduce Fiorenza's argument:

> Above all, why is there a thousand year reign of the resurrected, when the *eternal* reign of the eschatologically redeemed will be spoken of in Rev. 22.5? Is not this prophecy in contradiction with its context, not only in terms of content, but formally as well, since it interrupts the flow of the visions in Rev. 20.1-10?[4]

In laying a careful exegetical foundation for the answering of these

---

1.   *God's Rule and Kingdom*, p. 346.

2.   The full title of the monograph is *Priester für Gott: Studien zum Herrschafts- und Priestermotiv in der Apokalypse*. No claim is put forward here as to the overall motivation behind this work, but only the observation that its section on the millennium (pp. 299-334) seems in fact to attempt what Schnackenburg said had to be done to present a full-fledged case for his assertion. Cf. also her article 'Die tausendjährige Herrschaft der Auferstandenen (Apk 20, 4-6)', *BibLeb* 13 (1972), pp. 107-24.

3.   For a helpful summary of her position in English, cf. now *Revelation: Vision of a Just World* (Proclamation Commentaries; Minneapolis: Fortress Press, 1991), pp. 104-109.

4.   *Priester für Gott*, p. 293.

questions, Fiorenza attempts to establish various points about the context, literary structure, content and religious background of Rev. 20.1-10. Among them are the following:

1. Rev. 20.4-6 is recognizable as an 'interlude' [*Zwischenstück*] between vv. 1-3 and vv. 7-10.[1]
2. Rev. 20.4-6, along with the other sections of the chapter (vv. 1-3, 7-10, 11-15), recounts a *judgment vision*, but this case, in contrast to those others, shows a positive and rehabilitating verdict being passed in favour of the saints who have resisted the beast.[2]
3. Those whom John sees sitting on the thrones (Rev. 20.4a) are none other than the resurrected overcomers who have been deemed worthy of receiving the authority to rule (*Herrschaft*) with Christ (cf. Dan. 7.22; Rev. 3.22).[3]
4. 'Gog and Magog' (Rev. 20.8) cannot be peoples who had survived the parousia, since 19.21 indicates that 'no human survivors' will be left. Gog and Magog are therefore to be identified as all the demons of the abyss (and, just conceivably, the unresurrected dead). In other words, Rev. 20.7-10 pictures Satan and his combined forces of the underworld launching a last assault on the eschatological community of the resurrected saints.[4]
5. Fiorenza compares the sequence of eschatological events in Revelation 19–22 (parousia, destruction of the earthly kingdoms, messianic kingdom, destruction of Satan, last judgment [*Weltgericht*], new world, City of God) with OT (Ezekiel, Daniel), 'old Jewish-nationalistic'[5] and apocalyptic models

---

1. *Priester für Gott*, pp. 295-96.
2. *Priester für Gott*, pp. 303-304.
3. *Priester für Gott*, pp. 303-304.
4. *Priester für Gott*, pp. 311-12. In this contention she agrees with Metzger, 'Zwischenreich', pp. 110-18; W.W. Reader, *Die Stadt Gottes in der Johannes-apokalypse* (doctoral dissertation, Georg-August-Universität, Göttingen, 1971), pp. 240-41; and Rissi, *The Future of the World*, pp. 35-36.
5. This terminology follows P. Volz, who uses it to characterize a kind of Jewish national eschatological hope shared by the books of the Apocrypha, [earlier] rabbinic sources, Jewish prayers, Dan. 7, *Pss. Sol.* 17, etc. Cf. *Die Eschatologie der jüdischen Gemeinde im neutestamentlichen Zeitalter* (Hildesheim: Georg Olms, 1966 [1934]), pp. 63-64.

(*4 Ezra* 7; *2 En.* 33) and shows that John's sequence does not correspond closely to any one of these.[1] Rather, John has incorporated from Ezekiel 37 (as did the rabbis) the idea of the saints' resurrection for the messianic age,[2] and the idea of Gog and Magog's final attack; from the old Jewish nationalistic eschatology he has taken over the idea of an eternal earthly reign of the people of God with messiah, and the idea of a universal judgment of individuals according to works; and from apocalyptic he appears to have taken the idea of a temporally bounded messianic age.[3] But, notes Fiorenza, John's model does not really fit in with any apocalyptic model, since for him the thousand years do not constitute the limit of messiah's reign with the saints (as, for example, in *4 Ezra* 7), nor do they signal a passive world-sabbath (as in *2 En.* 33). The limitation indicated by the thousand years is *only* on the imprisonment of Satan, and on the delay of the resurrection and judgment of the 'rest of the dead'.[4]

The force of all these points may perhaps be added together as follows: on literary analysis, John's description of the thousand year reign of the saints with Christ (Rev. 20.4-6) does not function simply as part of a unified eschatological sequence (20.1-10), but rather as an interlude which steps out of a given sequence (in this case 20.1-3, 7-10) in order to give a contrasting look at the church. In terms of content, this interlude is strongly parallel with the last section of the chapter (20.11-15), but looks at judgment as the rehabilitation and rewarding of the saints, as opposed to the condemnation of the unjust. Both by the way that Rev. 20.4-6 recalls Daniel 7 (esp. vv. 18, 22), and by the way Rev. 20.7-10 recalls Ezekiel 38, it also becomes evident that the millennium is not intended as a transitional age of incomplete blessing or temporally limited sovereignty as regards the saints. In Daniel, the saints inherit the kingdom forever, and in Ezekiel, there is no hint of any qualitative difference for the elect that distinguishes their condition before the final attack of Gog from that

1. *Priester für Gott*, pp. 316-23.

2. Fiorenza observes that the original force of the 'dry bones' passage will have been to promise a miraculous national recovery, rather than to predict literal resurrection: cf. *Priester für Gott*, p. 318.

3. *Priester für Gott*, p. 323 (her summary).

4. *Priester für Gott*, p. 323.

which holds afterwards.[1] Similarly, Rev. 19.21 shows that the saints alone are pictured as inheriting the kingdom of the world at the parousia, and Rev. 22.5 shows that their reign with Christ is not limited to the thousand years. Furthermore, since the millennium is not even given significance as a world-sabbath or some other world-age of special character, the whole question of its purpose and meaning as an age separate from the final eschaton seems to be left without an answer.[2]

It is from this apparent lack of a discernible meaning for the millennium as a distinct period of time that Fiorenza draws her conclusion:

> The author of Revelation thus seemingly intends to discourage a temporal understanding of the vision of 20.4ff. . . In fact, it is obvious that the number 'one thousand' has lost its quantitative-temporal character in Rev. 20.4-6, since on the one hand it has lost its connection with the messianic world-age speculations, and on the other hand, it does not have the function of limiting the reign of the resurrected ones.[3]

Fiorenza fills out these statements by affirming that the picture of the first resurrection is intended to convey not chronological-sequential information, but rather theological promise. Agreeing with Schnackenburg, she sees the resurrection and active rule of the millennium as an attempt to picture a just reward for the true saints who have actively witnessed to Christ in this life in the face of the beast and his deadly persecutions.[4]

---

1. I have taken the liberty of drawing in this point about Ezek. 37–40 even though it does not function explicitly in this way in Fiorenza's argument: cf. *Priester für Gott*, pp. 318-19. Fiorenza has slightly understated the force of her own case.

2. *Priester für Gott*, pp. 322-23.

3. *Priester für Gott*, p. 323.

4. *Priester für Gott*, pp. 324-25; cf. the quotation from Schnackenburg on p. 35, above. Having stated her view in a literary and exegetical context, Fiorenza next proposes that it may be supported further by looking at three larger theological themes which develop throughout Revelation, namely the war for sovereignty over the earth, the establishment of the rule of God and Christ over the whole universe, and the role of the redeemed in the conflict for sovereignty over the earth (cf. pp. 325-32). A full survey of these points is inappropriate here, because it becomes evident that at least the first and third points do not add weight to her thesis about the non-sequential course of events in Rev. 20 *per se*: they may fit comfortably with it, but they are also equally coherent with such sequential interpretations as those of Metzger and Rissi (see below). Fiorenza's second point will be discussed shortly.

It remains now to attempt an evaluation of the evidences Fiorenza has proposed in favour of an a-temporal interpretation of the millennium, and to assess their cumulative weight.

First, regarding point 1 above, on close examination it appears incorrect to say that Rev. 20.4-6 functions as an 'interlude' (*Zwischenstück*) between vv. 1-3 and vv. 7-10. For each of the other sections that she rightly classes as 'interludes' qualifies as such by the fact that it can be removed from its context without leaving an obvious gap or ill-fitting pieces on either side.[1] But this is *not* the case with Rev. 20.4-6. It is to be noted that taking these verses out leaves an uncharacteristic redundancy between the emphasized portions of vv. 3 and 7:

> and bound him for a thousand years, and threw him into the abyss, and shut it and sealed it over him, so that he should not deceive the nations any longer, until the thousand years were completed; **after these things he must be released for a short time** [...] *And when the thousand years are completed, Satan will be released from his prison,* and will come out to deceive the nations which are in the four corners of the earth. . .

As it stands reconstructed, this passage suffers from meaningless repetition at the seam between its two halves. In order for it to read smoothly, one would have to do something like excise either the bold or the italicized portion. However, the repetition between the two verses makes perfect sense, assuming the integral function of vv. 4-6. Verse 6 ends with a reference to the thousand year reign of the saints, so v. 7 both links with this and serves to recall the situation as it was presented in v. 3 before a new subject was introduced. In other words, Rev. 20.1-10 functions elegantly as a whole, but it shows marked clumsiness when analysed as two halves of a single vision separated by an independent interlude. Further, the lack of a new 'And I saw' at v. 7, rather than showing that verse's connection to v. 3 (as Fiorenza asserts that it does),[2] actually underlines its unbroken contextual connection with v. 6.[3] Indeed, it would have been precisely the kind of

---

1. Cf. Rev. 5.9-14; 7.1-17; 11.1-14; 12.10-11; 14.1-5; 15.2-4; 16.7; 19.1-8. The section 11.1-14 is a less obvious choice than the larger section 10.1–11.14, which Fiorenza labels an interlude in 'Composition and Structure', p. 361. The reader is invited to confirm this pattern.

2. *Priester für Gott*, pp. 295-96.

3. The positive force of the connection between vv. 6 and 7 will be discussed in Chapter 7 below (on Rev. 20.7-10).

evidence needed for Fiorenza's contention about the interlude status of vv. 4-6 for v. 7 to have begun with something like 'And I saw Satan coming out of his prison...'

Second, regarding point 2 above on Rev. 20.4-6 functioning as a positive counterpart to 20.11-15, although it is indisputable that the *emphasis* in vv. 4-6 is on the verdict in favour of the martyrs, the present study will show that the double-edged character of the passage is also not to be missed. Fiorenza herself rightly notes that this scene, in that it pictures a partial resurrection, is to be described as a 'judgment of the dead'.[1] When 'judgment was given' to those on the thrones (v. 4), the outcome was that '*they* [the martyrs] lived and reigned'; however, 'the *rest* of the dead did *not* come to life until the thousand years were completed'.

Along these lines, Fiorenza's point 3 above must be supplemented as well. She asserts that the thrones John sees in Rev. 20.4a are royal thrones on which he sees seated the vindicated martyrs, whom he will describe in v. 4bc. In the analysis offered in Chapter 6, an attempt will be made to show that this paradoxical interpretation of the vision is well founded, but also that it is equally important to see an inbuilt double meaning here: it is precisely the phrase 'I saw thrones' that first ties Rev. 20.4 to Dan. 7.9 and implies that what follows is to be pictured as a courtroom scene (cf. Rev. 20.4-6; Dan. 7.9-10, 22). In support of this (and contrary to Fiorenza's assertion),[2] key references to thrones in Revelation are set in context of a heavenly courtroom scene.[3]

Moreover, in Revelation God is pictured (following the OT conception) as the heavenly king in his role as judge *par excellence,* so no opposition need be posed between a royal throne and a judgment throne.[4] Further, it will be demonstrated in Chapters 4 and 6 below that the overcomers are promised a share in Christ's and the Father's

1. Cf. *Priester für Gott,* p. 321.
2. 'In Revelation, θρόνος is never understood as a judgment seat' (*Priester für Gott,* p. 304). She admits Rev. 20.11 as a 'possible' exception.
3. It is arguable (cf. the following chapter) that the authorization of the Lamb by the Enthroned One in Rev. 5, and the subsequent unsealings of the seven-sealed document in 6.1–8.5, are precisely courtroom proceedings (Rev. 20.11-15 hardly needs to be mentioned).
4. So Reader, *Die Stadt Gottes,* p. 139.

role of royal judgment,[1] and that this idea must consequently be considered as a probable nuance of Rev. 20.4-6.

Third, in regard to point 4 above, I am in entire agreement with Fiorenza that the reader is not intended to picture ordinary people surviving the parousia judgment of Rev. 19.11-21.[2] In fact, it will be demonstrated in the following chapter that 19.21 is only one in an extensive chain of references that underline, and underline with the greatest possible clarity, the idea that no non-Christian (or lapsed Christian) survives the parousia. On the other hand, however, Fiorenza's proposal regarding the identity of 'Gog and Magog', which is a consequence of this point, remains problematical.

On this view, Gog and Magog are interpreted as hosts of demonic beings.[3] Thus the description in Rev. 20.7-9 supposedly parallels that of a demonic horde coming up out of the abyss in 9.1-11. But in the latter passage, the attacking armies are described as *locusts*, whereas in the former, they are described in human terms.[4] In particular, it

---

1.　Cf. Rev. 2.26-27; 3.21; 17.14; 19.14.

2.　Fiorenza is by no means alone in observing the apparent universality of 19.19-21: e.g. Beckwith (*The Apocalypse of John*, p. 745) begins his comments on the attack of Gog and Magog (Rev. 20.7-10) with the following remark: 'The victory described in 19.19-21 over the Antichrist and his subjects, who included all the kingdoms of the world (13.7f.), seems to leave no place for the hostile armies of this passage'. Rissi insists on the same idea in his comments on 20.4-6: 'the conclusion of the parousia vision (19.21) suggests that he intends to speak of the death of all unbelievers, and that any notion of the resurrected and the non-resurrected ones standing side by side in the millennium is completely foreign to him' (*The Future of the World*, p. 33).

3.　Fiorenza, *Priester für Gott*, pp. 311-12. For the same opinion, cf. A. Wikenhauser, *Die Offenbarung des Johannes übersetzt und erklärt* (RNT, 9; Regensburg: Pustet, 3rd edn, 1959 [1947]), pp. 75-80, followed by Lohse, *Offenbarung*, p. 58, and, more recently, Kraft, *Offenbarung*, pp. 259-60 and A. Pohl, *Die Offenbarung des Johannes* (Wuppertal Studienbibel; 2 vols.; Wuppertal: Brockhaus, 1983), II, p. 283. Similarly W. Bousset, *Die Offenbarung Johannis* (MeyerK, 16; Göttingen: Vandenhoeck & Ruprecht, 9th edn, 1966 [1906]), p. 399.

4.　On the face of it, the expression 'the nations which are in the four corners of the earth' (Rev. 20.7) obviously denotes people. Bousset's speculation that John has taken over from Ezek. 38–39 (both here and in 16.16) a myth about an attacking demonic army without understanding it does nothing to further this discussion (*Offenbarung*, pp. 397-99, 438-39). For it does not matter from what *source* Ezekiel may be speculated to have taken his material: the essential fact in any case is that, *in the form in which John presumably read it*, Ezek. 38–39 explicitly deals with human

seems very unlikely that John should choose to describe demonic forces from the underworld with the term 'nations' (20.8), when the term is elsewhere unattested as referring to demons, and he has in 20.3 used the term with unequivocal reference to human beings.

This brings up a second and equally crucial point. In Rev. 20.3 the reason given for Satan's imprisonment is 'so that he should not deceive the nations any longer, until the thousand years were completed' (i.e., that he should not be able to deceive the human race at large). When one is warned that Satan will be released for a short time at the end of this period (v. 3b), the natural implication is that he will be allowed once again briefly to deceive the nations. Thus when vv. 7-8 says Satan will be released and will 'go out to deceive the nations. . .', there is an immediate connection with v. 3, establishing the same context,[1] and confirming the expectation that a renewed deception of the human race would follow his imprisonment. It stands as highly implausible that John should have written this way if he had intended his readers to imagine a *demonic* horde in vv. 7-10.

Fourth, in reference to Fiorenza's point 5 above, about the unique character of Revelation's millennium, in my estimation much of what Fiorenza says under this point is both valid and important. Revelation 20 is indeed different from all other earlier and contemporary models for the messianic age. Unlike any OT model, it is bounded by an explicit resurrection and last judgment of humanity (Rev. 20.11-15), yet unlike apocalyptic models, its character completely transcends that of the present age. There seems to be no difference between the millennium and the age which follows it, as far as the saints are concerned. Its beginning signals a complete end to the present world-age with its flow of history (since the glorified saints alone live and reign on the earth during the millennium), and its end signals neither an end to the reign of the saints nor any explicit improvement in the character of their (already resurrected) life.[2]

---

armies (cf. Ezek. 32.26; 38.2-3). Further, as Bousset admits, John is following (in Rev. 20.7-10) a more or less standard model which has come out of Ezek. 38–39 (cf. *Offenbarung*, pp. 438-39), and that model as exemplified in Jewish literature uniformly interprets the hosts of Gog as human beings (cf. the discussion in A. Schlatter, *Das Alte Testament in der Johannesapokalypse* [BFCT, 6; Gütersloh: Beutelsmann, 1912], pp. 93-95).

1.   Cf. the discussion of Fiorenza's point 1, above.

2.   One can see at this point the logic of such early church interpreters as

On this final point, in fact, I will go somewhat further than has Fiorenza. Whereas her model assumes a (non-literal) picture of the millennium in which the creation remains un-renewed and the heavenly Jerusalem has not yet descended to earth,[1] it will be demonstrated in the following chapter that the re-creation of the world and the descent of the New Jerusalem (Rev. 21.1–22.5) are each described in a way that makes them virtually inseparable from the parousia. At first sight, one might well expect the proof of this contention to add considerable strength to the case for Fiorenza's a-temporal model. For first, it seems to take away the last vestiges of a qualitative difference between the millennium and the age that follows it. And second, by seeming to indicate that the last judgment and resurrection of the 'rest of humanity' are to be understood in the context of the parousia after all (cf. 20.13; 21.1), it appears to reduce the millennium from an aeon to no more than a symbolic episode within the parousia event.[2]

Irenaeus, who made a distinction between the renewal of the world at the parousia and a radical new creation after the millennium, and looked to the millennium as a training period during which the resurrected saints were to be prepared for an ultimate state of communion with God (cf. *Adv. Haer.* 5.36.1-3, cited in *The Writings of Irenaeus*, II [trans. A. Roberts and W.H. Rambaut; ANCL, 9; Edinburgh: T. & T. Clark, 1878]). For the earliest interpreters of Revelation, as well as Fiorenza, there seem to have been no models both ready to hand and capable of supplying a distinct salvific purpose for the millennium. Given this lack of perceived purpose, combined with the unavailability of an a-temporal interpretation, it is not hard to imagine the temptation to *create* a purpose for the millennium by speculating about an exalted state of things beyond that age.

1.   Fiorenza suggests rather vaguely that the New Jerusalem will be 'earthly' in a fuller sense than in Rev. 20.4-6: 'This "earthly" reality is described as a "new heaven and a new earth" in Rev. 21.1. It is different from the "earthly" reality of 20.4-6 in the fact that now the "sea" as the place of the wicked (Rev. 13.1) and the underworld (Rev. 20.13) no longer exists' (*Priester für Gott*, p. 328 n. 160).

2.   Arguing similarly, Fiorenza says that John has put forward various images from the traditions he has taken over in order to display the one eschatological event 'kaleidoscopically':

> This becomes obvious when one sees that his descriptions of the eschatological age of salvation, whether in the picture of the new earth, or the New Jerusalem, or Paradise, or the worship of the servants of God as priests and kings—that these do not show separate situations of salvation. . . Rather, the same eschatological salvation is being shown in ever new pictures ('Die tausendjährige Herrschaft', p. 124).

The exegetical analysis in Chapter 9, below, will show that this statement can in fact be endorsed without undermining the temporal *raison d'être* of the millennium.

It is arguable, however, that a different viewpoint is needed in order to put these considerations into a correct perspective. In particular, it needs to be recognized that even seeing the re-creation in the context of the parousia will tend to undermine the temporal significance of the millennium only if one focuses exclusively on the meaning of that age in the life of the saints. And as will become evident, to do this is to miss what should be immediately recognizable as the emphasis not only of the millennial passage itself (Rev. 20.1-10), but equally of its surrounding context.

In Rev. 19.11–20.15, the theme that is consistently dwelt upon is that of *judgment*, and, in particular, that negative form of judgment which deals with the eschatological encounter between God and his Christ on one side, and the unrepentant on the other.[1] Thus the analysis presented in this study will reveal that Fiorenza (along with Schnackenburg and others) has in effect looked in the wrong place for the heart of the millennium. The question that holds the key to the intelligibility of the millennium is not 'Why are the saints said to receive resurrection and reign for a thousand years?' (as she suggests), but rather, 'Why are those who are *not* saints said to be *denied* resurrection for a thousand years?' (20.6).[2] As will be argued in the chapters below, this is the question to which the book of Revelation offers a coherent (and perhaps irreducibly temporal) answer.

It may be worthwhile to summarize the main points of the foregoing response to Fiorenza's view. Fiorenza (as will become progressively more apparent) has contributed many important insights to the study of the millennium, but her a-temporal interpretation will have to be laid aside (at least to begin with) for the following reasons. (1) Her formal literary analysis of Rev. 20.4-6 fails as it relates to vv. 1-3 and vv. 7-10, and thus cannot even indirectly support an a-temporal argument. (2) Although her assertion of a common context between

---

1. In the exegetical study of Rev. 20.11-15 in Chapter 8, below, the majority view (that this passage is written so as to suggest an entirely negative application) will be defended.

2. Fiorenza comes close to seeing the force of this: 'Furthermore, it is to be noted that the expression ἄχρι τελεσθῇ τὰ χίλια ἔτη is not primarily related to the Messiah and those who reign with him, but rather to the "rest" of the dead, who are not given a part in the first resurrection, and to the binding of Satan in the underworld' (*Priester für Gott*, p. 321; cf. similarly p. 313 n. 99).

the various salvation scenes (including 20.4-6) in the final chapters of
Revelation is well supported (and will be developed further in the present study), this does not in itself undermine the temporal significance
of the millennium. For she has not shown that the millennium has
no temporal significance, but rather that it cannot easily find its
significance as a distinct *period of salvation*. And this leaves out
the question of its possible significance as a period of *judgment* or
punishment.

Given the context in which the millennium stands,[1] the matter cannot be closed without a full discussion of this last question. And
although Fiorenza herself devotes considerable attention to treating
the subject in these terms, her discussion of the millennium in relationship to the forces of evil seems to play little part in her reasoning
in favour of an a-temporal understanding.[2] Furthermore, there is a
serious shortcoming in the way she analyses the millennium as it
describes the interaction between God and his 'enemies'. But since she
has probably taken this shortcoming on board along with a larger
view inherited from Metzger,[3] it should be discussed in the context of
his work, which will now come under discussion.

---

1.   'All three vision units of Rev. 20 have judgment as their theme [meaning
vv. 1-3, 7-10, 4-6, 11-15]' (*Priester für Gott*, p. 312).
2.   Fiorenza begins the section that studies the place of the millennium in
Revelation's theology of judgment (and God's victory over his enemies) with this
assertion: 'It becomes obvious that a literary-theological arrangement characterizes
Rev. 19.11–22.5, and that no temporal assertions are to be made, when one lays out
the "theological centre" of Revelation and its visions in more detail' (*Priester für
Gott*, p. 325; cf. pp. 325-32, and esp. 325-29). As was mentioned previously, the
subsequent sections fail to deliver the sense of obviousness that is promised by this
remark: on the contrary, certain doubts are raised (see pp. 325-29). For example,
how is it that the relationship between the first and second stages of God's victory
over Satan (12.5; 20.1-3) is a temporal one (since the two stages coincide with the
beginning and ending points of the kingdom of the Beast), whereas the relationship
between the second and third stages (20.1-3, 7-10) supposedly is not?
3.   The opening paragraph of Fiorenza's section 'Die Durchsetzung der
Herrschaft Gottes und des Christus über den ganzen Kosmos' (*Priester für Gott*,
pp. 327-29) summarizes the 'three stage' model through which Metzger interprets
the changeover to the realization of God's full sovereignty in Revelation, and
Metzger is duly cited on p. 327 n. 157. The section as a whole follows Metzger
very closely. Cf. *Priester für Gott*, pp. 327-39, with Metzger, 'Zwischenreich',
pp. 112-16.

6. *W. Metzger*

W. Metzger's engaging essay, 'Das Zwischenreich', appears to be his only direct contribution to Revelation studies. The piece is full of conviction, and seems to draw its motivating power from the theological lessons of World War II and the fall of the Third Reich (it was published in 1948).[1]

Metzger's point of departure is the OT picture of the messianic age, and in particular Ezekiel 37–48. He argues that to understand John's use of the OT is to repudiate the idea of a millennium that belongs essentially to the present age:

> In the OT model, it will have been important for John's understanding that the judgment would see a complete break, such that the return to Palestine would issue in an entirely new beginning. The former stage is completely wrapped up. This is the breaking point of every interpretation of the messianic interregnum that looks for it in the context of the present age.[2]

Comparing Revelation 19–21 with Ezekiel 37–48, Metzger makes the claim that in both cases the full description of the messianic age is suspended until after the narration of the final war (Ezek. 38; Rev. 20.7-15):

> By portraying the interregnum of 20.4ff. in an intentionally terse manner, John holds back the description of the nature and content of God's kingdom there at first, until he has seen it through to its last conflict (21.1ff.). Thus for John, the point of transition to the new age cannot (as ordinary chiliasm assumes) lie between Rev. 20.10 and 11.[3]

Just as in Ezekiel 40–48 the author returns to the description of the good things of the messianic age which had been promised briefly in ch. 37, so also in Revelation. To put it explicitly, Metzger is saying that the new creation and the descent to earth of the New Jerusalem (Rev. 21.1–22.5) are to be understood as connected with the parousia

---

1. Hitler, it will be recalled, had explicitly claimed for the Reich the epithet 'the thousand year reign'. In a speech given at Nuremburg in September 1934, he asserted that there would be no new 'Reich' in Germany for the next thousand years, and from that point on, the expression 'das tausendjährige Reich' was popularized by his administration. On this, cf. L. Snyder, *Encyclopedia of the Third Reich* (London: Robert Hale, 1976), p. 346.

2. 'Zwischenreich', p. 105. Similarly, cf. Fiorenza, *Priester für Gott*, p. 327.

3. 'Zwischenreich', p. 107.

and the inauguration of the millennium.[1] He thus interprets the millennium as a distinct period of time, but he does not see a qualitatively new situation being introduced with the first verses of Revelation 21. In seeing the glories described in Rev. 21.1–22.5 as describing the millennial age, Metzger is reasserting Revelation's earliest interpretative tradition as reflected in the *Epistle of Barnabas*,[2] the works of Hippolytus and Methodius,[3] as well as the *Apocalypse of Elijah*[4] (and

1. More explicitly, cf. 'Zwischenreich', p. 111, and this quotation from p. 117: 'Jesus will triumph, and in his triumph the old earth will flee, in order to make room for the new earth of the millennium. This is unquestionably the earth of the new age.'

2. Cf. *Barn.* 15, cited in *Apostolic Fathers*, I (trans. K. Lake; LCL; London: Heinemann, 1977 [1912]). (The author of this epistle has traditionally been called 'Barnabas'. No claim about identity is intended.) For Barnabas, the seventh millennial day (reckoned in terms of the present creation) begins at the parousia, and is at the same time the inauguration of the eighth day of God's new creation. Cf. A. Hermans, 'Le Pseudo-Barnabé: Est-il millénariste?', *ETL* 35 (1959), pp. 849-76, who builds an extremely thorough case for the identification of the sabbath and the eighth day of the new world (*contra* W.H. Shea, 'The Sabbath in the Epistle of Barnabas', *AUSS* 4 [1966], pp. 167-68). In Barnabas's thinking, the millennium is God's final sabbath rest from creating the world, in the sense that the course of human history itself has been part of his creative activity. But at the same time, the millennium is an eighth day, in the sense that it is the first day in a new week of ages, the beginning of a flawless new creation. That is, the seventh and eighth millennia *overlap one another*. Hermans overstates the case when he claims Barnabas has 'suppressed' or 'cancelled' the seventh millennium in favour of the eighth ('Il *supprime* tout simplement le septième millénaire' [p. 876]). Agreed, Barnabas is no chiliast in the typical sense, for his millennium belongs completely to the new creation. But what Hermans does not appear to have considered is the concept of a distinct millennium beginning at the parousia, set in the new creation, and bounded by the resurrection and judgment of unrepentant humanity.

3. Cf. Hippolytus, *Schol. on Dan.* 7.17, 22, cited in *The Writings of Hippolytus*, I (trans. S.D.F. Salmond; ANCL, 6; Edinburgh: T. & T. Clark, 1887); Methodius, *Banquets of the Ten Virgins* 9.1, cited in *The Writings of Methodius, &c.* (trans. W. Clark: ANCL, 14; Edinburgh: T. & T. Clark, 1906). Cf. also Methodius, *De Creatis* 9.

4. Cf. *Apoc. Elij.* 4.26–5.39. The date of this document, which seems to be a composite of Jewish and Christian materials, is impossible to determine precisely, but estimates usually fall between 150 and 250 CE. For editions with comments on dating, cf. O.S. Wintermute (ed.), in J.H. Charlesworth (ed.), *The Old Testament Pseudepigrapha*, I (Garden City, NY: Doubleday, 1983), pp. 729-30, and the translators' introductory remarks in A. Pietersma, S.T. Comstock, with H.W. Attridge (eds. and trans.), *The Apocalypse of Elijah based on P. Chester Beatty 2018* (SBLTT, 19, Pseudepigrapha Series, 9; Chico, CA: Scholars Press, 1981).

to a lesser degree Tertullian, Commodianus and Victorinus).[1]

All these early interpreters see in Rev. 21.1-2 realities which are to be experienced at the parousia. But whereas the first four fully affirm the appearance of both the new creation and the New Jerusalem in the context of the parousia, the three within the parentheses expect the appearance of the New Jerusalem at the parousia, but see the radical new creation being held back until after the millennium.[2]

1.   These three only partially align with Metzger's interpretation, since although they place the descent of the New Jerusalem (and therefore the major application of Rev. 21) in the context of the beginning of the millennium, they nonetheless hold back expectation of a fully fledged new creation until after the millennium and the last judgment. E.g. see Tertullian, *Adv. Marc.* 3.24, cited in *The Writings of Tertullian*, I (trans. P. Holmes; ANCL, 15; Edinburgh: T. & T. Clark, 1884); Commodianus, *In Favour of Christian Discipline against the Gods of the Heathens* 43–44 (trans. R.E. Wallis; ANCL, 18; Edinburgh: T. & T. Clark, 1895). At 21.1, the 'unedited' version of Victorinus's commentary on Revelation reads: 'In regno ergo et in prima resurrectione exhibetur ciuitas sancta, quam dicit descensuram de caelo. . .' Most editions of Victorinus's commentary have been carefully edited by Jerome to remove all traces of chiliasm (cf. F.F. Bruce, 'The Earliest Latin Commentary on the Apocalypse', *EvQ* 10 [1938], pp. 352-66). However, the original and the edited version (Latin) are set out side by side in the edition of J. Haussleiter (ed.), *Victorini Episcopi Petavionsensis Opera* (CSEL, 49; Vienna: F. Tempsky, 1916). Although no complete English edition of the 'unexpurgated' version is available, Bruce's article supplies translations of key extracts.

2.   In agreement with these latter three is T. Zahn, who asserts that it is 'entirely unthinkable' that Jesus will go back to heaven after having reigned on earth for a thousand years in the New Jerusalem (*Die Offenbarung des Johannes* [Kommentar zum Neuen Testament, 17; 2 vols.; Leipzig: A. Deichertsche Verlags-buchhandlung, 1924, 1926], II, p. 599). Cf. also his comments on 11.15-19 *in loc.* Zahn, like Irenaeus (whose understanding of the millennium he highly respects; cf. *Offenbarung*, II, pp. 624-25 and p. 43 n. 2, above), posits a renewal of the earth as opposed to a radical new creation at the parousia. In Zahn's case, this is presumably because of his acceptance of the mainstream view that some ordinary nations are spared to participate in the millennial age. In other words, it is presumably necessary to imagine the full dissolution and new creation complex being put off until after the millennium if one is to imagine (mortal) people surviving the parousia. Irenaeus, on the other hand, does not expect anyone except the resurrected saints to inherit the millennium (*Adv. Haer.* 5.35.1), so his reasoning probably runs along different lines (cf. p. 16 n. 1, above): on the one hand, he takes prophecies such as Isa. 6.12 and 55.20-25 (which mention childbearing) as literal pictures of the new economy of the world in the millennium, but on the other hand, he knows Jesus' teaching (Mt. 22.30 par.) that in the ultimate economy of resurrection, there will be no place for marriage and child-bearing. Therefore, the millennium must constitute a transitional stage between the

Metzger sees the dissolution and re-creation of the world bringing human history to a full stop at the parousia and not at the end of the millennium, and so he does not have the option of viewing Gog and Magog as nations of ordinary human beings. But neither does he immediately follow the line which sees them either as demons[1] or as a combined army of demons and unresurrected human ghosts.[2] Instead, he asks if the two sections, Rev. 20.7-10 and 20.11-15, might not conceivably be seen as alternative ways of expressing the single idea of a last judgment:

> For Ezekiel, the annihilation of Gog and Magog accomplishes Jahweh's last judgment. . . For John, has not this single unified event in the original been split up into two visions (judgment on Gog and Magog on the one hand, last judgment on the other)? And does not John hereby say the same thing as Ezekiel, but simply in two passages, such that the revelation of God's justice before the nations (Rev. 20.7ff.) and that before the dead (Rev. 20.11-15) essentially resolve into one?[3]

As will be discovered in Chapter 8, below, this question raises many others in its wake—questions that go straight to the centre of the meaning, nature and purpose of the millennium as narrated by John. Nonetheless, for his part Metzger chooses to leave the matter open, neither clarifying nor arguing for the possible merits of his suggestion. In fact, he seemingly abandons this line of thinking. In its stead, he goes on to develop an interpretation of the millennium that identifies it as the second of three stages in Christ's victory over Satan and the forces of rebellion.

Metzger argues that Revelation pictures Christ's kingdom prevailing over the world in three successive steps corresponding to the three great realms of creation: heaven, earth and underworld.

First, in Revelation 12 (vv. 7-9), Satan and all his forces are seen being expelled from heaven. That is news for which rejoicing is called

---

present world and the final economy of things. Cf. *Adv. Haer.* 5.34.2; 5.35.1; 5.36.3. The view of Justin Martyr appears to be similar: *Dial. Tryph.* 80–81, cited in *The Writings of Justin Martyr and Athenagoras* (ed. A. Roberts and J. Donaldson; trans. G. Reith; ANCL, 2; Edinburgh: T. & T. Clark, 1892).

1. So e.g. Bousset, Wikenhauser, Lohse, Kraft, Pohl, commentaries *in loc.*

2. So Rissi, *The Future of the World*, pp. 35-36; Fiorenza, *Invitation to the Book of Revelation* (Image Books; Garden City, NY: Doubleday, 1981), pp. 193-94 (tentatively).

3. 'Zwischenreich', p. 109.

for in heaven (12.12a), but not on earth and sea, to which Satan has been forced to retreat (12.12b). Now, according to Metzger, Satan only has claim over the remaining two realms, earth and underworld.[1]

Secondly, at his parousia, Christ and his armies march forth from heaven (which has already been secured for his kingdom), and the ensuing battle extends the boundaries of his kingdom yet further: now Satan and all his forces are pushed out of the earth, and are left only with the underworld abyss as their last bastion.[2]

Thirdly, after the millennium, Satan and his confederates (the demons and those among the spirits of the dead who are willing to be led astray by him)[3] will give up even the underworld. They may come out fighting, but they will be defeated (Rev. 20.7-10):

> 'They came up on the plain of the earth' (20.9)—this does not simply mean coming up over the horizon, but coming up out of the abyss (for the expression, e.g. 9.2) onto the expanse of the earth. The 'nations at the four corners of the earth', who go to war at Satan's instigation. . . are the denizens of the last realm of the universe that still belongs to him, the inhabitants of the underworld. . . Just as Satan and his angels were forced out of heaven, and as he, with all those loyal to him, was forced to disappear from the earth, so now he and his underworldly confederates are forced to evacuate their last bastion.[4]

Thus, in the final state (Rev. 20.11-15) God is seen as the one and only Lord on his throne. Earth and heaven (that is, the old earth and heaven) have disappeared before him at the parousia, and so now must the sea, the realm of the underworld, also disappear (21.1). But first, suggests Metzger, at least some of those among the dead who will not have listened to Satan's deception (20.7-10) will be raised to eternal

1.   'Zwischenreich', p. 112: 'He has now only the earth and the underworld (the latter represented by the sea, 12.12) as territory under his control. He has no more say in heaven.' The suggestion here that in Rev. 12.12b the 'sea' refers to the underworld may have definite merits in view of 13.1.

2.   'Zwischenreich', p. 115; cf. also the following statements: 'The power of Satan is. . . restricted to the underworld. . . Satan is above all banned for a thousand years from the earth, which now belongs to Christ, just as heaven certainly belonged to him from 12.10' ('Zwischenreich', p. 113).

3.   Metzger, for reasons to be discussed shortly, wants to see some of those in the underworld as being due for a resurrection to eternal life, and so he cannot allow the idea that all the spirits of the dead follow Satan when he is freed (Rev. 20.7). Cf. 'Zwischenreich', p. 114.

4.   'Zwischenreich', pp. 114-15.

life (20.12). In talking about Rev. 20.11-15, he adds this parenthetical comment:

> If anywhere, this is the place where the biblical idea of a second choice of the generations of people who never got to hear of Christ is to be thought of. For that matter, it is also not least a meaningful place to include the hope that Paul the apostle held out for Israel (Rom. 9–11), a hope certainly not limited to the last living generation of the present age.[1]

On first look, Metzger seems to have achieved a great deal: he has proposed an alternative interpretation of the millennium that ties it in harmoniously and plausibly not only with the relevant background chapters in the book of Ezekiel, but equally with the whole movement of Revelation since ch. 12. Reference was made above, however, to a central shortcoming of this model, and this shortcoming must now be addressed. On close examination, Metzger's model of the three-stage expansion of God's kingdom turns out to be somewhat distorted, and, in particular, it falls apart when applied to the millennium and its outcome. The following points should be noted.

a. *War in Heaven*

It is not first in Revelation 12 that God's kingdom is pictured as established in heaven. In Revelation 4 and 5 the complete and unlimited authority of God and the Lamb is acknowledged (4.11; 5.11-13). Not a word of Revelation 12 or any other passage in Revelation implies (as does Metzger[2]) that Satan either has had, or pretends to have had, any ongoing claim to rulership in heaven. He is simply called the constant accuser of the brethren before God (12.10). In other words, Satan's role in heaven prior to his expulsion is described as that of a legal adversary who operates within the economy of God's royal court. No conflict of sovereignties is implied in this model. If Satan is to be pictured as being expelled, it will by no means be because God is enlarging the borders of his kingdom and capturing the territory of heaven: God's sovereignty in heaven has already incontestably been established.

---

1.   'Zwischenreich', p. 115.
2.   Cf. the quotation, p. 51 nn. 1 and 2, above. The picture of the dragon with its seven crowns in Rev. 12.3 could only have spoken in favour of Metzger's position at this point if some other passage could be produced to back it up as a symbol of (pretended) kingly authority *in heaven per se*.

Satan's expulsion will instead presumably be because Satan (and his confederate angels) have in some way disobeyed God and are now being banished from heaven as punishment. And although Rev. 12.7-8 makes it look relatively certain that the crime in question is *revolt*, it also makes it look as though Satan's party is beaten and banished the moment they try to oppose God's kingship. Revelation 12, in sum, does not picture God's assertion and acquisition of full rulership over the realm of heaven (Metzger's stage 1). It instead pictures Satan's abortive attempt at a revolt from under that (actually incontestable) rulership.

b. *Revolt on Earth*

A similar distortion lies in Metzger's way of discussing the stage of Satan's supposed earthly (and under-earthly) hegemony. Much of the problem here involves weighing matters of complexion as opposed to simply labelling statements true or false. For example, Metzger overstates the situation when he says in the context of Rev. 12.12 that Satan is forced to retreat, and that the boundaries of his kingdom now encompass only the earth and the sea. Rev. 12.12 in fact says nothing about Satan's kingship over those realms, but rather that his anger will be felt by those realms. And from 5.13 the readers are in a position to know that sovereignty over all realms of the created order belongs to God, who created them. When therefore Satan is confined to the earth, he is not being restricted within the boundaries of his own kingdom, but rather shut out of one portion of God's kingdom.

Satan's attempt at revolt is expressed on earth as well, to be sure. He tries to persecute the woman (Rev. 12.13), but the earth (naturally loyal to God, its true king) helps the woman (12.16). Satan makes war on the saints through the agency of the 'beast' (12.17; 13.7), but the beast does so only because he is 'allowed to'. He is allowed by God the king, who decrees the limits not only on the scope, but also on the time of the dragon's activity through the beast (13.5; cf. 12.12).[1]

It is true that the very widest scope is given to the beast to incite a rebellion (13.7; cf. above on ch. 12), but the battle remains a rebellion that occurs on God's turf.[2] The beast's divinely specified authority, so

---

1.   In support of this point, cf. Beasley-Murray, *Revelation*, pp. 212-13, and Sweet, *Revelation*, p. 210, who correctly calls the verb ἐδόθη a 'passive of divine action'.

2.   Undeniably, as it expresses itself on the earth, Satan's 'revolt' is virtually

far as it extends to the saints, is not authority to rule, but authority to kill (13.15). And even killing God's servants is paradoxically a defeat for him, because it proves that he cannot even by deadly force con-script the earthly witnesses of God's Anointed over to his rebellion (12.10, 11; 15.2). It is thus from the standpoint that the creation belongs to God that a last appeal is made to the whole of breakaway humanity in 14.6-7:

> And I saw another angel flying in mid-heaven, having an eternal gospel to preach to those who live on the earth, and to every nation and tribe and tongue and people; and he said with a loud voice, 'Fear God, and give Him glory, because the hour of His judgment has come; and worship Him who made the heaven and the earth and the sea and the springs of waters'.[1]

It is also clear from the victory song of the martyrs in Rev. 15.3-4 that even while the beast is at the zenith of his activities, God is still the only one who can truly be named king over the nations. And from the way that the seven bowls of God's wrath follow on from this song (and from the passage above),[2] it is equally clear that God is disciplin-ing them not as a king who is attacking the territory of another, but as the king who punishes his own rebellious subjects.

In Rev. 17.14 and 19.16-19, it is the beast who has mustered an army of rebels to fight against the 'Lord of Lords and King of Kings', and not vice versa. Seen in its larger context, the battle of Har-

---

universal. In human terms therefore (at least for the beast's career), the earth and its peoples can be said to be under his domination. Fiorenza is thus not far wrong in saying that the great theme of Revelation is 'the establishment of the kingdom of God and of Christ over. . . the whole earth, which at present for a short period belongs to and is ruled by the powers hostile to God' (*Priester für Gott*, p. 325). But W. Thüsing is more accurate when he says that Revelation's great theme is the unveiling or the public demonstration of God's full, actual and present sovereignty before the world ('Die theologische Mitte der Weltgerichtsvisionen in der Johannesapokalypse', *TTZ* 77 [1968], pp. 1-16, esp. 8).

1.   On the OT background of the concept that God's rulership of the world fol-lows from his role as its creator, cf. F. Mussner, '"Weltherrschaft" als eschatologis-ches Thema der Johannesapokalypse', in *Glaube und Eschatologie* (Festschrift W.G. Kümmel; ed. E. Grässer and O. Merk; Tübingen: Mohr, 1985), pp. 209-27 (209-10).

2.   It is those very aspects of God's good creation catalogued by the angel in Rev. 14.7 which are subsequently allowed to be disturbed in order to discipline people when the bowls are poured out in 16.2-11.

Magedon is decidedly *not* the picture of Christ taking over Satan's territory, but the picture (cf. ch. 12) of Christ expelling the would-be rebels from his own territory. Christ rules his own kingdom and disciplines his own subjects with a 'rod of iron' (19.15-16). And when the shout 'God reigns' goes up (cf. 11.15-18; 19.6), it is not because God has at this point won the kingship over a further realm, but because now for the first time he has completely asserted his rightful kingship over his own realm by putting down the rebels once and for all (cf. Ps. 2.1-12; Rev. 11.15-18).

c. *Imprisonment in the Abyss*

This discussion of the parousia brings us to what Metzger calls the 'second stage', and the place where his model breaks down completely. Metzger says that when Christ presses his claim of sovereignty over the earth, Satan is forced to retreat a further step so that the underworld becomes his 'last bastion'. But Milton's *Paradise Lost* notwithstanding, there is nothing whatever in the book of Revelation which either says or implies that the underworld is or has been part of Satan's kingdom. In Revelation, the underworld is always pictured as a *prison*: a place of confinement to which God, and in particular Jesus, owns the keys (cf. 1.18; 9.1; 20.1).[1]

Thus there is no ambiguity about what is narrated in Rev. 20.1-3. An angel who has received the keys of the underworld prison binds Satan with chains and imprisons him there. The angel then locks and seals the entrance of the abyss after him. It is contrary to the text to suggest that the parousia signals something analogous to a forced military retreat on Satan's part. What is pictured is arrest and imprisonment. The idea is certainly not that from this point on Satan will be restricted to expressing his rule over the abyss and its inhabitants.[2] On

---

1. Even if (as is barely possible) Satan himself is to be identified both as the star who falls from heaven in Rev. 9.1 (cf. 12.4, 9) and as the angel of the abyss in 9.11, it is obvious that he receives the key to the prison of the abyss from God (cf. again, above, the divine passive: 'he was given' [9.1]). And obviously whoever the 'messenger of the abyss' may be, he can only fill the role of kingship (9.11) in the sense of having authority to release and/or conscript the hostile beings who have been trapped there, rather than in the sense of asserting his authority over the abyss as the territory of his rule.

2. A number of scholars besides Metzger ('Zwischenreich', p. 115) also make this mistake: e.g. Fiorenza, *Priester für Gott*, p. 312: 'The partakers of the first resurrection are exempted from Satan's lordship over the dead'; D'Aragon, 'The

the contrary, v. 3 explicitly says that Satan is imprisoned in the abyss in order to take away his ability to deceive the nations (20.3). And if the nations whom he can no longer deceive are his former worshippers and subjects, in other words, *the dead* (as Metzger will have to admit),[1] then his imprisonment in chains, and his inability to deceive the nations any longer, can only spell the complete loss of any pretended kingship for the duration of the thousand years.[2]

When Satan therefore reappears in Rev. 20.7-8, one does not see him sally forth from his subterranean fastness with his army of subjects who have remained loyal over the course of the millennium. On the contrary, one sees him being released from prison, and being permitted 'for a short time' (v. 3) to deceive people into becoming his subjects once again, and so to gather together (i.e. recruit) a rebel army for the war. Metzger's model for the transition to the 'third stage' of God's dealings with Satan is thus entirely incorrect. God is not forcing Satan to give up his last stronghold, but rather the reverse: Satan is being released from a long and impotent period of incarceration in God's own dungeon.

If the reader should sense that Metzger's view has something irresistible about it in spite of the foregoing criticisms, it is no doubt for good reason. One cannot deny that Metzger's model is in an overall way very close to expressing the actual dynamics of Revelation 12–20.

Apocalypse', p. 490: '[in 20.1-3 Satan is] driven from earth and restricted to his proper sphere of influence'; Rissi, *The Future of the World*, p. 68: 'the dragon will be imprisoned in this [the abyss], his very own kingdom. . .'; similarly Sickenberger, *Erklärung*, p. 184.

1.   Metzger does not see mortal nations surviving into the millennial period on earth, nor would he want to identify the nations Satan deceived with the saints, who were not deceived by him, but rather were accused and persecuted by him. In fact, the saints lost their lives through being the only ones on earth who *refused* to be deceived by him and to acknowledge his lordship. The 'nations' he can no longer deceive must therefore be the inhabitants of the abyss who formerly worshipped him through his agent the beast. Cf. 'Zwischenreich', p. 115 n. 32.

2.   Further attention will be given to this theme in the development of the positive thesis espoused in the present study. For an instructive parallel to the idea presented here from John's favourite OT book, cf. Isa. 14.9-17. In this passage, various kings who had once been in awe of the king of Babylon jeer at him when they find him cast into Sheol just as dead and impotent as themselves. They marvel to themselves that this person, who had once wielded such power, has now lost everything—he who formerly possessed ultimate might and prestige now has nothing but weakness and disgrace.

But the central shortcoming of his approach lies in his assumption of an overly dualistic relationship between the kingdoms of God and Satan. Revelation 12–20 shows three progressive stages in God's judgment of angelic and human rebellion in his kingdom. In the first stage, angelic rebellion in heaven is exposed and expelled (ch. 12). In the second stage, human rebellion on earth is exposed through the catalyst of rebellious angelic beings, and then both are expelled and sentenced to the prison of the underworld (13.1–20.3). In the third stage, human and angelic rebellion are exposed for the final time when both are released from prison, but this time the sentence is irrevocable and everlasting (20.7-10, 13-15).

Metzger is right, insofar as he sees the sphere of the forces of rebellion successively restricted. But that restriction is not presented in Revelation under the dynamic of territorial struggle between two competing realms or kingdoms. Rather, it is presented as God's progressive exposure and punishment of rebellion within his own kingdom.

7. *Concluding Perspective: Questions That Need Answers*

If Fiorenza is now brought back into the discussion, it becomes understandable that she should have considered Metzger's model coherent with an a-temporal interpretation of the millennium. For on his 'progressive expansion' model, there does not seem to be any particular reason why God should delay to conquer the third sphere of the creation, the underworld. And, as Fiorenza has indeed proven, there is no obvious independent rationale for the millennium from the point of view of its application to the saints. She is thus perhaps well within her rights to suggest that the positing of a time span between the conquering of the second and third spheres might encourage interpretations on lines more literary and theological than eschatological and temporal.

But given the above criticism of Metzger, the whole question is raised afresh. A *prison term* (which is manifestly what the millennium signifies for Satan and the unresurrected dead) has meaning precisely in terms of time. Among the many questions which now arise are therefore these. Why should there be a lengthy but limited prison term for the rebellious (Rev. 20.1-10)? What relationship holds between this limited sentence and the second, radical sentence that befalls the released prisoners at the end of the millennium (20.7-15)?

If the rebellious deserved more punishment than a thousand years of imprisonment in the underworld, then why were they released; or, conversely, if the prisoners had paid the full penalty God had decreed, then why were they judged and punished again (20.11-15)? The most pressing question that remains concerns the relationship between Rev. 20.7-10 and 20.11-15. Can Metzger be right in his virtually unexplored suggestion that the two passages might merge into a single context?[1] If so, what effect has this on the overall meaning of the so-called 'last judgment', and on the millennium as a whole?

These, it may be argued, are the key issues in the question of an alternative interpretation of the millennium. It will nonetheless be prudent to postpone their treatment at this stage, because they can neither be framed nor resolved adequately apart from an exegesis that gives fresh consideration to the way Revelation is composed and interpreted. Such an exegesis will form the burden of the following chapters of this study.

---

1.   Cf. the quotation on p. 50, above.

Chapter 4

REVELATION 19.11-21:
THE PAROUSIA OF CHRIST AS KING AND JUDGE

1. *Methodological Strategies*

Before entering into the discussion of specific texts, it will be prudent to offer a brief introduction to the method to be employed in this and the following chapters. It was argued above that a valid and convincing interpretation of the millennium of Revelation 20 would have to incorporate an examination of that passage's literary ties with other parts of Revelation. Two different strategies will be employed to bring out such literary ties.

The first strategy will be to broaden what might be called the primary exegetical section of Rev. 20.1-10 to include the material from 19.11 to 21.8. This means that the core text of 20.1-10 will not be isolated by giving only passing attention to surrounding material; instead, it will have to be seen functioning organically in its native setting. Having said this, it would have been unworkable within the aims of this study to attempt a continuous close exegesis of such an extensive passage. As a result, close attention will be given only to those exegetical issues which impinge significantly on the interpretation of 19.11–21.8 as a whole. To give a single example, the fact that Christ 'has a name written on him which no one knows except himself' (19.12; cf. 2.17) will be left undiscussed, not because it is unimportant or uninteresting, but because discussion of it would distract from the presentation of the main thrust of the larger passage.

Furthermore, for the sake of convenience, treatment of this larger section will be divided into chapters dealing with the following subsections: the Parousia (Rev. 19.11-21), the Imprisonment of Satan (20.1-3), the Resurrection and Reign of the Martyrs (20.4-6), the Final Attack (20.7-10), the Final Judgment (20.11-15), and the New Creation and the New Jerusalem (21.1-8). The organic relationship among these subsections will be given full force by carrying over the exegetical results from each subsection into the following ones. Thus, for example, conclusions from Rev. 19.11-21 will help form the foundation for interpreting 20.1-10; likewise, cumulative results from 19.11–20.10 will help form the foundation for the exegesis of 20.11-15, and so on. In this way, the millennium will have to make sense not only in terms of internal consistency within the passage 20.1-10, but also in terms of a generous portion of immediate context on either side.

As the introduction will have made clear already, however, this conventional sort of 'putting in context' is not all that will be required. Revelation is a book in which the question of context is never addressed adequately by reference to a passage's relationship with the immediately surrounding material. And so a second methodological strategy becomes necessary. Because of the unique way in which Revelation employs pre-announcements, promises, cross-references and multiple representations of the same events, establishing the context for each of the four sections just mentioned will involve both selecting the key elements or themes of the passage, and tracing forward through the text from the beginning of Revelation, and up to the passage being considered, the literary preparation that has been made for each key element or theme. This will establish as far as possible (from the reader's point of view) the context of a given element as it appears in the passage.

Where relevant, this process will be extended to the end of Revelation as illustration or confirmation of a given pattern or theme. However, passages which *follow* a given section will not normally be appealed to directly in exegeting that section. The reasoning behind this restriction is that it forces one to begin by interpreting sections on the basis of the information that would have been available to a consecutive reader (hearer).[1] Subsequent material may indeed be intended to force the reader to change his or her understanding of a passage in many cases. But it is obviously wiser (where possible) to discuss a

---

1.   Revelation was composed with a view to being 'consumed' as a text by being read aloud (cf. Rev. 1.3). That its author intended it to be studied carefully and in detail is also beyond serious doubt. As A. Farrer states, 'St John even studies to inlay the plainer outline of his vision with riddles and mysteries, so that his book may be an inexhaustible mine of truth to those who ponder it' (*A Rebirth of Images* [Westminster: Dacre Press, 1949], pp. 21-22).

passage's alleged need for re-interpretation in the context of discussing the subsequent passage that requires such re-interpretation, rather than in the context of one's exegesis of the first passage. Thus the reader *of the exegetical argument* is invited to evaluate its success in making sense of the text at each step. Exegetical sleight-of-hand by mixing levels of interpretation is discouraged.

Finally, some remarks must be made about the relevance of the OT in the interpretation of Revelation. If few other things are beyond question about the author of Revelation (who shall be referred to as 'John' because he so names himself in 1.1), it is at least clear that he had an intimate knowledge of the OT. Few would want to dispute Sweet's remark that John

> had an astonishing grasp of the Jewish Scriptures, which he used with
> creative freedom. He never quotes a passage verbatim, but paraphrases,
> alludes and weaves together motifs in such a way that to follow up each
> allusion usually brings out further dimensions of meaning.[1]

Such comments are difficult to criticize in the case of a book whose OT reminiscences, references and allusions are sometimes said to outnumber its verses.[2] The OT will often be invoked to supply significant interpretative context for a passage in Revelation. But as in the case of passages subsequent to a given text in Revelation, so in the case of the OT. Given the fact that a reference to an OT passage is placed so as to affect or supplement the reader's understanding of what is being read, the following questions must be asked in this order. How does the text read on its own; in other words, how does it read without recourse to an OT context or contexts? and in what way might a reader's awareness of an OT reference affect his or her interpretation of the passage?

Without arguing for the point, it will be assumed as a likelihood that John composed Revelation in the anticipation that his readers would have a wide range of levels of familiarity with the OT. His awareness that those who had relatively little familiarity would have to interpret the text largely on its own is implicit in this assumption. A

---

1. Sweet, *Revelation*, p. 40.

2. For example, 'There are more than 500 allusions to the Old Testament in Revelation. Out of 404 verses in the book, 278 contain one or more references to Old Testament texts' (M.D. Ezell, *Revelations on Revelation: New Sounds from Old Symbols* [Waco, TX: Word Books, 1977], p. 20).

related split between a non-OT assisted and an OT assisted reading would develop in any case if, as is common in Revelation, an allusion or reference were relatively obscure. In such instances, the reader might only be expected to confirm, supplement or change an interpretation upon encountering an OT reference later on its own. Such is probably the sort of process Sweet is referring to in the above quotation.

To sum up, the procedure will be to examine six sections: 19.11-21, 20.1-3, 20.4-6, 20.7-10, 20.11-15 and 21.1-8. In each section, key exegetical issues will be addressed and solutions proposed on the following basis: by looking at the way in which central elements of the passage find their place in a contextual system that has built up from the very beginning of Revelation. Appeal will also frequently be made to the role of the OT or to subsequent passages in Revelation in forming a context for a passage, but such material will usually fill a confirmatory or illustrative role. The central aim of the method is to base the interpretation of each passage on its relationship with everything in the text that has paved the way for it.

2. *Revelation 19.11–21.8: Remarks on Formal Structure*

I begin with some observations about the place of Rev. 19.11–21.8 in the structural development of the book.

C.H. Giblin has demonstrated that Rev. 19.11–21.8 stands as the middle element in a larger A–B–A´ structure.[1] This structure begins with 17.1, and sets the harlot Babylon against the New Jerusalem in antithetical visions, each of which is mediated by an angelic guide (cf. 17.1-3; 21.9-10; 19.9-10; 22.6-9). If 19.11–21.8 can be seen in such a schema as functioning as the middle (B) section between the antithetical framing members A and A´, and if these latter members may be

---

1. 'Structural and Thematic Correlations in the Theology of Revelation 16–22', *Bib* 55 (1974), pp. 487-504. For other recent works touching on the place of chs. 19–22 in the larger structure and context of Revelation, cf. Fiorenza, 'Composition and Structure', pp. 344-66; F. Hahn, 'Zum Aufbau der Johannesoffenbarung', in *Kirche und Bibel* (Festschrift E. Schick; Paderborn: Ferdinand Schöningh, 1979), pp. 145-54; J. Lambrecht, 'A Structuration of Revelation 4.1–22.5', in J. Lambrecht (ed.), *L'Apocalypse johannique et l'apocalyptique dans le NT* (BETL, 43; Leuven: Leuven University Press, 1980), pp. 77-104; Shea, 'Parallel Literary Structure', pp. 37-54.

described respectively as 'The Judgment of the Harlot' and 'the Glorification of the Lamb's Bride',[1] then how is the central section to be described? And in what way does it form an appropriate middle element between the surrounding sections? An answer to these questions is implied by the announcement of the wedding theme in 19.5-8:

> And a voice came from the throne, saying, 'Give praise to our God, all you His bond-servants, you who fear Him, the small and the great'.
> And I heard, as it were, the voice of a great multitude and as the sound of many waters and as the sound of mighty peals of thunder, saying,
> 'Hallelujah! For the Lord God, the Almighty, reigns. Let us rejoice and be glad and give the glory to Him, for the marriage of the Lamb has come and His bride has made herself ready.'
> And it was given to her to clothe herself in fine linen, bright and clean; for the fine linen is the righteous acts of the saints.
> And he said to me, 'Write, "Blessed are those who are invited to the marriage supper of the Lamb"'.
> And he said to me, 'These are the true words of God'.

These words come immediately on the heels of the final announcement of Babylon's destruction in Rev. 19.1-4. The sense of the passage is that the final rejection and removal of the idolatrous 'prostitute' have made way for the final acceptance of the true and faithful bride. In a similar way, 19.11–21.8 can be seen as devoted to the theme of the final replacement of all that is old, false and rebellious, with all that is new, true and reconciled to God. Giblin's 'B' section (19.11–21.8) could thus appropriately be titled 'The Final Transition'.

Serving as framing elements within this section are the subsections Rev. 19.11-21 on the one hand, and 21.1-8 on the other. The first deals with the final ousting of rebellious humanity as a whole at the parousia (cf. 19.17-18),[2] and the second with the final appearance of the reconciled community of God under the figure of the New Jerusalem.

Revelation 20 may therefore be seen as the core of the inner 'B' section. As the central subsection, its role is to portray the eschatological events of resurrection and judgment as working out the rationale for God's final acceptance and rejection of people.

---

1. The terms are mine as opposed to Giblin's.
2. The question of the universality of this judgment will be dealt with below.

This divine election, or choosing, is a theme that stands as a strong undercurrent throughout the whole of Rev. 19.11–21.8. In the verses leading up to 19.11, the *announcement* of the choosing of a bride and of the invitation of wedding guests has introduced this idea (19.7-8). But within the section, it is the stately *picture* of the bride on her wedding day in 21.2, and the interpretation, 'he shall dwell among them, and they shall be his people[s]'[1] (21.3), which fill it out. The sense is that God is choosing a people which uniquely belongs to him, and to which he in turn uniquely belongs. The pictures of judgment in the core subsection 20.1-15 also embody the theme of God's choosing some for life and refusing others (20.4-6, 11-15), particularly since the 'book of life' (20.15) has already been linked twice before not only to the question of who worships the beast, but also to the idea of eternally predestined election of those who hold fast their allegiance to God (cf. 13.8; 17.8; 20.4).

Finally, some concluding comments may be made about the literary relationship between Rev. 19.11-21 and the larger body of 19.11–21.8. Attention has been drawn to a certain kind of antithetical balance between the outer subsections, 19.11-21 and 21.1-8: they embody respectively the rejection of the old and rebellious humanity, and the acceptance of a new and reconciled humanity. But there is another, and more parallel, balance to be observed as well between these two sections.

If it seems odd that Rev. 19.5-8 should announce the *wedding* theme only to have the appearance of the bride postponed until 21.1, then this oddity clears up when one recognizes in 19.11-21 the theme of the groom as victor-king. Attention has rightly been drawn[2] to the rapport between the first vision in 19.11-21 and Psalm 45, which has been entitled 'The Royal Wedding Psalm'.[3] The psalm not only celebrates the beauty of the king's bride and the joy of the occasion, but begins by praising the handsome appearance and valour of the king, and by blessing him with victory in battle:

> Thou art fairer than the sons of men;
> Grace is poured out upon Thy lips;

---

1. The text-critical question of whether *people* or *peoples* is to be read (λαός or λαοί) will be discussed below.

2. Cf. A. Farrer, *A Rebirth of Images*, pp. 170-71; Sweet, *Revelation*, p. 281.

3. A. Weiser, *The Psalms* (trans. H. Hartwell; OTL; London: SCM Press, 1962), p. 360.

Therefore God has blessed Thee forever.
Gird Thy sword on Thy thigh, O Mighty One,
In Thy splendor and Thy majesty!
And in Thy majesty ride on victoriously,
For the cause of truth and meekness and righteousness;
Let Thy right hand teach Thee awesome things.
Thy arrows are sharp;
The peoples fall under Thee;
Thy arrows are in the heart of the King's enemies (Ps. 45.2-5).

That John had this passage in mind as he wrote Revelation 19 seems clear, even though the ties are not to be found so much on the verbal level, as on the level of theme: the marriage of the warrior-king who rides forth triumphantly, and 'in righteousness judges and wages war' (19.11).

Thus it is appropriate to see Rev. 19.11-13 as paralleling 21.1-2 in the following sense: Jesus Christ stands on one side of Revelation 20 as the valiant groom who comes for his bride, and the New Jerusalem stands on the other as the bride who is prepared to meet him. Once again Revelation 20 stands in the middle: between the pictures of the rejected and the chosen, and between groom and bride. It would be fair, therefore, to say of that chapter that it answers the question of who will (and who will not) be invited to the final wedding of the Lamb and his people.

3. *Revelation 19.11-21: Main Elements and their Context*

Three broad themes find themselves intertwined in Revelation 19, but the background and development of each needs to be taken into account separately. The discussion of context for the section will thus be carried out under the following headings: a. Christ as Agent of God's Judgment; b. the Objects of Judgment, including the Parousia as Judgment on Babylon, and the Parousia as Judgment on Humanity as a Whole; and c. the Parousia as an Event of Eschatological Salvation.

a. *Christ as Agent of God's Judgment*
What context has been developed for the representation of Christ's parousia as judge in Rev. 19.11-21? In terms of imagery, one immediately notes that in 19.11-16 two images are brought forward from the 'inaugural vision' of ch. 1 (1.14-16), having been underlined once already as to their judgmental significance in the letters to the

churches at Pergamum and Thyatira (2.12, 16, 18, 23-27).[1] These images are the sharp sword seen coming out of Christ's mouth, and his eyes 'like a flame of fire'.

In Rev. 1.14-15 (cf. 2.18), as here in ch. 19, the fiery eyes of Christ are given prominence in the description of his appearance. This imagery is clearly to be interpreted as indicating the searching gaze of the omniscient Christ (cf. 2.23: 'I am He who searches the minds and hearts'[2]).

In Rev. 19.21 the beast's followers are slain by the sword that comes out of the mouth of Christ, even as in 2.16 Christ has warned those who follow the teaching of the Nicolaitans that, if they do not repent, 'I am coming to you quickly, and will make war against them with the sword of My mouth'.[3]

These two elements in the description of the returning Christ are to be linked with a key christological motif in Revelation. This motif develops Christ's role as the witness whose testimony before God is instrumental in convicting the guilty.[4]

In Revelation 5, which sets the stage for the 'judgments' of the seven seals, Christ receives, on the basis of his sacrificial death, the authority from God to reveal in the heavenly courtroom the contents of the seven-sealed document.[5] It is arguable that the concept of

1.   So, e.g., R.H. Preston and A.T. Hanson, *The Revelation of Saint John the Divine* (Torch Bible Commentaries; London: SCM Press, 1968 [1949]), p. 120.

2.   This reference is significant because it occurs at the end of the letter to Thyatira, and apparently interprets the imagery of the 'eyes like a flame of fire' which is to be found at the beginning of that letter.

3.   This reference follows the pattern by which the glorified Jesus refers in a letter to a feature of himself encountered in the inaugural vision. Cf. Rev. 2.2, 1.16; 2.8, 1.17-18; 2.12, 1.16; 2.18, 1.14-15; 3.1, 1.16; 3.7, 1.18.

4.   Already in ch. 1, for example, the whole of Revelation is called 'the testimony of Jesus Christ' (1.2), and in the epistolary address, he is called 'the faithful witness' (1.5). Correspondingly, each of the letters to the seven churches begins with the formula 'I know your deeds. . .', or something similar. In other words, the glorified Jesus is the omniscient witness of his people's behaviour, and, consequently, each of the letters is to be received as his authoritative testimony concerning the spiritual condition of the church being addressed. Support for this idea is to be found in the address of the Laodicean letter. In this, the strongest of the critical letters, Christ begins by introducing himself as 'The Amen, the faithful and true Witness' (3.14). Cf. B. Dehandschutter, 'The Meaning of Witness in the Apocalypse', in J. Lambrecht (ed.), *L'Apocalypse johannique*, pp. 287-88.

5.   Cf. Rev. 5 and Dan. 7.9-10, 13-14. I follow O. Roller ('Das Buch mit sieben

judgment functions no differently in this context than it does in the seven letters. In other words, from ch. 5 on in Revelation, judgment is still to be understood primarily in the sense of proving someone guilty by revealing the facts of the case, as opposed to the sense of punishing someone for a crime.

The first four seals (Rev. 6.1-8), for example, far from revealing divine chastisements, reveal the catalysts through which sinful and murderous humanity is brought to witness against itself. The four horsemen thus represent demonic agencies whose release into the arena of nations and societies tempts them to express their true nature.[1]

The central theme of Revelation 5–6, that judgment is God's sovereign activity of bringing into the open (through Christ) the true character and disposition of human beings, clearly stands as common ground between Revelation and the Fourth Gospel (cf. Jn 3.19; 9.39). The presence of this theme also tends to corroborate Roller's thesis that the seven-sealed scroll is intended as a certificate of debenture. Christ, the Son of Man and the Redeeming Lamb, has the unique right to make public the truth about mankind which is contained in the scroll. For as the Son of Man, he is a firsthand witness of humanity's debt of sin, and as the sacrificial Lamb, he has paid that debt in full on the cross (cf. Rev. 5.9-10).[2]

In the sixth seal of Rev. 6.12-17, Christ is revealed along with the Enthroned One in confrontation with 'the kings of the earth and the great men and the commanders and the rich and the strong and every

---

Siegeln', *ZNW* 26 [1937], pp. 98-113) in seeing the seven-sealed scroll as a *certificate of debenture*, i.e., a legal document that gives an accounting of one party's indebtedness to another. Other suggestions as to its identity are: (1) the OT: Christ has the right to reveal its judgments because he is the central subject of its prophecies (e.g. Prigent and Sweet, along with many of the earliest commentators on Revelation); (2) a testament: Christ inherits the kingdom of the world from the Father, but judgments (the unsealings) are the necessary precursors to his final acquisition of the inheritance (e.g. Zahn, Beasley-Murray); (3) a book of destiny revealing the predetermined end of the world (e.g. Barclay, Caird, Mounce).

1.   The idea that God uses (evil) spirits to accomplish this kind of judgment (i.e. the revelation of true motives) is an old one (cf. Job 2.2, 7; 2 Kgs 22.19-23, and the term *satan*, i.e., prosecutor). It is also to be found in the eschatology of 2 Thess. 2.8-12.

2.   For a closely related idea from the Pauline corpus, cf. Col. 2.13-14.

slave and free man'.[1] The fact that they attempt to hide themselves (6.15-17) recalls Gen. 3.7-10, and underlines the judicial character of the passage.[2] In the fifth seal, the souls of the slain had been heard crying before God, 'How long, O Lord, holy and true, wilt Thou refrain from judging and avenging our blood on those who dwell on the earth?' (Rev. 6.10). Now, in the sixth seal, the sense is that the prayer is being answered, and that all humanity is being 'caught red-handed'. Thus people are represented as having a sense of guilt so great that they prefer death to standing face-to-face with a just God and his Christ: ' . . . they said to the mountains and to the rocks, "Fall on us and hide us from the presence of Him who sits on the throne, and from the wrath of the Lamb, for the great day of their wrath has come, and who is able to stand?"' (Rev. 6.16-17).

After the sounding of the seventh trumpet, there is a further revelation of Christ's co-appearance with God in judgment:

> And the seventh angel sounded; and there arose loud voices in heaven, saying, 'The kingdom of this world has become the kingdom of our Lord, and of His Christ; and He will reign forever and ever'. And the twenty-four elders, who sit on their thrones before God, fell on their faces and worshipped God, saying, 'We give thanks, O Lord God, the Almighty, who art and who wast, because Thou has taken Thy great power and hast begun to reign. And the nations were enraged, and Thy wrath came, and the time came for the dead to be judged, and the time to give their reward to Thy bond-servants the prophets and to the saints and to those who fear Thy name, the small and the great, and to destroy those who destroy the earth' (11.15-18).

One notes here a striking (and certainly intentional) ambiguity of reference in the singular pronoun of the phrase 'he will reign',[3] which makes it clear that Christ is full co-regent with God (cf. Rev. 3.21).

The theme of Christ as king is extended in Revelation 12 (whose overall interpretation does not concern us here), where he is described

---

1.   This is, in fact, a list not far from being identical to that given to the birds of prey in Rev. 19.18, except that in the latter passage the 'kings of the earth' are left out in order to be mentioned immediately afterwards in 19.19.

2.   So, e.g., Mounce, *Revelation*, pp. 162-63.

3.   The christological significance of this special phrasing will be underlined by its reappearance in Rev. 22.3-5 (cf. 21.23). As Beasley-Murray comments on 22.3-5, 'God and the Lamb are viewed as a unity in so real a fashion that the singular pronoun alone is suitable to interpret them' (*Revelation*, p. 332). Cf. similarly Holtz, *Die Christologie der Apokalypse des Johannes*, pp. 202-203.

as 'a male child, who is to rule all the nations with a rod of iron' (v. 5). This recalls Ps. 2.8-9 for the second time in Revelation,[1] and underlines the fact that Christ's kingly role has within it his right to execute God's eschatological judgment.

This theme is also found in Rev. 17.14, where a final battle is predicted between the Lamb and the kings allied to the beast:

> These will wage war with the Lamb, and the Lamb will overcome them, because He is Lord of lords and King of kings, and those who are with Him are called and chosen and faithful.

All of this prepares for Rev. 19.11, in which Christ is 'called Faithful and True; and in righteousness He judges and wages war'. But in the context of ch. 19, it is the whole of humanity that comes into confrontation with Christ's convicting testimony.[2]

It is to be recalled that Christ 'wages war' (πολεμεῖ) precisely with the sword of his mouth (Rev. 2.16)—in other words, by revealing the deeds of his enemies for what they are. If such a revelation is to be pictured as fatal (19.21), this is arguably rooted in the OT idea that God deals with the murderous enemies of his people by causing them to destroy one another.[3] Revelation clearly uses this concept: Babylon is pictured as the ultimate enemy of God's people, and she is to be judged and destroyed by God. Yet her destruction comes about not through direct miraculous intervention, but through the agency of the beast himself, who shows his true character by betraying her to the kings from the east (17.16-17). John's descriptions of a subsequent gathering together of these kings, along with all the other rulers of the world, for a great 'war', hint at the same concept (cf. Rev. 14.19-20; 16.12-16). In other words, the murderousness of God's enemies is to be revealed and punished in the process of that murderousness being deflected away from his people and onto one another.[4] That this may

---

1. Cf. Rev. 2.26-27, which will be treated below.

2. As Caird says, 'here the witness judges because it is on his evidence that the legal victory turns' (*A Commentary on the Revelation of St John the Divine* [BNTC; London: A. & C. Black, 1966], p. 241).

3. E.g. Judg. 7.22; 2 Chron. 20.23-24.

4. Schlatter notes that Ps. 7.12 ('If a man does not repent, He will sharpen His sword') lies behind the sword of Christ's mouth which people will encounter unless they repent in 2.16 (*Alte Testament*, p. 35). What the psalmist expects to happen when God applies his sword is relevant (Ps. 7.14-16):

be the case is strengthened upon recognizing in Rev. 19.17-18 a reference to the battle of judgment pictured in Ezekiel 38–39.[1] There it is prophesied against Gog and his hosts who have come to attack Israel that '"I shall call for a sword against him on all My mountains", declares the Lord God'. As Ezek. 38.21 says, 'Every man's sword will be against his brother'.

b. *The Objects of Judgment*
From ch. 14 on in Revelation, the setting for Rev. 19.11-21 begins to be revealed in ever clearer images. Up to this point, the readers have received more or less veiled intimations of a final and decisive confrontation between God and his Christ on the one hand, and wicked humanity as a whole on the other. From now on, however, the outworking of this conflict is pictured more and more as having a realistic and historical shape. In other words, the reader is given more and more information that adds up to the prediction of relatively specific events, transpiring in a clear chronological order and in identifiable geographical locations. Specifically in terms of the parousia, there are two kinds of context, which may be pictured as large historical movements, and it will be wise to put these in relation to one another and to the parousia as judgment. The first is the destruction of Babylon, and the second (as usually termed) is 'the battle of Har-Magedon' (from Rev. 16.16).

The Parousia as Judgment on Babylon. The following statements can be made about the destruction of Babylon: it will be associated with the judgmental aspect of the parousia;[2] it will be by fire;[3] it will be at the hands of the treacherous beast (Babylon's own king[4]) and certain hostile

> He [the unrepentant] has dug a pit and hollowed it out,
> And has fallen into the hole which he made.
> His mischief will return upon his own head,
> And his violence will descend upon his own pate.

1. Cf. Ezek. 39.17-20; *1 En.* 100.1-13; *4 Ezra* 15.35.
2. Cf. Rev. 14.7-10; 16.17-19; 19.1-7.
3. Cf. Rev. 17.16; 18.8-9, 18; 19.3. A likely but not certain addition to this list may be found in Rev. 9.13-18.
4. Commentators usually assume this whether or not they hold the tempting contemporary-historical interpretation of the beast as a treacherous 'Nero redivivus' (e.g. R.H. Charles, *The Revelation of St John* [ICC; 2 vols.; New York: Charles Scribner's Sons, 1920], II, pp. 77-87, *pro*; Beasley-Murray, *Revelation*, pp. 256-

kings (Rev. 17.16); and the 'kings of the earth' (and presumably many of their subjects) will survive both to witness and regret Babylon's destruction at their hands.[1]

The great harlot Babylon experiences the judgment of the parousia as a conflagration at the hands of the beast (her traitor-king) and her enemies. And in Rev. 19.19, the kings of the earth, who are free at last from her dominance (and now regretting it), appear on the battlefield in common cause with the beast.[2] Tracing the previous intimations of this final alliance and its defeat by Christ will supply the next major element in the contextual background of Rev. 19.11-21.

The Parousia as Judgment on Humanity at Large. In Rev. 1.5, Christ is named 'the first-born of the dead, and the ruler [ἄρχων] of the kings of the earth' (cf. Ps. 89.27).

Already in Revelation 6 the reader is supplied with proof of that claim, when the kings of the earth head the list of ranks and classes of humankind who are terrified in the presence of the Enthroned One and the Lamb (cf. 6.15).

It is arguable that this passage falls into a pattern according to

---

58, *con*). Whereas in Rev. 17.18 the harlot is interpreted as 'the great city, which reigns over the kings of the earth', the beast himself can claim complete and worldwide political and economic control (13.3-4, 7; 11-17). Thus,

> The seven heads are seven mountains on which the woman sits, and they are seven kings; five have fallen, one is, the other has not yet come; and when he comes, he must remain a little while. And the beast which was and is not, is himself also an eighth, and is one of the seven, and he goes to destruction (17.9-11).

If the seven mountains are the harlot's own mountains, then the seven/eight kings (including the beast) are most naturally her own kings. This idea is strengthened by the fact that she is pictured riding on his back (17.3, 7). This seems to symbolize the relationship between the two. The fact that he is a wild 'beast', together with the absence of any mention of reins or the like, would seem to suggest that, as opposed to her directing him, he is carrying her wherever he wants to go, i.e., he is her leader.

1. Cf. Rev. 18.9, 11, 15, 17. Cf. also 9.20, which probably is a veiled reference to this.

2. One senses a situation full to the brim with irony here: have they learned nothing about the character of the beast they had *worshipped* (Rev. 13.7-8) from the fact that he was willing to betray his own people to fiery destruction? Later in this study attention will be drawn to the final irony of self-deception of which this is but the second-to-last example (cf. Rev. 20.7-10).

which things are revealed for the first time in a partially veiled way, and then are progressively brought into sharper focus as the narrative moves forward. In other words, this first representation of the parousia as judgment assures the readers that God and the Lamb will come, and that humanity's overdrawn account of hidden sin will be revealed. But it is only later in Revelation that one will be introduced to the more or less specific roles of the beast and the kings of the earth in this judgment.

Similarly, the aftermath of mass slaughter of the sixth trumpet (Rev. 9.13-21) sees revealed for the first time humanity's corporate attitude of stubborn unrepentance and self-deception, which is to build up steadily until it issues in the out-and-out confrontation of 19.19:

> And the rest of mankind, who were not killed by these plagues, did not repent of the works of their hands, so as not to worship demons, and the idols of gold and of silver and of brass and of stone and of wood, which can neither see nor hear nor walk; and they did not repent of their murders nor of their sorceries nor of their immorality nor of their thefts (Rev. 9.20-21).

When the seventh trumpet sounds, the 'twenty-four elders' celebrate the final inbreaking of the kingdom of God and of the Lamb in terms strongly reminiscent of Psalm 2. More importantly, the sentence 'and the nations were enraged' (Rev. 11.18) recalls the first verses of that Psalm.[1]

The point illustrated by the way in which Rev. 11.15-19 and 19.19 grow out of their OT background is this: the author of Revelation stands in the line of a strong prophetic tradition that looks to the eschatological judgment as a *battle*. The battle is a final conflict in which God and his messiah must prosecute their claim to sovereignty for the final time, and against a humanity adamant in its refusal to acknowledge the truth. The trumpets of Revelation, harsh as they may be, are in the very nature of their symbolism gracious danger signals that warn the human race to stop sinning before the final confrontation comes. Yet, even when the third part of humanity perishes (at the sixth trumpet), the rest do not turn from their ways. Thus even though all is veiled in generality in the sweeping 'pre-announcement'[2]

---

1. The next words in Rev. 11 are also evocative of the last verses of the Psalm (and 19.19 the more so). Caird (*Revelation*, p. 141) calls 11.15-19 'an exposition of Psalm ii, to which he [John] will return more than once in the following chapters'.

2. For this term, cf. Fiorenza, 'Composition', p. 359.

of 11.18 (the seventh trumpet), one is still hard-pressed to imagine anything short of a complete polarization between God, his Christ and his servants on the one hand, and the rest of humankind on the other. As in the sixth seal of ch. 6, there seems to be no hint of repentance, no hint of further patience on God's part, and no hint of any un-involved party.

In Revelation 13, when the beast comes on the scene, what formerly has remained a strong suggestion (i.e. that the end will see a situation of absolute polarity between those who will and will not own God and his Christ as their Sovereign) is now predicted in a more or less definite form:

> And it was given to him [the beast] to make war on the saints and to over-come them; and authority over every tribe and people and tongue and nation was given to him. And all who dwell on earth will worship him, every one whose name has not been written from the foundation of the world in the book of life of the Lamb who has been slain . . . And there was given to him [the second beast] to give breath to the image of the beast, that the image of the beast might even speak and cause as many as do not worship the image of the beast to be killed. And he causes all, the small and the great, and the rich and the poor, and the free men and the slaves, to be given a mark on their right hand, or on their forehead, and he provides that no one should be able to buy or to sell, except the one who has the mark. . . (Rev. 13.7-8, 15-17).

Even as in Revelation 6 John deliberately insisted on the fact that all classes of people, and indeed all people, were terrified at the appear-ance of the Enthroned One and the Lamb, and as in ch. 9 he stated that 'the rest of men' did not repent even at the unparalleled catastrophe of the sixth trumpet, so here in ch. 13 he paints the picture in equally universal terms. One need not be concerned here to ask the question of realism, of how John could have expected the appearance of an administration capable of enforcing emperor-worship on an absolutely universal scale. To think in that direction would be to ignore the intentional pattern of absolutes which John has taken care to establish. If his picture of the end idealizes the polarity between the servants of Christ and the servants of the beast to the maximum degree possible, it is nonetheless that idealized picture, and not some other which the narrative is challenging its readers to accept.

The claim being pressed in Revelation 13 is thus to be seen as giving focus to that which has previously been asserted: all those who do not give full allegiance to God through Christ will choose complete enmity

with God and his Christ, and indeed with his servants. This enmity is
so structured that there remain exactly two options, once the beast
comes on the historical scene: worship God and face death by martyrdom, or worship the beast and face God in judgment.

In Revelation 14, the second of these options is spelled out in stark
clarity by angels, the address of whose warnings has the now familiar
ring of universality:

> And I saw another angel[1] flying in mid-heaven, having an eternal gospel
> to preach to those who live on the earth, and to every nation and tribe and
> tongue and people; and he said with a loud voice, 'Fear God, and give
> Him glory, because the hour of His judgment has come; and worship Him
> who made the heaven and the earth and sea and springs of waters'.
>
> And another angel, a second one, followed, saying, 'Fallen, fallen is
> Babylon the Great. . .'
>
> And another angel, a third one, followed them, saying with a loud
> voice, 'If anyone worships the beast and his image, and receives a mark
> on his forehead or upon his hand, he also will drink of the wine of the
> wrath of God, which is mixed in full strength in the cup of His anger; and
> he will be tormented with fire and brimstone in the presence of the holy
> angels and in the presence of the Lamb. And the smoke of their torment
> goes up forever and ever; and they have no rest day and night, those who
> worship the beast and his image, and whoever receives the mark of his
> name' (Rev. 14.8-11).

Strikingly, 'Babylon the Great' is introduced here for the first time
with a pre-announcement of her destruction. More important, however, is the fact that the meaning of her horrible end (cf. Rev. 17.16;
19.3) is already being foreshadowed here in ch. 14: her end is only a
graphic example of what must befall everyone who worships the
beast.[2] Later on in ch. 14, there appear (in a passage noted for its
enigmatic character) the first hints of a geographical setting for the

---

1. 'Another angel' (ἄλλος ἄγγελος) seems to refer (*pace* A.P. van Schaik,
'ἄλλος ἄγγελος in Apk 14', in J. Lambrecht [ed.], *L'Apocalypse johannique*,
pp. 217-28) back to the eagle also seen flying in mid-heaven (Rev. 8.13). The
eagle's proclamation of three woes comes after the first four trumpets have issued in
judgments on the earth, sea, springs of waters, and heaven, respectively—precisely
those elements that are to be singled out for mention by the 'other' angel of 14.6-7.
Angelic beings are often represented as living creatures in Revelation (cf. below), so
picturing the former messenger as an angel in the form of an eagle is without
difficulty.

2. Cf., for example, Beasley-Murray, *Revelation*, p. 226.

great eschatological battle prophesied after the seventh trumpet (11.18):

> And another angel, the one who has power over fire, came out from the altar; and he called with a loud voice to him who had the sharp sickle, saying, 'Put in your sharp sickle, and gather the clusters from the vine of the earth, because her grapes are ripe'. And the angel swung his sickle to the earth, and gathered the clusters from the vine of the earth, and threw them into the great wine press of the wrath of God. And the wine press was trodden outside the city, and blood came out of the wine press, up to the horses' bridles, for a distance of two hundred miles (Rev. 14.18-20).

It seems more than probable that Jerusalem is to be identified as the city outside whose gates the wine press is trodden.[1]

In both the sixth seal and the seventh trumpet, reference is made to the wrath of God (Rev. 6.16; 11.18). In each case, it has been argued, the context is of universal judgment on the whole wicked human race. Now, in Revelation 15, reference is made for the third time to God's wrath: seven angels are given seven 'last plagues, because in them the wrath of God is finished' (15.1). The polarity between 'saved' and 'unsaved' is expressed here not by assurance of protection and salvation (as in ch. 7, following on the sixth seal), nor by reference to a positive 'reward' (as in 11.18, after the seventh trumpet), but by reference to the Exodus theme of the crossing of the Red Sea (15.2-4). This is interesting, because mention of the seven last 'plagues' (15.1) will already have recalled the theme of the plagues on Egypt.

In Revelation, playing the role of the Israelites safe on the far side of the Sea are 'those who had come off victorious from the beast and from his image, and from the number of his name' (Rev. 15.2). In a fascinating *double entendre*, they are said to be standing 'on the sea of glass' (cf. 4.6), which now appears to be 'mixed with fire'. The words 'standing on' (ἵστημι ἐπί) can mean that one stands on something,

---

1. Cf. Joel 3.9-17, whose context is the eschatological judgment/war outside Jerusalem, and whose imagery is precisely that of Revelation: 'Put in the sickle, for the harvest is ripe. Come tread, for the wine press is full. The vats overflow, for their wickedness is great' (Joel 3.13). An alternative approach is taken by Caird (*Revelation*, p. 192; followed hesitatingly by Sweet, *Revelation*, p. 232), who rather unconvincingly argues that the grape harvest symbolizes the martyrdom of the saints 'outside the city' (cf. Heb. 13.12-13). Confirmation of the view taken here comes in Rev. 19, when Jesus appears as the one who treads the winepress and clear reference is made to Ezek. 39 and a Palestinian context.

but in the context of the word 'sea' (θάλασσα), it (ordinarily) means standing on the shore. In this case the expression can simultaneously mean one thing in the symbolism of the heavenly sea as a kind of floor, and another in the symbolism of the crossing of the Red Sea. Just as the inhabitants of God's throne-room presumably stood before him on the glassy sea, now these victorious ones stand before God and sing 'the song of Moses. . . and the song of the Lamb' (15.3, 4).[1]

The effect of this mixed symbolism is to underline further the absoluteness of the polarity mentioned above: the servants of Christ are now standing victoriously in heaven, while the rest of humanity is left on earth, to drown in the fiery 'red sea' of God's wrath, as did the armies of Pharaoh. The theme of the eschatological battle clearly is being presented once again. Moreover, in the description of the seven last plagues, emphatic attention is given (as in Rev. 9.20-21) to the allied theme of total unrepentance (which is at home in the Exodus typology as well):

> they blasphemed God who has the power over these plagues; and they did not repent, so as to give Him glory (16.8);

> and they blasphemed the God of heaven because of their pains and their sores; and they did not repent of their deeds (16.11);

> and men blasphemed God because of the plague of the hail, because its plague was extremely severe (16.21).

Two key texts remain to be discussed in order to complete the tracing of contextual preparation for the eschatological battle of Revelation 19. The first follows the pouring out of the sixth bowl in 16.12:

> And the sixth angel poured his bowl upon the great river, the Euphrates; and its water was dried up, that the way might be prepared for the kings from the east. And I saw coming out of the mouth of the beast and out of the mouth of the false prophet, three unclean spirits like frogs; for they are spirits of demons, performing signs, which go out to the kings of the whole world, to gather them together for the war of the great day of God, the Almighty. (Behold, I am coming like a thief. Blessed is the one who stays awake and keeps his garments, lest he walk about naked and men see his shame.) And they gathered them together to the place which in Hebrew is called Har-Magedon (Rev. 16.12-14, 17).

---

1. Kraft suggests insightfully that the implied 'crossing of the Red Sea' is the martyrdom of the victors, and their crossing over into God's presence through death (*Offenbarung*, p. 201).

One notes that it is not only the 'kings of the East', but 'the kings of the whole earth' who are gathered into Palestine for the great eschatological battle.[1] This war is connected by Rev. 16.15 with the coming of Jesus, and the hint is that what will happen in this battle is an exposure of motives and deeds. Such an interpretation is not unexpected, and will be confirmed by the reappearance (from chs. 1 and 2) of the highly-charged symbol of the 'sword of Christ's mouth' in ch. 19.

The final text to bring into consideration is Rev. 17.12-14:

> And the ten horns which you saw are ten kings, who have not yet received a kingdom, but they receive authority as kings with the beast for one hour. These have one purpose and they give their power and authority to the beast. These will wage war against the Lamb, and the Lamb will overcome them, because He is Lord of lords and King of kings, and those who are with Him are called chosen and faithful.

Many commentators identify the ten kings with the 'kings from the east' in Rev. 16.12, and this seems by far the most likely interpretation, since (as Beasley-Murray points out) ch. 17 is offered as an explanation of the concluding vision of ch. 16 (cf. 16.19; 17.1).[2] These kings, after having destroyed Babylon with fire (17.16), will appear on the battlefield opposite Christ and his faithful and chosen ones. But the kings of the east will not be alone: all the kings, generals and armies of the world will be there (cf. 16.12-14; 19.15-19).

c. *The Parousia as an Event of Salvation*

In the foregoing sections, three kinds of contextual preparation for Revelation 19 have been traced: the context for the presentation of Christ as Judge, the context for the fall of Babylon and, finally, the context for the appearance of a universal alliance against Christ and those with him. A last important element of context has yet to be traced, namely, that of Christ's parousia as salvation for his people. Nearly all the passages that contain references to this theme have already been treated in the foregoing sections, but the focus has been on the judgmental side. The task which remains, therefore, is to

1. The place name 'Har-Magedon' (Mountain of Megiddo?) is impossible to interpret with any confidence, since it does not occur anywhere in the OT, or for that matter in extant ancient literature (cf. the summaries of positions in Mounce, *Revelation*, pp. 301-302; J. Jeremias, 'Har Magedon [Apc. 16.16]', *ZNW* 31 [1932], pp. 73-77).

2. *Revelation*, p. 258.

explore the extent to which Christian readers have been prepared, by hearing what has gone before, to imagine a participatory role for themselves in Rev. 19.11-21.

For example, are those seen following Christ on white horses angels, who are perhaps coming to rescue the saints (cf. Mt. 24.31), or are they the saints themselves, returning as Christ's armies?[1] In view of the frequent association of angels with God and Christ in Revelation (e.g. 14.10) on the one hand, and the strong tradition of angelic participation in the eschatological judgment of God on the other,[2] it would be foolhardy to attempt to prove that angels are not meant to be seen as involved here. But are the saints involved, and if so, how?

The answer—which has been developing since ch. 1 of Revelation —is that the saints *are* to be pictured here, and their role is to be co-witnesses with Christ in the judgment and conviction of the beast and his followers.[3] This becomes apparent as the theme of co-judgment and co-regency with Christ is developed as part of the idea of eschatological salvation. Because many of the texts to be treated here have already been quoted, summaries will be given of most passages.

Salvation as Participation with Christ in Judgment. In Revelation 2, Christ promises the overcomer a share in his authority to judge and subdue the nations. The language is graphic and violent:

---

1.   Commentators are fairly evenly divided on the issue. For the view that those on white horses are angels, cf. Beasley-Murray, *Revelation*, p. 281; for the view that they are saints, cf. Sweet, *Revelation*, p. 283. Many scholars find it likely that both are in mind: e.g. E. Lohmeyer, *Die Offenbarung des Johannes* (HNT, 16; Tübingen: Mohr, 2nd edn, 1953), p. 159: 'The hosts are obviously angels and martyrs'. The last may be the safest position. Given the fact that angelic beings are often represented as various living creatures in Revelation (cf. 4.6-8; 8.13; 9.7-10; 12.9; 16.13), angels may be being represented here by the horses which carry the saints (cf. Ps. 91.8-12; Mk 13.27 par.).

2.   E.g. *T. Levi* 3.3; *2 En.* 17; Mt. 25.31; 2 Thess. 1.7; *4 Ezra* 19.6.

3.   The reluctance of many commentators to see the saints in this battle is arguably based on a misunderstanding of the kind of warfare they wage. For example, Kraft says, 'The martyrs are exempt from every sort of fighting' (*Offenbarung*, p. 250). Has he realized that the witness of the martyrs is their one and only offensive weapon, that standing up for the truth with Christ is precisely what constitutes them as warriors and conquerors (e.g. Rev. 12.11)?

And he who overcomes, and he who keeps My deeds until the end, to him
I will give authority over the nations; and he shall rule[1] them with a rod of
iron, as the vessels of the potter are broken to pieces, just as I also have
received authority from My Father (Rev. 2.26-27).

In Revelation 3, Christ promises the overcomer the role of
co-regency with him (3.21):

He who overcomes, I will grant him to sit down with Me on My throne,
as I also overcame and sat down with My Father on His throne
(Rev. 3.21).

In Rev. 12.10-11, a pivotal passage for the question of Christians'
participation, Satan's fall to earth is announced, and the outcome of
the ensuing war between him and the Christian martyrs is expressed in
this way: 'they overcame him because of the blood of the Lamb and
because of the word of their testimony, and they did not love their life
even unto death'. The victory of the saints over Satan is, first, through
the atonement of Christ and, secondly, through their role as *witnesses*,
including the witness of their willingness to face death as the ultimate
expression of their allegiance to Jesus.

In Rev. 15.2, John sees in heaven those who 'had come off victorious from the beast' (who have presumably been martyred), and, in
17.14, those who are with Christ when he overcomes the ten kings
who oppose him are 'called chosen and faithful'. They are *chosen*
because they have been written 'from eternity in the book of life of
the Lamb who has been slain' (13.8; cf. 12.11), and they are *faithful*
because they have been 'faithful unto death' (2.10; cf. 12.11).

In Rev. 19.8, the bride of Christ is said to be clothed 'in fine linen,
bright and clean; for the fine linen is the righteous acts [sic] of the
saints'.[2] The meaning is that the saints display the credentials recog-

---

1. In Hebrew, the same consonants spell the verbs to *shepherd* and to *break*.
Thus John's use of the Greek verb ποιμαίνω (shepherd) here harks back to the
ironic sense of Ps. 2.9.

2. Most translations, such as the NASB quoted here, significantly obscure the
point of this verse: the word δικαιώματα normally means 'valid legal claims' or
'just decrees', and it is not attested in the Greek of the period to mean 'righteous acts'
in the sense of 'good deeds'. For example, cf. the entry under δικαίωμα in
J.H. Moulton and G. Milligan, *The Vocabulary of the Greek New Testament: Illustrated from the Papyri and Other Non-Literary Sources* (Grand Rapids: Eerdmans,
1974 [1930]), p. 163. BAGD erroneously cites under the meaning 'righteous deed'
(1) 3 Kgdms 3.28, which refers to Solomon's decree concerning the child of the

nized by God himself as those which make one worthy of acquittal in his court: faith in Christ's atonement, and a life lived in consistent profession of that faith, even to the point of death (cf. 3.4-5; 7.14).

Thus Rev. 19.8 will thematically (as well as verbally)[1] form the immediate context for the description of 19.14: 'And the armies which are in heaven, clothed in fine linen, white and clean, were following Him on white horses'. By having persevered in faithfulness to Christ, the saints have 'proven their case' before God, and now they are to exercise the right of bearing witness to the truth with Christ at his coming. It is exactly (and exclusively) in this sense that they will join him in 'waging war' against all the nations. Such is also the meaning of what was promised to them figuratively in 2.26.

The promise to the overcomers that they will be Christ's co-assessors at his coming is a theme that is appealed to and developed a number of times in Revelation, and this ongoing process of confirmation and extension serves to prepare the reader to recognize the theme's presence when it appears for the first time in imagery in ch. 19. But this judgmental role vis-à-vis the beast and his followers is clearly not the most emphasized aspect of the eschatological role which is offered to the saints. Not unexpectedly, the eschatological role which *is* most emphasized is that which the overcomers are to enter in relationship to God and Christ. This theme deserves a discussion of its own.

Salvation as Ultimate Communion with Christ and God. The appearance of Christ as the *groom* in Rev. 19.11-16 (see above) comes on

---

two prostitutes; (2) Bar. 2.19, in which Baruch declines to base his plea to God for mercy on the δικαιώματα of figures in the past, i.e., on claims they would have been able to make; (3) *Barn.* 1.2, and (4) Rev. 15.4, in both of which the subject is God's just decrees; and (5) Rom. 5.18, which may fairly be translated (my translation): 'So therefore, as one person's transgression resulted in conviction in everyone's case, so also through one person's valid claim (δικαίωμα), everyone received a life-saving acquittal'. This closely parallels the nearby Rom. 5.16, which also contains the term, and may be rendered thus: 'And the gift is not like [what happened] through one person having sinned, for the decision in the case of (lit. *from*) the one resulted in conviction, but the one favour in the case of (lit. *from*) many transgressions resulted in a [favourable] sentence (δικαίωμα)'. The central force of the term in both statements is clearly legal, not moral.

1.   Rev. 19.14 (fine linen, white and clean) closely echoes 19.8 (fine linen, bright and clean), and recalls 3.4-5, 18; 4.4; 6.11; 7.9, 14.

the heels of an announcement that the Lamb's wedding is at hand (19.7). This role obviously complements that of the *bride* and the *wedding guests*, both of whom are referred to for the first time in ch. 19. In other words, the wedding, the bride and the guests are figures of speech that contain the promise of a new, eschatological relationship (in one case as a community, and in another case as individuals) between the overcomers and the returning Christ. Thus the following survey will show how Revelation's readers have been given previous promises without appeal to that specific imagery, promises that will serve as the interpretative material by which they can, as it were, fill in the new figures with appropriate content.

In Rev. 1.5-6, Christ is praised as 'Him who loves us, and released us from our sins by His blood, and He has made us to be a kingdom, priests to His God and Father'. A relationship is being expressed here as already established between the hearers and Christ, and this relationship will be the unspoken basis of many promises for the future that come later in the text. The key aspects of the relationship may be summarized as being his loved ones, being citizens in his (and God's) kingdom, and being priests to God the Father.[1]

When John has seen a vision of the risen Jesus, he reports this reaction:

> And when I saw Him, I fell at His feet as a dead man.
>
> And He laid His right hand on me, saying, 'Do not be afraid; I am the first and the last, and the living One; and I was dead, and behold, I am alive forevermore, and I have the keys of death and of Hades' (Rev. 1.17-18).

For the readers, Christ's action here will create a symbol of his complete personal involvement with their hope of resurrection from death. It is the touch of Christ's hand which revives the 'corpse-like' John and prepares him to act as a scribe of the visions (cf. Dan. 10.8-10). Further promises and visions will fill out this hint of intimacy more and more as the account progresses.

In Rev. 2.7 Jesus gives the first eschatological promise to the over-

---

1. The idea that this passage affirms the present kingly status of the believers has already been refuted in the introduction. Fiorenza rightly says that the sense in which believers are now a kingdom is that they acknowledge and live under God's kingship in the present evil world. The consistent promise is that they will take up the kingship if they persevere in this commitment. See *Priester für Gott*, p. 334.

comer: 'To him who overcomes, I will grant to eat of the tree of life, which is in the Paradise of God'. On the face of it, this is a promise of everlasting life in God's presence. Everything else from now on will be seen to build on this basic promise.

In Rev. 2.10-11, Jesus promises, 'Be faithful until death, and I will give you the crown of life... He who overcomes shall not be hurt by the second death.' The promised eternal life is once again to be conferred on the overcomer by Jesus, under the figure of a victor's wreath (στέφανος). With the second part of the promise, the following equation becomes understandable: to be allowed to eat of the tree of life *equals* to receive the crown of life *equals* to be invulnerable to the 'second death'. Two things are noteworthy here: first, the reader is being trained from the start to expect the same reality to be re-expressed under different figures and to be viewed from different aspects.[1] Secondly, the reader is being required to pick up a piece of terminology, 'the second death', which will only much later (in 20.6, and finally 20.15; 21.8) be given an explicit context.[2]

All this points again to the fact that context in Revelation is broadened to the point that any part of the text, before or after a given passage, may need to be consulted in order to interpret it.

In Rev. 2.17, Jesus promises, 'To him who overcomes, to him I will give of the hidden manna, and I will give him a white stone, and a new name written on the stone which no one knows except he who receives it'. There is little doubt that the 'manna' promised here relates directly to the Johannine tradition that Jesus himself is the true manna.[3]

1.   On this characteristic of Revelation, cf. R. Bauckham, 'The *Figurae* of John of Patmos', in *Prophecy and Millenarianism* (Festschrift Marjorie Reeves; ed. A. Williams; Harlow, England: Longman, 1980), p. 113.

2.   This is not to claim that they would necessarily be unfamiliar with the term or its significance, but only that they would be forced to wait to see exactly how it would be developed in Revelation. On the rabbinic use of 'the second death', cf. Beasley-Murray, *Revelation*, p. 83.

3.   Zahn, *Offenbarung*, pp. 274-75. Cf. also P. Prigent, *L'Apocalypse de Saint Jean* (CNT, Deuxième Série, 14; Paris: Delachaux & Niestlé, 1981), p. 53, and Sweet, *Revelation*, p. 90, who recognize here a reference to the eucharist as a foretaste of the final communion that the saints will enjoy with Christ. For a recent study of many points of contact between John's Gospel and Revelation (including this one), cf. O. Böcher, 'Das Verhältnis der Apokalypse des Johannes zum Evangelium des Johannes', in J. Lambrecht (ed.), *L'Apocalypse johannique*, pp. 289-301.

> Truly, truly I say to you, it is My Father who gives you the true bread out
> of heaven. . . Your fathers ate the manna in the wilderness, and they died.
> I am the bread of life. This is the bread which comes down out of heaven,
> so that one may eat of it and not die. I am the living bread that came down
> out of heaven; if any one eats of this bread, he shall live forever (Jn 6.32,
> 48-51).

In Rev. 2.17, eternal life is being promised for the third time, but
this time it is through Jesus figuratively promising himself to the
overcomer. The hope of eternal life has thus been made inseparable
from the hope of coming into a special relationship with Jesus as the
source of that life.[1]

In Rev. 2.28, the above interpretation of the hidden manna is
strengthened significantly by the next promise: 'I will give him the
morning star'. In a similar case to that of the expression 'the second
death', the reader must wait patiently all the way up to the sixth-to-last
verse in Revelation to find out that Jesus himself is the one who can
say, 'I am the root and the offspring of David, the bright morning
star'. Now for the second (or third) time Jesus has figuratively
promised the overcomer the gift of himself. In Rev. 3.5 Jesus says,

> He who overcomes shall thus be clothed in white garments; and I will not
> erase his name from the book of life, and I will confess his name before
> My Father and before His angels.

Two brief comments may be made. First, the promise of white garments is yet one more way in which the readers are being prepared to
see themselves in Rev. 19.14 (cf. 3.3-5; 16.13-16). Secondly, having
one's name retained in the book of life is both to partake of eternal
life and to be exempted from the second death (cf. 20.12, 15).

In Rev. 3.12, Jesus promises,

> He who overcomes, I will make him a pillar in the temple of My God, and
> he will not go out from it any more; and I will write upon him the name of
> My God, and the name of the city of My God, the New Jerusalem, which
> comes down out of heaven from My God, and My new name.

To be a permanent pillar in the temple of God seems at first to be a
figure of speech suggesting a greater future dimension to the present
priestly role of the saints spoken of in Rev. 1.6. But later in Revelation it becomes clear that more is involved than the notion of priest-

---

1. The 'white stone' is difficult to interpret, but it is just conceivable that it also
in some way represents Jesus himself (cf. Zech. 3.8-9; Rev. 5.6; 2.16; 19.12b).

hood. The community of the saints actually becomes fully identified with the heavenly tabernacle of God (13.6): to overcome so as to be made part of God's temple is thus to be a member of the eschatological community of God, the intimacy of whose experience of his presence can only be suggested by the way in which God's glory used to fill his tabernacle/temple in times past.

In Rev. 3.21, Christ promises, 'He who overcomes, I will grant to him to sit down with Me on My throne, as I also overcame and sat down with My Father on His throne'. This can be seen as an eschatological extension (even as 3.12 extends the priestly idea) of the present reality of the saints' present citizenship in God's kingdom (1.6). It is at the same time a promise of intimate communion, which continues the invitation offered immediately before (3.20).

It should be observed before proceeding any further that these promises (which have come at the end of each of the letters to the seven churches) have reached out to all the readers, strongly encouraging them to be overcomers. There is no hint that status as an overcomer is some kind of special position among Christians, but quite the contrary: *not* to overcome is to lose one's eternal life and receive instead the opposite of the promises, that is, to be hurt by the second death, to be outside God's temple (cf. 22.15), and to be erased from the book of life. The promises contained in the seven letters are thus intended to spur the Christian readers on toward becoming overcomers at any cost, and toward seeing themselves throughout the text as those who stand to receive the blessings promised to the overcomer alone. This needs to be emphasized here for reasons which will only later become clear (see Chapter 6, §3 on Rev. 20.4-6, below).

In Rev. 5.9-10, a hymn is sung to the Lamb, which contains these words:

> Thou wast slain, and didst purchase for God with Thy blood men from every tribe and tongue and people and nation. And Thou hast made them to be a kingdom and priests to our God; and they will reign on the earth.

As in the relationship between Rev. 1.6 and 3.21, the present status is *citizenship*, and the future promise is *kingship*. And as in 1.5-6, the basis of both the present state and the promise is the redemption accomplished through Christ's shed blood.

In Revelation 7, John sees a 'great multitude, which no one could

count' (7.9), from every nation and group in the world—just as
universal a list as that of the beast's worshippers (cf. 13.8). These
worship God and the Lamb, dressed in white robes, and carrying
palm branches in their hands. The picture evokes a sense of victory
and vitality, as distinct from the passivity of the souls pictured in the
fifth seal, whom John sees in heaven. They are presented under the
figure of blood pooled in the channel around the base of the heavenly
altar of sacrifice. In 6.10, the souls had been heard to cry out,

> 'How long, O Lord, holy and true, wilt Thou refrain from judging and
> avenging our blood on those who dwell on the earth?' And there was
> given to each of them a white robe; and they were told that they should
> rest for a little while longer, until the number of their fellow servants and
> their brethren who were to be killed even as they had been, should be
> completed also (6.10-11).

It is clear in Rev. 7.9-12 that the waiting is over, the number of the
fellow martyrs is full,[1] and the Parousia has come.[2] Because those in
the great international multitude have 'washed their robes in the blood
of the Lamb' (7.14), in other words, because they have steadfastly
clung to the atonement of Christ, in spite of the pressure of the 'great
tribulation' (7.14), they receive great promises:

> For this reason they are before the throne of God; and they serve Him day
> and night in His temple; and He who sits on the throne shall spread His
> tabernacle over them. They shall hunger no more, neither thirst any more;
> neither shall the sun beat down on them, nor any heat; for the Lamb in the
> centre of the throne shall be their shepherd, and shall guide them to
> springs of the water of life; and God shall wipe every tear from their eyes
> (7.15-17).

Underlined here are the previously developed ideas of God and
Christ's full and intimate eschatological presence, the extension of the
relationship of priestly service, and the fullness of eternal life. As in

1.   Recent commentators (e.g. A. Feuillet, 'Les martyrs de l'humanité et
l'agneau égorgé: Une interprétation nouvelle de la prière des égorgés en Ap 6, 9-11',
NRT 99 [1977], pp. 189-207; Kraft, *Offenbarung*, pp. 119-20) have suggested per-
suasively that the martyrs of the fifth seal are those who have been killed for their
witness to the truth before the coming of Christ. (Cf. especially the conspicuous
absence of the stock phrase 'the testimony of Jesus' in Rev. 6.9.)
2.   Fuller reasons for seeing Rev. 7.9-17 as a representation of the Parousia will
be offered in Chapter 9, §2, below.

2.11 and 3.12, the promise is viewed under both positive and negative aspects.

In Revelation 11, after the sounding of the seventh trumpet, a great liturgy in heaven celebrates the Parousia as the coming of the kingdom of God and Christ (11.15-18; cf. 10.5-7). On the face of it, this passage affirms that the Parousia is the occasion of the great eschatological battle (see above), the time for the judgment of the dead, the time for their reward to be given to all God's people without exception, and a time of retribution upon those who have 'destroyed the earth'.

Of notable importance in the interpretation of this passage is the fact that the hope of reward for the faithful has previously in Revelation been tied both implicitly and explicitly to the Parousia (esp. Rev. 2.25-28; 3.3-5). It should therefore be assumed (barring the discovery of clear evidence to the contrary), that each of these eschatological events, and the rewarding in particular, belongs in the chronological context of the Parousia.[1]

In Revelation 12, with the expulsion of Satan and his armies from heaven, comes a further intimation of impending martyrdom for the saints:

> Now the salvation, and the power, and the kingdom of our God and the authority of His Christ have come, for the accuser of our brethren has been thrown down, who accuses them before our God day and night. And they overcame him because of the blood of the Lamb and because of the word of their testimony, and they did not love their life even unto death (12.10-11).

If the Christian readers of Revelation have been conscious up to this point of the possibility that becoming 'overcomers' might involve their facing martyrdom (cf. Rev. 2.10-11; 6.11; 7.14), that possibility will now seem all the more real. The atonement of Christ assures them of victory over Satan, but achieving that victory will involve maintaining their testimony to the point of death.

In Revelation 13, the final life-and-death stakes of the battle with Satan come to the surface in the polarity between the people of the Lamb and the people of the beast:

1.	This is more apparent when one notes that in the Greek the word καιρός (time) occurs only once (this is obscured by NASB and most translations), and is most naturally taken as tying together all of the clauses of Rev. 11.18.

> And it was given to him to make war with the saints and to overcome them [cf. 12.11]; and authority over every tribe and people and tongue and nation was given to him. And all who dwell on the earth will worship him, every one whose name has not been written from the foundation of the world in the book of life of the Lamb who has been slain. If anyone has ears to hear, let him hear (13.7-9).

It is as though the readers are being told: 'Be forewarned. There will soon be no more middle ground.' And in Rev. 13.15, the issues at last become entirely clear. To choose eternal life (and all the promises of God's presence associated with it) will mean refusing worship of the beast's image, which in turn will mean undergoing martyrdom. In facing the seemingly sure prospect of martyrdom, the readers are encouraged to hang on to their faith by appeal to the poetic justice that will be done to their murderers:

> He who leads into captivity, into captivity he goes. He who kills with the sword must himself be killed with the sword. Such is the endurance and the faith of the saints (Rev. 13.10).[1]

In Rev. 14.9-11, it is not just those who have physically lifted the sword against the saints, but all who worship the beast (and so become accessories to the saints' persecution), who are graphically assured of a violent end. Once again, this is put forward as an encouragement to perseverance:

> And the smoke of their torment goes up forever and ever; and they have no rest day and night, those who worship the beast and his image, and whoever receives the mark of his name. Here is the perseverance of the saints who keep the commandments of God and their faith in Jesus. And I heard a voice from heaven, saying, 'Write, "Blessed are the dead who die in the Lord from now on!"' 'Yes', says the Spirit, 'that they may rest from their labors, for their deeds follow with them' (14.12-13).

John seems to be saying, 'When you are tempted to capitulate to worship of the beast by the threat of violent death, keep in mind that you will not escape violent death by giving in—the most you will do is to put it off temporarily. In time to come, everyone will either face violent death for Jesus (followed by rest and blessedness), or face it in his presence at the Parousia (followed by torment). You must choose

---

1. This is R. Lattimore's translation in *The Four Gospels and Revelation* (New York: Farrar, Straus & Giroux, 1979), p. 272. NASB margin is equivalent.

one of the two, for there is no third option.'[1] The blessing of Rev. 14.13 promises the readers that beyond death lies rest from persecution, but also that their suffering will not be forgotten by God, for their deeds of perseverance under trial will go with them into his presence in heaven.

In Rev. 15.2 (as discussed above), John sees those who have been overcome by the beast (13.7), but who have actually 'come off victorious' through death. They are henceforth immune to the threats of their persecutors, who are now hopelessly trapped beneath the waters of the heavenly 'Red Sea'.[2] In their hands are 'harps of God', indicating that they are privileged to worship God in his heavenly temple like a choir of levitical singers.[3]

In Revelation 22,[4] Jesus will say,

> Behold, I am coming quickly, and My reward is with Me, to render to every man according to what he has done. I am the Alpha and the Omega, the first and the last, the beginning and the end. Blessed are those who wash their robes, that they may have the right to the tree of life, and may enter by the gates into the city (22.12-14).

As was clear in Rev. 11.17-18, the reward that Christ promises to those who obey him is to be given at his Parousia. When he comes, those who have 'washed their robes' (by trusting in his atoning death)

---

1.   This may be seen to go hand in hand with the conclusions reached above, which traced the theme of the judgment of humanity as a whole. Apart from the saints, humanity is seen as completely unified in rebelling against God.

2.   That no one else from now on will be able to cross the barrier of the 'sea of glass' (cf. Rev. 4.6; 15.2) into heaven and God's presence is stated with different imagery in 15.8: 'And the temple was filled with smoke from the glory of God and from His power; and no one was able to enter the temple until the seven plagues of the seven angels were finished'. The unrepentance with which the earth-dwellers respond to the bowls of ch. 16 (see above) both confirms and extends this idea by making it clear that, from now on, no one on earth *desires* to enter God's temple. This pointed development of the theme of unrepentance cuts across Caird's attempt to find notes of universal salvation in the words of 15.4-5 (*Revelation*, p. 199). The words of 15.4-5 affirm that all nations will submit to the sovereignty of God and admit the righteousness of God. But only the context will determine whether they are to be pictured as doing so willingly or under the constraint of having every refuge of self-deception removed from them (cf. Ps. 2.5-12, which John refers to more than once).

3.   Cf. Rev. 5.8; 14.2-3; 2 Chron. 5.11-14 (cf. Rev. 15.8).

4.   Discussion of this passage is included to illustrate and confirm concepts that the reader will already have been taught in the passages above.

will enter the 'city' (in context, the New Jerusalem), and will be given
the right to eat of the tree of eternal life (cf. 2.7).

To summarize, in the above paragraphs, the book of Revelation has
been seen to be creating an extensive context of both *promise* and *cost*
for its portrayal of the Parousia in 19.11-21. The promises amount to
various ways of picturing a blessed eternal life in which the saints
corporately enjoy the full presence of God and his Christ. The cost is
in one sense already paid, since those who receive the promises are
those who have 'washed their robes' by accepting their redemption
purchased by the blood of the Lamb (5.9). In equally strong terms,
however, the cost of inheriting the promises is the highest that can be
paid by a human being: maintaining one's testimony to that redemption to the point of being murdered. The promises have been firmly
linked with overcoming, and overcoming has in turn been firmly
linked with martyrdom under the beast. Assumed throughout, and
stated explicitly on occasion, is the idea that the Parousia constitutes
the occasion for the righting of all wrongs, and the giving of all
rewards, both positive and negative.

4. *Exegetical Conclusions for Revelation 19.11-21*

In the foregoing sections, four major strands of contextual background for Revelation 19 have been traced: Christ as Judge, the
Parousia as judgment on Babylon, the Parousia as judgment on
humanity as a whole, and the Parousia as an event of eschatological
salvation. In the discussion of this last strand, special attention was
given to the relationship between promises offered to the readers on
the one hand, and the cost of receiving them on the other. In the present section, the results of this study in context will be applied to key
exegetical questions of Rev. 19.11-21. This completed, it will remain
to apply the same method to the following sections in their turn, but
this will be done by building the interpretation of these subsequent
sections on the context already firmly established for them both in and
behind ch. 19.

a. *Identifying the Human Participants in Revelation 19.11-21*
To begin with, one may ask, who are the earthly participants in the
scene of 19.11-21? On the surface of it, 'the beast and the kings of the
earth and their armies' (Rev. 19.19) is the answer. But who follows

the beast? The investigation above revealed an insistence on John's part that (aside from the saints) all people on earth followed the beast. Coupled with this was his insistence that no one repented throughout the seven trumpets and the seven bowls, but all insisted on following their idols and blaspheming God. In the first revelation of Christ's Parousia in ch. 6, a pointedly universal list of ashamed (and by impli- cation condemned) humanity was given, ending with the inclusive cat- egories 'every slave and free man'. Now in 19.17-18, in immediate preparation for the revelation of the beast and his armies, the final inclusive statement is made:

> And I saw an angel standing in the sun; and he cried out with a loud voice, saying to all the birds which fly in mid-heaven, 'Come, assemble for the great supper of God; in order that you may eat the flesh of kings and the flesh of commanders and the flesh of mighty men and the flesh of horses and of those who sit on them and the flesh of *all men*, both free men and slaves, and small and great'.

Who participates in the battle against the returning Christ and his armies? The answer to this question is both clear and consistent with everything that has gone before: every single person remaining on earth participates. The reader must therefore conclude that all those belonging to Christ will be with him as he comes at the Parousia. But if any of them have achieved his presence by some other means than undergoing martyrdom, Revelation has not been willing to say clearly what that means is.

To be fair, however, there are in fact passages that may indicate exceptions to the totally pessimistic outcome of the 'great tribulation' (Rev. 7.14), in which absolutely all who refuse to worship the beast are killed. The first is the sealing of the 144,000 (7.1-9), which seems to imply the possibility of that group's continued presence well into the period during which plagues would be poured out on the human race. Similarly, the two witnesses of 11.1-13 at least manage to sur- vive to the very end of the beast's three-and-a-half year career (cf. 11.3; 13.5). Once again, in 12.14, the woman (hinting at a remnant of ethnic Israel?)[1] survives the beast's career, but nothing more is said of

---

1.   Rev. 12.14-17 seems to contain echoes of such OT passages as Hos. 2.14- 16; Exod. 19.4 (cf. the echo of the equation Egypt = Rahab, the chaos dragon who is kept from drowning the redeemed: Job 26.12-13; Ps. 89.10; Isa. 30.7; 51.9); Mic. 5.7; Isa. 40.2-3. Though significant in itself, the question of the woman's identity does not affect our argument, and so is not discussed.

her. Finally there is the mysterious figure of the wheat harvest in 14.14-16. Coming before the clearly judgmental picture of the vintage (14.17-20), it can conceivably be linked to Synoptic and Pauline traditions, and interpreted as the eschatological ingathering of the surviving saints which saves them from the judgment of the whole world.[1]

Given these considerations, my impression is that John's pessimism stems not from an expectation of absolutely universal martyrdom, but from his awareness of traditions indicating the survival of only a small group of saints (e.g. Obad. 17; Mk. 13.20 and parallels). Given this kind of background, it begins to look as though he is deliberately painting the bleakest picture possible. Why? His purpose is to strengthen his readers by preparing them for the worst. For in the coming conflict with the beast, false hopes of survival could well make one more vulnerable to the deadly temptation of giving up one's testimony. It is better, so John appears to be saying, to be resolved to face martyrdom and then to be spared, than to have one's hopes set on survival, and be cowed into silence, or worse.

Thus, although the matter of realism suggests itself in Revelation 19, there is no escaping the intent of the words: when Christ is revealed, the remaining inhabitants of the earth will be absolutely united in opposing him.

b. *The Fate of the Human Participants*
What will be the fate of earthly humanity which is met in judgment by Christ and his army? The relevant text is Rev. 19.20-21:

> And the beast was seized, and with him the false prophet. . . these two were thrown alive into the lake of fire which burns with brimstone. And the rest were killed with the sword which came from the mouth of Him who sat upon the horse, and all the birds were filled with their flesh.

The sense of these words is as plain as it is consistent with the pattern leading up to them: no one on earth survives the confrontation with the returning Christ.[2] Moreover, granted that the idea of such

1. Cf. Mt. 3.12 par. (common wheat imagery); 24.30-31 par.; 1 Thess. 4.15-17 (common imagery of clouds, angel); 2 Thess. 1.6-8. For this opinion, see e.g. Ford, *Revelation*, p. 250; Ladd, *Revelation*, pp. 199-200; Holtz, *Die Christologie der Apokalypse des Johannes*, p. 133.

2. To quote Fiorenza, 'As verses 17-18 and 21 above all imply, no one is left on earth after this judgment, but all humanity belongs to the dead' ('Die tausendjährige Herrschaft', p. 112).

universality is jarring, it nonetheless is one for which John will have had ample OT prophetic precedents. Isaiah prophesies that, on the day of the Lord, 'I will make mortal man scarcer than pure gold, and mankind than the gold of Ophir' (Isa. 13.12). Zephaniah is even more pointed: '"I will completely remove all things from the face of the earth...and I will cut off man from the face of the earth", declares the LORD' (Zeph. 1.2-3). Later Zephaniah repeats the same idea: 'For He will make a complete end, indeed a terrifying one, of all the inhabitants of the earth' (Zeph. 1.18).

c. *The Special Fate of the Beast and the False Prophet*
What is the difference between the fate of the beast (and his cohort the false prophet) and the rest of unrepentant humanity? This is a question that will only be given a full answer by bringing in extensive arguments regarding Revelation 20, but a start may be made. Of immediate note, for instance, is the fact that the beast and false prophet seem to receive a unique punishment (Rev. 19.20). They are cast alive into the 'lake of fire', whereas the 'rest' are simply 'slain' by Christ. Does this difference of description indicate a difference of fate, or does it simply dramatize the fate of the beast for effect?

On the surface, there does seem to be a fundamental difference of fate. For in Revelation, ordinary bodily death is pictured as issuing in one's taking up residence in Hades, the temporary abode of the dead, whereas the 'lake of fire' is described as that state into which those brought *out of* Hades (for judgment) are cast.[1] Thus the lake of fire is

---

1. Cf. (1) Rev. 1.18, where Christ's resurrection is connected with his having possession of 'the keys of death and Hades', which presumably means that he has the authority to decree who will and will not be resurrected from the state of physical death; (2) Rev. 2.10-11, where Christ predicts that some will experience the bodily death of martyrdom, but promises them that they will not be hurt by the 'second death', which will later be interpreted as the lake of fire (20.14); (3) Rev. 6.8, where Death goes out with the authority to 'kill with the sword', and Hades follows him, presumably to receive the spirits of those slain. Cf. also Rev. 11.7, where the beast is introduced for the first time with the statement that he 'comes up out of the abyss'. Later on, it is discovered that he had a 'fatal wound which was healed' (13.3, 12), and that he 'was and is not, and is about to come up out of the abyss and to go to destruction' (17.8). Regardless of whether some kind of coming back from the dead on the part of an individual person is being signified here (which does seem likely), these passages serve to give further testimony to the *conception* that one who is 'slain' goes into a state of confinement in the 'abyss'. Cf. Rom. 10.7, where Paul

called 'the second death' (Rev. 20.14), implying something subsequent to and qualitatively different from the bodily death that is the normal human experience. The fact that the beast is cast into the lake of fire will recall the fact that he 'comes up out of the abyss and goes to destruction', that he 'had a fatal wound which was healed', and that he 'was and is not and will come'. That is, because the beast has already come back from the realm of the dead,[1] he is seemingly being sent straight to his final perdition, as opposed to being consigned for a second time to the abyss.

The question of whether the 'false prophet' is committed immediately to the lake of fire along with the beast because of his prodigious wickedness, or perhaps because he himself has also come back from the realm of the dead, is left without an explicit answer.[2] Nonetheless, his 'coming up out of the earth' on his first appearance in Rev. 13.11 has visually suggested the idea of rising from the grave. It has also contained a potential allusion to the idea of coming up from the realm of the dead, since the same phrase occurs in 1 Sam. 28.13, where the medium sees the departed Samuel in a vision as 'a divine being coming up from the earth'. If this allusion is intentional, then he and the beast may be intended to correspond antithetically to the two witnesses of Revelation 11 (Moses and Elijah sent to earth from the realm of the righteous departed?).[3]

As for the 'rest' of the beast's followers and their fate, Farrer's comment describes a scenario which is entirely plausible, given what the readers are already in a position to know:

> The rest of the host being killed, that is, parted from their bodies, lead a shivering half-life until resurrection shall restore them to bodily being, divine judgment, and everlasting fire (xx. 12-15).[4]

uses the word ἄβυσσος in reference to the realm of the dead.

1. One notes that the sea is one of the realms of the dead mentioned in Rev. 20.13, and that the beast's 'coming up out of the sea' (13.1) quite intentionally parallels his 'coming up out of the abyss' (11.7; 13.11; 17.8).

2. The first of these options has in its favour the parallel with Num. 16.28-33, where the false prophets Dathan and Abiram go down alive into Sheol, rather than 'suffering the fate of all men' (Num. 16.29).

3. Cf. the argument for this identification in Charles, *Revelation*, I, pp. 281-82. Beasley-Murray has helpful remarks on the tradition that Moses and Elijah would be 'sent back' in the end times, although he thinks that the tradition has been remodelled by John to refer to the church (*Revelation*, pp. 183-84).

4. *Revelation*, p. 201. Ford (*Revelation*, p. 325) notices the similarity between

5. *Concluding Methodological Remarks*

At this point, an appropriate observation must be made before proceeding: previously in Revelation, the readers have been given more and more information enabling them to see that the population of the earth will follow the beast right up to a final confrontation with Christ at his Parousia. In the absence of any previous overt sign in the text that those following the beast in Rev. 19.19 are (or include) people who have died and are now appearing for judgment in a resurrected state, the assumption must for the moment be that, when Christ slays them in v. 21, they are being consigned to Hades to await resurrection and judgment.[1]

It is also to be recognized that reading further (e.g. to the end of Rev. 20) may conceivably force the *abandonment* of this assumption. For example, in *retrospect* Rev. 19.11-21 could appear to be a veiled picture of what is finally interpretable as a resurrection and judgment occurring at the Parousia.[2] But if this is to be argued convincingly, it will have to be shown exactly when, how and why it becomes impossible to keep reading through ch. 20 without beginning to alter one's assumptions about ch. 19, rather than showing that it is possible to interpret the imagery of both chapters more or less consistently by taking as foundational the assumption (brought into the text from elsewhere) that a general resurrection must attend the Parousia. It is only the former strategy that treats the text as literature to be read, as opposed to a specimen to be examined for the purpose of proving or disproving points in NT theology.

---

this picture and Dan. 7.12, in which the 'beast' is burned alive with fire, but the rest of the 'beasts' are spared for a certain interval, after having been stripped of their sovereignty.

1.   John *could have* said that the beast and his armies were consigned together to the lake of fire (cf. *4 Ezra* 13.9-11; *Asc. Isa.* 4), and it is arguable that his decision not to do so is significant. On the consistent difference between *Hades* and *Gehenna* (to which *the lake of fire* corresponds) in NT usage, cf. J. Jeremias, 'γέεννα', *TDNT*, I, pp. 657-58.

2.   I anticipate here the possibility that conclusions reached in following sections (about resurrection and judgment as battle in Rev. 20.7-10) will find welcome application within models that see in Rev. 19.11-21 and 20.7-10 separate pictures of what is finally to be understood as a single judgment event (cf. esp. the views of Schnackenburg and Fiorenza).

Chapter 5

REVELATION 20.1-3: SATAN'S IMPRISONMENT

In the foregoing discussion of Rev. 19.11-21, it seemed advisable to gather together all the major strands of context for the section before raising any particular exegetical question. This point of organization was especially recommended by the fact that a large volume of previous material in Revelation had to be consulted in order to solve a small number of interpretative issues. By reserving the combined exegetical remarks on 19.11-21 for the conclusion of the chapter, the relatively concise exegetical discussion was kept from being fragmented and scattered among discussions of sometimes disparate background materials. In contrast to this, however, common sense seems to indicate that the flow of the argument hereafter would often be obscured, rather than simplified, by attempting to establish *all* the background for a given section before trying to gain any exegetical ground. Consequently, maintaining an understandable presentation will often require that the interpretation of each new element in the text be built upon a reasonably secure interpretation of those elements that immediately precede it. From this point on, therefore, contextual backgrounds will usually be sought for new elements as they appear in the text, and the results of such background inquiries will be drawn into an ongoing exegetical discussion. This is not so much a substantial change of methodology as it is a change of *pace*.[1]

1. Revelation 20.1-3: Context for the Imprisonment of Satan

Since the opening verses of Revelation 20 concern the fate of Satan, it will be necessary to trace the background information concerning his

---

1.   The goal is not to gather together all the strands of hermeneutical information necessary to interpret a passage before beginning to exegete it, but rather to establish as far as possible from the reader's point of view the context of each element *as it appears in the passage.*

career which the readers will be expected to have in their possession as they encounter him at this point in the narrative. In other words, Satan's reappearance in Rev. 20.1 will be seen to grow out of a contextual system analogous to those systems which have been uncovered in the sections above for other persons and groups.

One may begin in Revelation 12,[1] where John saw Satan and his fellow rebellious angels being expelled from heaven after a battle with Michael and his colleagues:

> And the great dragon was thrown down, the serpent of old who is called the devil and Satan, who deceives the whole world; he was thrown down to earth, and his angels were thrown down with him (12.9).

In the next verses, woe is pronounced upon the earth, because the devil knows that his time is short, and he is angry. The first thing he does is to try to persecute the 'woman who gave birth to the male child', who for the present purposes may be taken as the ideal mother, Zion (Rev. 12.12-13).[2] Frustrated in his attempt to persecute the woman, he goes off 'to make war with the rest of her offspring, who keep the commandments of God and hold the testimony of Jesus', in other words, Christians (12.14-17). He is next seen in the company of the 'beast', who becomes his agent for the persecution of Christians (13.1-7).

Comparing the fact that the woman is protected from Satan for 'time, times and half a time', that is, three and one half equal lengths of time (Rev. 12.14), with the fact that the beast's career is to last for 'forty-two months', that is, three and one half years, one strongly suspects that Satan's association with the beast begins more or less immediately upon his expulsion from heaven to earth, and that it runs concurrently with that period during which the beast is 'given authority to act' (13.5).

In other words, excepting the time of his first abortive attempt to persecute the woman, Satan's 'little time' (Rev. 12.12) seems to coincide with the time of his association with the beast. For it is expressly

---

1.   The following references may be included for completeness, but are not relevant to the present discussion: Rev. 2.9-10, 13, 24; 3.9.

2.   For a careful discussion of issues of interpretation (especially those regarding comparative religions), cf. Beasley-Murray, *Revelation*, pp. 191-206. The question of the woman's identity is not crucial to the present study.

because of the protection of the woman, and by implication for its duration, that the dragon applies his alternative strategy of persecuting Christians (12.16-17). Therefore the reader will expect the end of the beast's career to signal some kind of apprehension and judgment of Satan.

During the following chapters, one recognizes a kind of devilish *troika* made up of Satan, the beast and a second beast. The second beast, which 'speaks like a dragon' (13.11), is finally named the 'false prophet' (16.13; 19.20; 20.10), presumably because he is the mouthpiece of Satan the dragon, and wields the power of Satan to impress people to worship the beast.[1] The express outcome of this treble partnership is a universal persecution of the saints, issuing in the successful extermination of all who will not worship the beast.[2]

In Rev. 16.13-14, 16, Satan is seen acting as part of this trio to gather all the kings of the world to the battle of Har-Magedon:

> And I saw coming out of the mouth of the dragon and out of the mouth of the beast and out of the mouth of the false prophet, three unclean spirits like frogs; for they are spirits of demons, performing signs, which go out to the kings of the whole world, to gather them together for the war of the great day of God, the Almighty. . . And they gathered them together to the place which in Hebrew is called Har-Magedon.

From this passage, the readers will have known enough to have placed Satan as a behind-the-scenes participant in the battle just described in Rev. 19.19-21. Thus, when the criminal careers of the beast and false prophet are brought to an end with their 'apprehension' (πιάζω) in 19.20, the question arises as to what will happen to Satan their chief, since his career on earth, during which 'his time was short', seems to be at an end as well: his two associates are burning in the lake of fire, and all of his followers are in Hades.

This is the context for Rev. 20.1-3:

> And I saw an angel coming down out of heaven, having the key of the abyss and a great chain in his hand. And he laid hold of the dragon, the serpent of old, who is the devil and Satan, and bound him for a thousand years, and threw him into the abyss, and shut it and sealed it over him, so that he should not deceive the nations any longer, until the thousand years are completed; after these things he must be released for a short time.

---

1. Cf. Rev. 13.11-18; 16.13. For a history of interpretation of this trio, see O. Böcher, 'Die teuflische Trinität', in *idem, Kirche in Zeit und Endzeit*, pp. 90-96.
2. Cf. esp. Rev. 13.2, 7, 11-12, 15.

2. *Revelation 20.1-3: Exegesis of the Imprisonment of Satan*

As was argued in Chapter 2, there is no question either of Satan's binding in respect to one sort of deception alone, or of this being a picture of some sort of forced military retreat on his part. The imagery is obvious, direct and decisive. Satan is taken prisoner, chained with a great chain[1] and confined to the prison of the abyss. Therewith, the entrance is shut, presumably locked,[2] and sealed with a seal so that no one may open it. His *binding* (with the chain) is for a thousand years, so the picture of the chain evokes not only the image of binding in the process of capture and transport to prison, but also that of Satan's being bound in irons inside the prison. Satan has been reduced to a state of complete impotence, and has no power whatever to deceive the nations even *within* the prison, if that were possible.

But what is the point of his thousand-year imprisonment? Why has he not been thrown into the lake of fire along with his partners? Further, is one not forced to conclude that Satan has been cast into the underworld along with all the slain 'kings of the earth and their armies' who have been his human followers? Such a conception is perhaps far less strange than would at first appear. For although in Revelation the abyss is usually the prison of demonic spirits,[3] and Hades the realm of the human dead,[4] yet in Revelation, Hades, no less than the abyss, is conceived of as an underworld *prison*,[5] and the beast, who is clearly identified as a man, is always referred to as coming from the abyss.[6] Given these observations, the most that can

1.   Presumably around the neck(s!), since he is pictured as a dragon. Commentators sometimes mention the idea of 'manacles' or 'handcuffs', but this is misleading, since the plural would be expected, and Rev. 20.1 has the singular (ἅλυσις).

2.   Cf. the *key* which John sees in the hand of the angelic jailor (Rev. 20.1). For the idea that the abyss is locked with a key and/or sealed, cf. *Pr. Man.* 3–4; *Odes* 24.7.

3.   Cf. Rev. 9.2, 11; 20.1; cf. Lk. 8.31.

4.   Cf. Rev. 1.18, where death and Hades are equated; 6.8, in which Hades follows behind Death to gather in his victims; 20.13-14, where Death and Hades give up those consigned to them at the resurrection. In popular thought, Hades was often imagined to be a place of fire (cf. Lk. 16.24), and although this idea is not explicit in Revelation in the case of Hades, it is in the case of the abyss (9.2).

5.   Cf. Rev. 1.18 (where Christ has the *keys* of death and Hades) with 9.1-2; 20.3.

6.   Cf. Rev. 11.7; 13.3, 12, 14, 18; 17.8, 11, from which one may conclude that the beast is a human being who has been killed, and who subsequently comes

be done to distinguish Hades from the abyss is to imagine that they form separate compartments of a larger underworld prison. But Revelation gives no distinct indication that even this differentiation is to be made.

All of this begins to make good sense when it is seen against the background of certain oracles of Isaiah (John's favourite prophet).[1] Isaiah describes the day of the Lord in the following way:

> The earth reels to and fro like a drunkard,
> And it totters like a shack,
> For its transgression is heavy upon it,
> And it will fall, never to rise again.
> So it will happen in that day,
> That the LORD will punish the host of heaven on high,
> And the kings of the earth, on the earth.
> And they will be gathered together
> Like prisoners in the dungeon [literally: the pit];[2]
> And will be confined in prison;
> And after many days they will be punished.
> Then the moon will be abashed and the sun ashamed,
> For the LORD of hosts will reign on Mount Zion and in Jerusalem,
> And His glory will be before His elders (Isa. 24.20-23).

The following case may be made for the supposition that John had exactly this passage in mind when he wrote Rev. 20.1-3.

First, as Caird has astutely shown,[3] reference has already been made to Isa. 24.21-23 in the description of Rev. 6.12-17, for in 6.13 John watched while 'the sun became as black as sackcloth made of hair, and the whole moon became like blood; and the stars of the sky fell to the earth'. Thereafter, he saw all people (headed by 'the kings of the earth') hiding from God's wrath. Since the expression 'hosts of heaven' in Isaiah is figurative for the sun, moon and (especially) the stars,[4] so in each passage the heavenly host and the 'kings of the earth' are being punished.[5]

---

back from the abyss and is restored to life. Cf. also Rom. 10.7, where ἄβυσσος stands for Hades.

1. Cf. for example Swete, *Apocalypse*, pp. cxlvi-cxlviii.
2. This term frequently refers to the realm of the dead, e.g., Pss. 28.1; 30.4; 88.5; Isa. 14.15; 38.18 (Hebrew בור). LXX here translates בור with δεσμωτήριον.
3. *Revelation*, pp. 89-90.
4. Cf. Isa. 34.4 (*bis*); 40.26; 45.12; similarly, e.g., Deut. 4.19; 17.3.
5. Cf. Caird, *Revelation*, p. 89: 'Israel came to believe that every nation had

Secondly, in Rev. 12.4, 7-9, Satan is pictured as a heavenly dragon who sweeps one third of the stars to earth. This is interpreted to mean that he is the leader of a rebellious host of angels who are banished from heaven. In some sense, therefore, already in ch. 12 God has punished the 'hosts of the height in the height' (Isa. 24.21).[1] There is correspondingly but a short while (ὀλίγον καιρόν) (Rev. 12.12) before the kings of the earth are punished on the earth (19.19-21), and all are gathered together into the pit.

Thirdly, the most decisive consideration is that in Isa. 24.1–27.1, one finds the following pattern: (1) Day of the LORD, punishment and imprisonment of heavenly and human powers (24.1-22); (2) Reign of God, messianic banquet (24.23; 25.6-9); (3) Resurrection for those in distress, but no resurrection for the wicked (26.14-19);[2] (4) Punishment of the inhabitants of the earth, which has apparently been predicted as fire sent from the LORD (26.20-21; cf. 26.11); (5) Intimation that the fiery destruction of enemies is because they are attacking Israel or Jerusalem (cf. 27.2-4 [5.1-7]; 26.1, 11-12); (6) Punishment, in other words, killing, of 'Leviathan the fleeing serpent' (27.1).

This tallies point by point with Rev. 19.19–20.10: (1) Parousia, punishment and imprisonment of rebellious human beings and Satan (19.19–20.3); (2) Reign of God, Christ and of the saints, previously referred to under the figure of the messianic banquet (20.4-6; cf. 19.9); (3) Resurrection for the saints persecuted under the beast, but no resurrection for 'the rest of the dead' (20.4-6); (4) Destruction of 'Gog and Magog' by fire from heaven (20.9); (5) Fiery end of Gog and Magog, because they have come to attack the 'camp of the saints and the beloved city' (20.7-9); (6) Final slaying by destruction in the lake of fire for Satan, who has been pictured as Leviathan in ch. 12,[3] and called 'the serpent of old' in 20.2 (20.10).[4]

been set by God under the authority of an angel ruler or guardian [e.g. Dan. 10.13], so that national punishment must involve the nation's angel as well as the nation's king'. For helpful notes on the stars as the hosts of heaven, see Böcher, 'Jüdischer Sternglaube im Neuen Testament', in *idem, Kirche in Zeit und Endzeit*, pp. 13-14.

1. NASB margin, literal translation.

2. The question of whether or not this passage 'originally' denoted the concept of bodily resurrection is not a matter of concern here: the relevant point is that John interpreted it that way.

3. So virtually all commentators.

4. Among many others, the following commentators agree in seeing Isa. 24.21-23 behind Rev. 19.19–20.3: Beasley-Murray; Charles; Ford; Kraft; M. Kiddle, with

On the basis of these arguments, it would appear reasonably certain that Isa. 24.21-22 lies behind Rev. 19.19–20.3. If these verses in Revelation create a reasonably plausible and coherent scenario as they stand on their own, they do so all the more when seen in the context of their OT background. By the time the readers have reached 20.3, they will be in a position to know that Satan and all the unrepentant are gone from the earth (presumably all demonic spirits as well, although this idea must be supplied by reading Isaiah from Revelation's point of view). They are trapped in the nether world for 'many days' (Isa. 24.22), together awaiting the divine summons for judgment.[1] That is, all wicked forces have been overcome and banished from the earth. All obstacles to Christ's claiming the kingdom of the world (Rev. 11.15) have been removed.[2]

M.K. Ross, *The Revelation of St John* (MNTC; London: Hodder & Stoughton, 1940); Lohmeyer, *Offenbarung*; P. Minear, *I Saw a New Earth* (Washington: Corpus Books, 1968); Preston and Hanson, *Revelation*; N. Turner, 'Revelation', in *Peake's Commentary on the Bible* (ed. M. Black; London: Nelson, 1962), p. 1057.

1. Cf. also *1 En.* 21–22; 90.24-27; 108.2-6. It is impossible to say confidently whether or in what form this composite book may have been available to John; nonetheless, together these passages seem to imply a cosmology and an eschatology in which the same chaotic abyss beyond the edges of the earth serves as the prison for both rebellious humans and angels until the final judgment.

2. Cf. Metzger, 'Zwischenreich', p. 113.

Chapter 6

REVELATION 20.4-6: THE REIGN OF THE SAINTS

This short passage is by common agreement one of the most difficult in the whole of Revelation. One would be hard pressed to demonstrate that the discussion has moved on significantly from the place it stood a decade ago when U. Vanni registered this note of dissatisfaction:

> The first resurrection... How should one understand it? The responses to this question are extremely varied, and their ingeniousness betrays the lack of an adequate solution.[1]

In the following analysis, the approach to the section will be broken into two stages. First, individual issues will be addressed as they become important, and secondly an overall perspective or re-reading will be proposed on the basis of the results of the first stage. As usual, a relationship of connectedness and dependency will be assumed to hold between this passage and the other parts of the text which the readers have met with previously.

1. Revelation 20.4a: The Judgment of the Enthroned Ones

> And I saw thrones, and they sat upon them, and judgment was given to them (Rev. 20.4a).

The first exegetical issue which needs to be addressed here is the role and identity of those who sit on the thrones. In terms of the imagery of thrones, it is more than likely that a reader's first tendency will have been to think of the 24 'elders'. These personages were first encountered in John's description of the heavenly court in ch. 4:

> And around the throne were twenty-four thrones; and upon the thrones I saw twenty-four elders sitting, clothed in white garments, and golden

---

1. U. Vanni, 'L'Apocalypse johannique: Etat de la question', in J. Lambrecht (ed.), *L'Apocalypse johannique*, p. 42.

crowns on their heads. . . And when the living creatures give glory and honor and thanks to Him who sits on the throne, to Him who lives forever and ever, the twenty-four elders will fall down before Him who sits on the throne, and will worship Him who lives forever and ever, and will cast their crowns before the throne, saying, 'Worthy art Thou, our Lord and our God, to receive glory and honor and power; for Thou didst create all things, and because of Thy will they existed, and were created' (Rev. 4.9-10).

As was argued above in setting the context for Christ's role as Witness, Revelation 4 and 5 depict a heavenly courtroom in which God is seen holding royal court in his role as supreme King and Judge.[1] From the fact that the elders wear crowns and sit on thrones before the divine throne, it becomes clear that God has in some important way shared with them his royal and judicial authority.[2] But who and what are these elders? Specifically, are they intended to be understood as angels, or as human beings? Although there does not seem to be any answer free from one difficulty or another, I am inclined to agree with those who identify them as worthies of the OT, as opposed to angels.[3] It should be noted, however, that nothing crucial in the interpretation of Rev. 20.4-6 hangs on the *identity* of the elders per se. It is their *role* which will prove significant.

Mounce observes that in their continuous act of offering the crowns back to the Enthroned One (Rev. 4.10),

> the elders acknowledge that their authority is a delegated authority. The honor given them is freely returned to the One who alone is worthy of universal honor.[4]

The same may be said of the gesture of prostrating themselves (Rev. 4.10a), since in performing this act of worship, they must give

1.   Schlatter cites as a parallel the fact that Solomon reportedly had 70 golden thrones arranged on either side of his own, where his 'elders' sat as his co-assessors (*Alte Testament*, p. 14).

2.   Cf., for example, A. Feuillet, 'The Twenty-Four Elders of the Apocalypse', in *Johannine Studies* (trans. T. Crane; New York: Alba House, 1965), pp. 183-214; Sweet, *Revelation*, p. 118; Prigent, *L'Apocalypse*, pp. 84-85. A parallel of possible interest is Exod. 24.9-11, in which the elders of Israel are given the privilege of eating and drinking before God's heavenly throne. In favour of an angelic identification are, e.g., Beasley-Murray, Lohmeyer, Mounce, commentaries *in loc.*

3.   For a clear presentation of the strong context for this imagery in OT and apocalyptic literature, cf. Ford, *Revelation*, pp. 76-79.

4.   *Revelation*, p. 139.

up their places on the thrones. Effectively then, the elders are pictured as continuously receiving, yet continuously releasing both of these symbols of their authority. The paradoxical image evoked is of an uninterrupted reciprocation between divine giving and creaturely giving back of authority. No one in the scene (not even God) stakes a claim to autocratic rule.

If the elders have been given executive and judicial authority, one also finds in Rev. 5.8-9 that they have a priestly role. In short, the elders both *reign* and *serve*:

> the four living creatures and the twenty-four elders fell down before the Lamb, having each one a harp, and golden bowls full of incense, which are the prayers of the saints. And they sang a new song. . . [1]

Further on in Revelation, the elders and their thrones are once again brought into view. They praise God and prophesy in response to the announcement of the parousia at the seventh trumpet:

> And the seventh angel sounded; and there arose loud voices in heaven, saying, 'The kingdom of this world has become the kingdom of our Lord, and of His Christ; and He will reign forever and ever'. And the twenty-four elders, who sit on their thrones before God, fell on their faces and worshipped God, saying, 'We give thanks, O Lord God, the Almighty, who art and who wast, because Thou hast taken Thy great power and hast begun to reign' (Rev. 11.16-17).

From the point of view of Rev. 20.4, this will have been the last time the readers have heard mention of thrones. The context is one of the exchange of world-sovereignties: the kingdom of the world has come into the hands of God and of his messiah in the fullest sense, and for the final time. As sovereign, God will now put down all enemies and execute judgment in favour of his loyal subjects:

> And the nations were enraged, and Thy wrath came, and the time came for the dead to be judged, and the time to give their reward to Thy bond-servants the prophets and to the saints and to those who fear Thy name, the small and the great, and to destroy those who destroy the earth (Rev. 11.18).

It seems indubitable that a return to this precise context is intended in Rev. 20.4-6. For shortly before in 19.11-21, Christ, acting as

---

1.   An OT echo is to be found in 1 Chron. 25.1-5 (cf. similarly 24.4-6), which enumerates 24 orders of Levites who were to prophesy with harps and lyres and cymbals. The 24 elders will clearly prophesy in Rev. 11.18.

God's agent in prosecuting his claim to sovereignty, has been seen slaying all the false pretenders. The earthly kings, including the beast, along with all their subjects, may well have been 'enraged' (11.18) when they 'assembled to make war against Him who sat upon the horse, and against His army' (19.19), but they were judged as rebels against the kingdom of Christ and God, and were seen being eradicated from the earth. Then in 20.1-3 one witnessed the overthrow of Satan, the would-be king, the age-old opponent (διάβολος) of God, and the real authority behind the beast (13.2, 4). He too was ousted, banished to the abyss for a thousand years. No one now remains to contest the rule of God on earth.

The question which therefore awaits an answer on the threshold of Rev. 20.4 is this: who will be allowed to take possession of the earth under the kingship of Christ and God, now that the earth's unworthy and rebellious inhabitants have been removed? It is thus natural and expected that the courtroom context should be evoked in 20.4, for a decision of universal proportions is to be made.

Given the facts that the readers already know (at least through the symbolism of crowns and thrones) that the 24 elders have been delegated juridical and executive authority, and that the elders' 'thrones' are the only ones which the readers have encountered, the most natural assumption will be that it is the thrones of the 24 elders, and the 24 elders sitting upon them, which John is seeing in Rev. 20.4a.[1] Likewise, the phrase 'judgment was given to them' (κρίμα ἐδόθη αὐτοῖς) will denote that God has specifically delegated to them the task of making a judicial decision in the present case.[2]

In view of Rev. 11.18, one's expectation will be that the issue to be decided must concern the judgment of the dead, and the reward of all God's faithful ones. For in 19.19 one presumably saw 'the nations enraged', and in 19.20-21 one saw the 'destroyers of the earth' (i.e., the murderous beast and his followers) destroyed. One therefore

---

1. For this view, cf. Düsterdieck, *Offenbarung, in loc.*; W.M.L. de Wette, *Kurze Erklärung der Offenbarung Johannis* (Leipzig: Weidmann, 1848), *in loc.*

2. E.g. Lohmeyer (*Offenbarung*, pp. 161-62), A. Pohl (*Die Offenbarung des Johannes* [Wuppertal Studienbibel; 2 vols.; Wuppertal: Brockhaus, 1983], p. 266) and Sweet (*Revelation*, p. 288) agree that judgment is being given to the enthroned ones in the sense of authorization to judge. They nonetheless think that those on the thrones are the martyrs (as also, e.g., Fiorenza). For discussion of this interpretation, see below.

expects the rest of the prophecy, which predicted what was to happen at the parousia, to be fulfilled.[1]

This is exactly what is to be encountered in Rev. 20.4-6. John will see the souls of those who have been killed because of their faithfulness to God, and who refused to capitulate to the beast, and they will come to life and reign. The rest of the dead will not be given life, but will be left incarcerated in Hades for a thousand years. Further, as will have been entirely expected in view of the promises discussed at length above (Chapter 4, §3), the reward mentioned in ch. 11 will turn out to be resurrection to eternal life as kings with Christ and priests to God (20.4, 6).

The OT allusion contained in the words 'and I saw thrones, and they sat on them' confirms this as well. Dan. 7.9-10 reads,

> I kept looking until thrones were set up, And the Ancient of Days took His seat. . . Thousands and thousands were attending Him, And myriads and myriads were standing before Him; The court sat, And the books were opened.

The picture is of God holding court with his heavenly co-assessors. The decision concerns the saints and the beast, both of which parties have a claim to the sovereignty of the earth. The outcome is as follows:

> I kept looking, and that horn was waging war with the saints and overpowering them until the Ancient of Days came, and judgment was passed in favour of the saints of the Highest One, and the time arrived when the saints took possession of the kingdom (Dan. 7.21-22).

In the previous vision, Daniel had seen the results of this decision in the images of the fiery destruction of the beast and the granting of the kingdom to the 'Son of Man'. Just as the marauding of the beast had symbolized the madness and 'brutality' of the fourth kingdom's imperialism,[2] so the orderly presentation of the Son of Man before God symbolized the reasonableness and the 'humanity' of the kingdom represented by the community of the saints.[3]

---

1. The Greek aorist verbs of Rev. 11.18 are equivalent to Hebrew 'prophetic perfects'.

2. The picture of the beast symbolizes not only the king (Dan. 7.17), but also his kingdom (7.23). In the latter, the king is represented by a horn (7.7-8, 11, 24).

3. On the symbolism of man and beast in Dan. 7 and its significance, see, e.g., D.S. Russell, *The Method and Message of Jewish Apocalyptic* (OTL; Philadelphia: Westminster Press, 1964), pp. 324-27.

The strong commonality between this passage in Daniel and Rev. 19.11-21 and 20.4-6 is evident. As has been demonstrated, Jesus stands in 19.11-21 not only as a warrior, but as the witness before the divine court, whose decisive testimony issues in the conviction and punishment of the beast and his armies. The saints who are present with Jesus bear witness as well, wearing white garments, the emblems of the justice of their cause in the dispute. And as in Dan. 7.11-12, Rev. 19.20-21 shows the beast himself being immediately given to fiery destruction, but with 'the rest' being in some sense spared for a specified amount of time.[1]

Correspondingly, Rev. 20.4 shows the court of God's co-assessors,[2] who decree in favour of the saints 'overcome' by the beast,[3] and they receive the kingdom with Christ. Admittedly, it will not be obvious why God's throne should not be pictured here as it had been in Dan. 7.9-10. But one will already have seen John separating out into *two* strands the scene which Daniel presents as one.[4] It will therefore not be surprising to see the *third* strand of Daniel's vision (the vision of the Enthroned One) brought in on its own at Rev. 20.11-12. In retrospect, the dominance of the vision of God in the latter passage of Revelation will be seen to have made sense of John's silence about it in the former.

In summary, the process of following up John's allusion to Dan. 7.9-27 has confirmed that the enthroned ones are to be identified as the elders in their role as God's co-assessors in judgment. As has been discovered before, and as will be found to be typical, the interpretation suggested through comparison with previous material in Revelation has been further supported and clarified by consulting an OT text to which John has alluded in his description.

1. In the case of Revelation, the period is a thousand years, during which the unrepentant nations suffer imprisonment in Hades, but receive a stay of execution vis-à-vis the 'second death' of the lake of fire. Cf. Chapter 4, §4.c, above.

2. Cf. H.J. Holtzmann and W. Bauer, *Evangelium, Briefe und Offenbarung des Johannes* (HNT, 4; Tübingen: Mohr, 3rd edn, 1908), p. 492.

3. Cf. Dan. 7.21, 25; Rev. 13.5-7; 20.4. These parallels are noted by Fiorenza, *Priester für Gott*, p. 306. Her point of view as to the identity of the enthroned ones will be treated below.

4. Rev. 19.11-21 // Dan. 7.11-12; Rev. 20.4 // Dan. 7.9-10, 18, 22, 27 (minus the vision of God).

But the question of who sits on the thrones cannot be left here. For there is a completely different set of connections which can be discerned, on the one hand between Rev. 20.4a and other parts of Revelation, and on the other between Rev. 20.4a and Daniel 7. These connections may well appear more oblique than the ones just discussed, but they nonetheless prove themselves far from imaginary. To frame the matter differently, the following remarks will demonstrate that John has supplied significantly more than the keys to a single, straightforward reading of his description. He has in fact provided keys to a second and paradoxical reading.

To begin with, if John had wanted to refer unambiguously to the elders in Rev. 20.4a, he could have mentioned them by that term. Yet he does not. Furthermore, as was demonstrated above, the readers will have tended to see themselves (even if martyred) already as Christ's colleagues in 19.14. If they have seen themselves pictured as coming back to *judge* with Christ, then they will be open to seeing a picture of themselves *reigning* as well. Both roles are promised equally in the letters (2.26-27; 3.11, 21), and the second has been prophesied in 5.10. As was noted above, the elders were cast in the double role of *reigning* and *serving as priests*. Thus, if one's tendency has been to begin by imagining the elders on the thrones in 20.4, then one should also discover in 20.6 that there is no difference between the role of the enthroned ones and that ascribed to those chosen for participation in the millennium.

All of this means that, in retrospect, Rev. 20.4a will have the potential to evoke not just a picture of the judicial role of the elders, but one of the enthronement of the overcomers as well. In terms of a progression of pictures, thrones of rule (20.4a) stand as the next logical step from the white horses of judgment and conquest (19.14).[1]

An altogether different allusion to Daniel 7 from that treated above may well be designed to encourage such an interpretation. The following passages make an instructive comparison:

and judgment was given to them (καὶ κρίμα ἐδόθη αὐτοῖς) (Rev. 20.4a).

and He passed judgment in favour of the saints of the Highest One. . . (LXX καὶ τὴν κρίσιν ἔδωκε τοῖς ἁγίοις τοῦ ὑψίστου) (Dan 7.22).

From this comparison, it is clear that giving judgment to someone

---

1.   So rightly Prigent, *L'Apocalypse*, pp. 302-303.

can mean passing judgment in their favour, and not just delegating judicial authority to them.[1] The common context between the two passages is also suggestive. In Dan. 7.22 the result of the decision is that the persecuted saints receive the kingdom; in Rev. 20.4c the result is that the martyrs 'live and reign with Christ'. Fiorenza and others are therefore correct to suggest that in Rev. 20.4 the martyrs are to be pictured as having God's judgment passed in their favour, being enthroned and being given the kingdom.[2]

Nonetheless, it must be stressed that this interpretation is not to be taken as primary. From the point of view of a consecutive reading, it only 'works' as a paradoxical overlay on the reading which had been most natural to begin with. That is, if a reader had tried to begin with the idea that the saints were those pictured on the thrones, the scene would have remained incoherent. For example: What need has someone who is sitting on a throne of rehabilitation? People on thrones give out verdicts, they do not receive them. Why were the souls of the slain pictured as coming to life and reigning *after* being seen enthroned? Would it not have been far more appropriate to say something like 'And I saw thrones, and the court sat. And I saw the souls...and judgment was given to them, and coming to life, they took up the thrones and reigned with Christ...'? The problem can be made yet more specific. Enthronement, reigning and resurrection have already been tied tightly together in Revelation (esp. 2.10; 3.11, 21; 5.10), and this implies that for a reader to imagine him- or herself on a throne is already to imagine a resurrected setting. Thus it simply will not have been one's immediate inclination as a reader to take the souls of the slain as the same group as the enthroned ones.

It is not an adequate rejoinder to these criticisms to observe that John is well capable of paradox and inconsistency. For even in Revelation one is not free to choose an incoherent reading in preference to a coherent one that stands ready to hand. What makes the best sense of the data in Rev. 20.4 is the notion of an *invitation*: an invitation to a possible paradoxical interpretation which adds layers of meaning on top of the straightforward reading. The analogy of the 'overtone' in harmonics is suggestive. Equally so is that of the

1. Lattimore's translation gives yet a third viable possibility for the phrase: 'judgment was given by them'.

2. Fiorenza, *Priester für Gott*, pp. 303-306; similarly, e.g., Prigent, *L'Apocalypse*, p. 310; Roloff, *Offenbarung*, p. 193.

kaleidoscope.[1] The interest of John's composition is that the same elements, when combined in different ways according to different sets of clues in the text, create new and often surprising patterns of meaning. There is no doubt that a paradoxical meaning is discernible in 20.4a. But to speak of that meaning as though it were intended as anything other than a 'surprise' is arguably to flatten something inherently multi-dimensional.

2. Revelation 20.4b: The Resurrection and Reign of the Martyrs

And I saw the souls of those who had been beheaded because of the testimony of Jesus and because of the word of God, and those who had not worshipped the beast or his image, and had not received the mark upon their forehead and upon their hand; and they came to life and reigned with Christ for a thousand years (Rev. 20.4b).

In this passage, there is one central exegetical issue, which splits interpreters more or less evenly.[2] That issue is the question of whether participation in the millennium is being presented as the exclusive right of people who have been killed for their faith, or whether John has made room for 'confessors'—in other words, for those whose confession of Jesus is genuine but does not issue in their martyrdom.

It is possible that this discussion has been sidetracked in the past by the assumption of a false dichotomy between the options of whether John does[3] or does not[4] split the participants of the millennium into two groups. The central question is not one of *division* between classes of participants, but of *inclusion*: who is the description designed to *include*?[5] As in the case of previous exegetical questions, a look at the

---

1. Cf. Fiorenza, 'Die tausendjährige Herrschaft', p. 124.

2. The issues of where and when the millennial reign takes place will not be addressed here, since these have already been treated (see Chapter 2, above). The present discussion will assume that the resurrection and reign of the saints (Rev. 20.6a) is pictured as commencing at the parousia, and as taking place on earth (cf. 5.10; 20.6, 9).

3. E.g. Swete, *Apocalypse*, p. 259: 'καὶ οἵτινες introduces a second class of persons, the confessors. . .'

4. E.g. Kraft, *Offenbarung*, p. 257: 'The idea of a distinction here between classes of martyrs and confessors is entirely misguided'.

5. Rejecting a distinction between martyrs and confessors, Fiorenza suggests that 'it ought much more. . .to be emphasized that all Christians—not only the mar-

contextual background of the passage will help put the issue in perspective.

First, John's expression 'And [I saw] the souls'[1] of those who had been beheaded[2] because of the testimony of Jesus, and because of the word of God. . .' clearly evokes the martyrs under the beast's regime, who will be explicitly recalled in the next phrase.[3] But it also deftly makes room for other Christian martyrs such as Antipas (Rev. 2.13), and for the martyred saints of the Old Covenant who appeared in 6.9: 'the souls of those who had been *slain* because of *the word of God, and because of the testimony* they had maintained'.[4] As 11.18 looks to the rewarding of the faithful of both covenants at the parousia, so here in ch. 20 the time has come when the martyred saints of whatever age will have to wait no longer for their vindication and reward, for 'the number of their fellow servants and their brethren who were to be killed even as they had been' has now been completed (6.11).[5]

---

tyrs—who have resisted the godless seduction [of the beast], and have refused to acknowledge its power, will take up the sovereignty with Christ' (*Priester für Gott*, pp. 305-306).

1.   The accusative ψυχάς depends on εἶδον ('I saw') in Rev. 20.4a.

2.   The verb πελεκίζω (axe), implies official execution, which recalls the false prophet's policy of inflicting capital punishment on those who refused to worship the image of the beast (Rev. 13.15—the announcement of this policy had cunningly been delegated to the 'enchanted' image of the beast).

3.   One recalls from Rev. 13.15-17 that those who would not worship the beast's image were killed, and that those who would not take the number of his name were deprived of the right to buy food. For the idea of being killed by the beast (or by the dragon) for one's 'word' or one's 'testimony', cf. 11.7; 12.11 (note the ironic reversal of who *conquers* whom); 12.17; 13.7.

4.   *Pace* H.W. Günther, who argues from the similarity of the witness formulas (Rev. 1.9; 6.9; 12.17; 20.4) that Christian martyrs are meant in 6.9 (*Der Nah- und Enderwartungshorizont in der Apokalypse des heiligen Johannes* [n.p.: Echter Verlag, 1980], pp. 78-79). In my opinion, however, noting the similarity of the formulas serves not to dampen, but to *enhance* a sense that the absence of 'the testimony of Jesus' in 6.9 is significant. In my view, this similarity is designed to emphasize the fraternity and the common cause that unite the witnesses of the two covenants: Christians (those who hold 'the testimony of Jesus') are 'brothers and fellow servants' not only with one another, but equally with all those who have preached and suffered for God's word in the past (6.9, 11; 11.18; 19.10).

5.   On Rev. 6.9-11 as a reference to OT martyrs, cf. Feuillet, 'Les martyrs de l'humanité', pp. 189-207; Kraft, *Offenbarung*, pp. 119-20. Also cf. Zahn's extensive discussion in *Offenbarung*, II, pp. 602-603.

But the next phrase, 'whoever did not worship. . .', also encompasses two other possible groups. First, it hints at the possibility of there being some people surviving through to the parousia, as does the carefully chosen expression 'they lived' (ἔζησαν), which can either mean 'they came to life', or simply 'they lived'.[1] Secondly, John's use of the indefinite[2] relative pronoun 'whoever' (οἵτινες)[3] opens the possibility that there could be some who are faithful to Christ, and who yet do not live long enough to face the 'incense test'. In particular, the fact that he has put the conjunction καί in front of the relative pronoun creates the effect of making room for the conception that the two groups, those killed for their faith on the one hand, and those who did not worship the beast on the other, might not be identical.[4]

Similar, for example, is the other occurrence of καὶ οἵτινες in Rev. 1.7, where it apparently distinguishes, rather than identifies, two groups:

> Behold, He is coming with the clouds, and every eye will see Him, *even those who* pierced Him; and all the tribes of the earth will mourn over Him. Even so. Amen.

Given this parallel, the expression καὶ οἵτινες in Rev. 20.4 may be seen as conceding a positive answer to the question, 'Suppose I and my loved ones testify openly to Christ, but end up dying before emperor-

---

1. On the double meaning of ἔζησαν, cf. Bousset, *Offenbarung*, pp. 437-38. Prigent cites G. Quispel, *The Secret Book of Revelation* (New York: McGraw–Hill, 1978), *in loc.*, and Cyprian, *Ad Fortunatum* 12, for this interpretation as well (*L'Apocalypse*, p. 311).

2. In Koine the distinction in meaning between the definite and indefinite forms was beginning to be lost, so the force of the indefinite here is ambiguous. (This may suit John's purpose!)

3. Ford (*Revelation*, p. 349) is puzzled over the fact that οἵτινες is in the nominative, rather than in the accusative following εἶδον τὰς ψυχάς, but this is explained (granting that τὰς ψυχάς is the antecedent) by the grammatical rule that the long forms of the relative are not attracted to the case of their antecedents (e.g. Rev. 1.7, 12; 9.4; 11.8; 19.2).

4. Bietenhard asserts, 'It is not said that all Christians perish in this tribulation. The second group of partakers in the millennium will be included with καὶ οἵτινες. Were only souls meant (as in the first group), then certainly καὶ αἵτινες would have to have been used' (*Das tausendjährige Reich*, p. 23). This is mistaken. As in Rev. 6.10, where the participle λέγοντες and the following pronouns derive their masculine gender implicitly from ἐσφαγμένοι as opposed to ψυχαί (6.9), so here οἵτινες may naturally derive its gender from οἱ πεπελεκισμένοι.

worship becomes enforced where I live. Will people such as ourselves have a part in the millennium?' In the context of Revelation as a whole, there is no doubt about the answer to this. As Sweet says, John views those resurrected as typically martyrs, but not exclusively, since the basis of entrance to the New Jerusalem is trust in the atonement, not managing to get oneself martyred (cf. 7.14; 22.14).[1]

Nonetheless, it may be said without hesitation that the passage looks calculated to leave as little room as possible for such non-martyr thinking.[2] But this makes perfect sense in the context of the thrust of the whole text up to this point in Revelation. The readers have progressively been forced to make an exclusive choice between worshipping the beast and losing their lives (cf. Chapter 4, §3.c, above). Given this context for Rev. 20.4, it seems clear that the same implication is being brought home yet again for the Christian reader. That is, each one is being told for the final time that there is no warrant for the hope of living through the beast's career. Behm puts it this way:

> The fact that it is only the martyrs who attain to new life and co-enthrone-ment with Christ accords with the character of Rev. as a book of encouragement for churches facing martyrdom [*Märtyrergemeinden*]: it is not the special distinction [*Auszeichnung*] of a few, but the final goal of all Christians in a time of universal martyrdom that is being pointed to here.[3]

According to this interpretation, Rev. 20.4 is to be seen as intentionally paradoxical. On the one hand, it manages to leave the reader with the strong impression that martyrs alone share in the millennium. On the other hand, it also leaves subtle clues that this may not strictly be the case. The paradox lies in the fact that even these clues remain

---

1.   *Revelation*, pp. 83, 288.

2.   Cf. the further exclusivity of Rev. 20.5: 'the rest of the dead did not come to life until the thousand years were completed'. It is not altogether certain that 'those who pierced Him' in 1.7 should be taken as other than the whole human race, and even if so, the phrase καὶ οἵτινες ('even those who') refers to a subclass of the first group, a parallel which might imply that the 'whoever' of 20.4 intends to distinguish a subclass within the larger company of martyrs throughout the history of the world.

3.   J. Behm, *Die Offenbarung des Johannes übersetzt und erklärt* (Göttingen: Vandenhoeck & Ruprecht, 3rd edn, 1937), p. 102. Similarly Fiorenza, *Priester für Gott*, p. 342; Roloff, *Offenbarung*, p. 193, who emphasize that it is the whole church, and not just a part of it, which is called to resist the pressure of the Imperial Cult. For discussion of possible hints that some may survive to the parousia, cf. pp. 90-91, above.

elusive. For example, the idea that people may be a part of the millennium without dying a martyr's death remains problematical for the following reason: if one allows the reference of the clause 'whoever did not worship. . .' to expand so as to include Christians or Israelites who lived and died in peace before the time of the beast, then it threatens to include too many people. In other words, if the relative οἵτινες is taken with indefinite force, meaning 'whoever' in a sense general enough to include all 'the faithful', then everyone in the history of the world up until the time of the beast seems to be included as well, which is senseless. On the other hand, to narrow the reference at all threatens to make it strictly refer to the martyrs in the previous clause. Given this state of affairs, one hesitates to find fault with Bousset, for example, who says that no one who dies a peaceful death has a part in the millennium.[1] Yet since Bousset himself broadens οἵτινες to include people who survive the beast's career as faithful 'resisters', what is it that keeps it from including still more? The apparent answer is that the *focus* of the passage is on people who live and/or die during the time of the beast, and not on previous generations. And this seems to be the most important point. As elsewhere, John is prophesying to his churches that the imminent 'great tribulation' will make it impossible to die both in faithfulness and in peace.

Such an approach admittedly requires one to see John doing something rather subtle and complex. But it is already in evidence (given the discussion of Rev. 20.4a above) that he is capable of such subtlety and complexity. Furthermore, this view is a definite improvement over the one that the first resurrection is some kind of special reward for martyrs as a sub-class of saints.[2] That view contradicts both the wording and the clear intent of a whole host of passages, not the least of which is 11.18. As has been demonstrated in Chapter 4, §3, above, in Revelation the time for rewards is the parousia, and uniquely the parousia. Thus the only real alternative to the present position is to hold John to the affirmation that all saints of whatever age (with the exception of those few who survive to the parousia) must have been martyred to gain eternal life. Although this radical notion is not ruled out by the text of Revelation, yet it is certainly not affirmed or suggested in any obvious way. It therefore seems wisest to look upon

---

1. *Offenbarung*, pp. 437-38.
2. As, e.g., Farrer, *Revelation*, pp. 206-207; Kiddle, *Revelation*, pp. 391-92; Mounce, *Revelation*, pp. 356-59.

John as a *theologian* who sees the conflict between God's people and the forces of evil as a rule resulting in the martyrdom of those who remain faithful; as a *pastor* who wishes to press this point home as forcefully as possible to his readers; and as a skilful *writer* who has the tools at his disposal to do so.

3. *The Blessings of the First Resurrection*

The rest of the dead did not come to life until the thousand years were completed. This is the first resurrection.

Blessed and holy is the one who has a part in the first resurrection; over these the second death has no power, but they will be priests of God and of Christ and will reign with Him a thousand years (Rev. 20.5-6).

The phrase 'the rest of the dead' resonates with the phrase 'the rest were killed' in Rev. 19.21, which illustrates the above point about the focus being on those who experience the time of the beast. One sees the saints (who were killed under the three-and-a-half year regime of the beast) being raised at the parousia for the millennium. Conversely, one hears that the rest of humankind (who followed the beast and were killed at the parousia) were denied resurrection. Thus the phrase 'the dead did not come to life'[1] unambiguously stands for the refusal of resurrection.[2] As if to underline this, the next sentence calls the former experience, the lot of those who come to life at the parousia, the 'first resurrection'. As far as the readers know at this point, there will be a 'second' resurrection at the end of the thousand years, in which the followers of the beast and the rest of (unsaved) humankind take part.

As the elders prophesied in Rev. 11.18, the parousia has seen not only the destruction of the earth's destroyers (19.11-21), and the rewarding of all God's servants and saints, but also *the judgment of the dead*. Their judgment in the court pictured in 20.4 is that they are not chosen to live and reign with Christ for the millennium. Instead, they remain in the prison of Hades for the whole aeon, 'until the thousand years are completed'.

Rev. 20.6, on the other hand, returns again to the partakers in the first resurrection. The blessings and promises given them to echo the

1. The Greek is οὐκ ἔζησαν. Cf. Rev. 20.4 for the converse.
2. Cf. ὃς ἐγένετο νεκρὸς καὶ ἔζησεν (Rev. 2.8), and οἱ λοιποὶ τῶν νεκρῶν οὐκ ἔζησαν (20.5).

major themes of reward that have grown up around the parousia in the letters, in 5.10, and in 7.11-17.[1] Yet it is noteworthy that in terms of concrete *pictures* the promises of the good anticipated for the parousia remain absent.[2] In preference to this, the *essence* of the promised role and status of the overcomers is expressed: they are blessed, they are holy, they are resurrected to life, they are invulnerable to the second death, they are priests and kings, and they are together with Christ.

This coheres with the fact that the focus of the vision is on the judgment: on the decision of who is and is not worthy of resurrection to life with Christ.[3] The scene was set in Rev. 20.4a as a court proceeding, and 20.4b-5 pictured the outcome of the trial. The blessing here in v. 6 therefore finishes off the scene on a purely positive note, by reminding the readers in brief of the surpassing promises that resurrection contains for them. First time readers may not know it yet, but the promises of eternal life are also due for their own luxurious *pictorial* development in later visionary sections of the book (21.1–22.5). At the present, however, 20.6 gives the readers enough key information for them to know that the millennium holds the full blessings of eternal life for them.

A final exegetical question must be posed. If the resurrected ones reign with Christ, over what do they reign? Given the fact that all the rebellious have been removed from the earth (cf. on Rev. 19.21, above), the obvious answer is that they reign over the earth itself (5.10). For when the resurrected fully worship God and fully join him in the management of his whole creation, they come at last into the purpose for which the Scriptures say they were originally created:

> Let us make man in Our image, according to Our likeness; and let them rule over the fish of the sea and over the birds of the sky and over the cattle and over all the earth, and over every creeping thing that creeps on the earth (Gen. 1.26; cf. also 1.28).[4]

1.   Cf. the survey above in Chapter 4, §3.c.
2.   E.g. the fruit of the tree of life (Rev. 2.7), the victor's crown (2.10; 3.11), the hidden manna and the white stone (2.17), the morning star (2.28), white robes (3.5), the springs of living water (7.17).
3.   Cf. the previous remarks on the place of the whole chapter in the literary structure of Rev. 17.1–22.5 (Chapter 4, §2, above).
4.   As R.H. Gundry says, 'As nations of kings, rather than kings of nations, the saints have finally fulfilled God's original commission to "be fruitful and multiply

The picture evoked by such passages as Rev. 2.7 and 7.16-17 coheres with this theme. The parousia is presented as the return of paradise, where all is unspoilt and free from the former cares caused by human sin. And to take an uncharacteristic look ahead in the text, Rev. 22.1-5 will confirm this all the more:

> And he showed me a river of the water of life, clear as crystal, coming from the throne of God and of the Lamb, in the middle of its street.
>
> And on either side of the river was the tree of life, bearing twelve kinds of fruit, yielding its fruit every month; and the leaves of the tree were for the healing of the nations.
>
> And there shall no longer be any curse; and the throne of God and of the Lamb shall be in it, and His bond-servants shall serve Him; and they shall see His face, and His name shall be on their foreheads.
>
> And there shall no longer be any night; and they shall not have need of the light of a lamp nor the light of the sun, because the Lord God shall illumine them; and they shall reign forever and ever.

According to Revelation, the saints will not just reign during the millennium—they will reign forever in (and over) paradise. These considerations show that scholars miss the point when they make comments such as the following:

> it would be a singularly empty recognition of their [the martyrs'] services if they were to reign over a world of which they were the sole inhabitants. If we take these statements [about reigning with Christ] seriously, as indeed we must, it inevitably follows that the commentaries are wrong which treat the battle of the previous chapter as the end of world history and the wiping out of all the members of the human race who have not lost their lives in the great martyrdom.[1]

and fill the earth and subdue it and rule over. . . every living thing that moves on the earth" (Gen. 1.28). As often in apocalyptic, *Endzeit* recaptures *Urzeit*' ('The New Jerusalem: People as Place, Not Place for People', *NovT* 29 [1987], p. 264).

1. Caird, *Revelation*, p. 251; similarly Bietenhard, who wishes to refute the idea that the millennium is set in the new creation: 'Reference to Rev. 5.10 ought rather to point to the idea that the saints take up their reign on earth. Beyond this, Rev. 2.26-27 promises the overcomers that Christ will grant them the authority over the nations which he will "lead with an iron rod" and "shatter like vessels of clay"—just as Christ himself has this complete authority. *On the new earth of the kingdom of God, there is no longer any occasion for such doings*' (*Das tausendjährige Reich*, p. 28). According to the analysis in Chapter 4, §3, above, the promise of shepherding/ smashing the nations with an iron rod, far from offering the overcomers despotic rule during the millennium, instead looks ahead to the power of their truthful testimony in the world judgment of the parousia. Although nothing in Rev. 20.1-6 gives a clue in

On the contrary, in comparison to enjoying the perfection of paradise, the idea of ruling over a world full of sinful people might well prove to be a severe disappointment in the eyes of all but those with a taste for positions of power.[1]

4. *Summary of Results on Revelation 20.1-6*

Before moving on to exegesis of the next four verses (Rev. 20.7-10), a summary of conclusions so far will be in order.

1. Just as the various images, words and themes of Revelation 19 were shown to have extensive contextual roots all through the previous sections of the book, so also with the first six verses of ch. 20. It was argued that Satan's downfall in 20.1-3 must be interpreted (at least to begin with) as an event which happens at the parousia. The basis of this argument was that such would be the obvious conclusion reached by a person reading Revelation consecutively. Equipped with the context supplied by the previous visions of Satan's expulsion from heaven, the indication that he had but a 'little time', and the apparent identification of that time with the career of the beast, the reader would know enough to expect to encounter some kind of definite judgment and defeat of Satan at the end of the beast's career. And since the beast's destruction happened at the parousia, it would have seemed entirely appropriate to see a clear and total defeat of Satan connected with the parousia as well.

2. Although it would certainly have been no surprise to see Satan thrown with his associates into the lake of fire at the parousia, it came as no more of a surprise to see Satan chained and imprisoned in the abyss at the parousia, since John had patterned a previous description of the parousia on Isaiah 24, and there one found the idea that the day of the Lord is not the time for the final destruction of wicked powers on earth and in heaven, but of their lengthy imprisonment in

either direction, nothing so far in the text contradicts the idea that the millennium might be set in the new creation (as e.g. Metzger, 'Zwischenreich', pp. 110-11, holds).

1. As Sickenberger notes, the absence of Satan is no guarantee of the absence of sin (*Erklärung*, pp. 181-82).

preparation for final punishment (Isa. 24.22-24).

3. It was argued that behind the *prima facie* exclusion of non-martyrs from the millennium in Rev. 20.4-6 lay an extensive contextual system in which varied promises of eternal life at the parousia were strongly coupled with repeated intimations that the achievement of eternal life would cost the reader his or her present life in the struggle with the beast. In this light, the distinctive wording of the passage was seen (consistently with the rest of the book) as designed to discourage the readers from seeking an escape-route from the threat of martyrdom, rather than as (inconsistently) predicting a special reward for the martyrs as a sub-class of the faithful.

4. It was noted that a prediction following the seventh trumpet (Rev. 11.15-18) had set up an expectation on the reader's part that the parousia would be pictured at some point as the occasion of the judgment of the dead.[1] It was then argued that 20.4-6 was to be seen as fleshing out this prediction, in view of its indication of a judgment scene whose outcome was the choosing of some of the dead for the reward of resurrection, and of the 'rest' for continued incarceration in Hades.

If the conclusions above be granted, then what expectations will the readers of Revelation be intended to entertain as they stand on the threshold of Rev. 20.7-10? First, they will be curious to see what happens when Satan is released to deceive the nations once more (20.3). Secondly, they will have been interested to see what happens when the 'rest of the dead' come to life (20.5).

---

1. No argument needs to be made at this point about the judgment scene of Rev. 20.11-15, and its relationship to 11.18. As has been stated, the idea behind the present method is to suggest how the readers would tend to interpret each new passage based on contextual information in hand, i.e., based on what could be gathered from a consecutive reading of the text to a given point. Thus if reading 20.11-15 is to force a re-thinking of assumptions about such matters as the timing, conditions and outcome of the judgment of the dead, then so be it. But whether or not this turns out to be the case, it must be recognized that the crucial question concerns not whether, but *how* the subsequent information of 20.11-15 is to be seen as affecting the interpretation of other texts such as 20.4-6. And the argument here is that such questions can only be validly addressed in the context of a study which gives a plausible account of one's acquisition of information through the consecutive reading of the text.

Chapter 7

REVELATION 20.7-10: THE FINAL ATTACK

> And when the thousand years are completed, Satan will be released from
> his prison, and will come out to deceive the nations which are in the four
> corners of the earth, Gog and Magog, to gather them together for the war;
> the number of them is like the sand of the seashore.
>
> And they came up on the broad plain of the earth and surrounded the
> camp of the saints and the beloved city, and fire came down from heaven
> and devoured them.
>
> And the devil who deceived them was thrown into the lake of fire and
> brimstone, where the beast and false prophet are also; and they will be
> tormented day and night forever and ever (Rev. 20.7-70).

The first and most obvious exegetical question of the section is this:
whence come the nations that Satan deceives? According to all that has
been demonstrated above about the relationship between the contextual
build-up and final outworking of the theme of judgment at the
parousia in Rev. 19.11-21 (see Chapter 4, §§3, 4, above), there is one
answer to this question that to all appearances must be immediately
and firmly excluded: they cannot be peoples (or the progeny of such
peoples) somehow left out of the final conflict—in other words,
nations that have been spared at the parousia.[1] At no point previously
has Revelation been willing to open the door to this sort of possibility,
but rather the reverse. But as Beckwith notes, a problem appears to be
created for the present passage:

> The victory described in 19.19-21 over the Antichrist and his subjects,
> who included all the kingdoms of the world (13.7f.), seems to leave no
> place for the hostile armies of this passage.[2]

1. So correctly, e.g., Rissi, *The Future of the World*, pp. 33-35; Fiorenza,
Priester für Gott, p. 311.
2. Beckwith, *Apocalypse*, p. 745. Beckwith goes on to assume that Rev. 20.7-
10 does deal with earthly nations, and that John was unaware of or unconcerned with
the inconsistency created by this.

On first glance, it might appear helpful to appeal at this point to a key dynamic uncovered above in Rev. 20.4-6. There, a situation apparently characterized by strict polarity (between those martyred and those denied resurrection) turned out to admit conceivable exceptions to that polarity, exceptions played down to the maximum degree possible for understandable pastoral reasons. Could not the very same pastoral concerns serve to explain the fact that exceptions appear only later (and in a negative context) to the rule that 'the parousia sees no earthly survivors'? The answer to this is that they could, provided it were demonstrable that Gog and Magog really were intended to be earthly nations.

Admittedly, casting about for possible hints of people being spared at the parousia could produce reasonably encouraging results. For example, one might consider Rev. 1.7, 11.13, and 15.4, where people are to respond to the parousia by mourning over Christ, and by glorifying, fearing and worshipping God. Given the assumption that people other than Christians *cannot* survive the parousia, these responses can without much difficulty be taken as evoking that involuntary recognition and acknowledgement of the truth which even the enemies of God must experience when put face to face with him. But then again, given the assumption that some *do* survive the parousia, such responses could easily hint at the possibility of at least partial repentance issuing in divine clemency at the parousia. Along similar lines, 2.26 *could* mean that ordinary nations survive to be ruled over by the saints,[1] 6.17 *could* be framed as a hint that some on earth will be able to stand before God and the Lamb, and so on.

To take this tack, however, is to get dangerously ahead of oneself. In the interpretation of Rev. 20.4-6 above, two clear lines of background information within the text were discovered to be in tension with one another: the first was that all God's servants would be rewarded at the parousia, and the second was that only the martyrs would be rewarded at the parousia. Because (and only because) the first line of information was strong elsewhere in Revelation, the door was opened to finding paradoxical hints of it in a passage dominated

---

1. This is not at all a likely reading of the promise, since in this context it would connote despotism, which is highly out of character for Revelation. (Cf. the comments in Chapter 6, §1, above, on the authority of the 24 elders, and on the meaning of Rev. 2.26 in relation to other promises of authority to judge in Chapter 4, §3, above.)

by emphasis on the second. But the issue of who survives the parousia on earth *is not analogous,* because as regards that issue, there is but *one* line of information in the chapters leading up to 20.7-10. That information tells the reader in almost the strongest language imaginable that no one survives the parousia except the faithful (who will be given resurrection). Therefore the interpreter has no business overturning this datum at the outset by mere appeal to elements that are at best potentially in tension with it.

Thus, if correct procedure in interpreting Rev. 20.4-6 is first to pursue the reading that responds to the loud and clear elements in the text, and next to follow up possible 'overtones', then here all the more so. The prudent course is to begin with a reading which assumes that Gog and Magog cannot be survivors of the parousia and participants of the millennium. Should there come a point where tensions, paradoxes or impossibilities become apparent on such a reading of 20.7-10, it is then (and not until and not unless that point is reached) that it will become appropriate to explore the idea that survivors might be hinted at elsewhere in Revelation.[1]

1. *Revelation 20.7: Identifying Gog and Magog*

As was shown in the introduction, the attempt to identify Gog and Magog as demonic hosts has its attractiveness because it solves the problem of people surviving the millennium. Nonetheless, in its turn this view encounters insuperable difficulties as well (see pp. 42-43, above). If the nations that Satan is prevented from deceiving in Rev. 20.3 are nations of human beings, then without a doubt the nations that he is allowed to deceive once again in 20.7 are nations of human beings.

What then about the proposition that the vision of Gog and Magog is to be interpreted as an attack by all the evil spirits and the spirits of the human dead?[2] This appears equally unworkable for at least two reasons.

---

1.   The same point of procedure applies to the suggestion that Rev. 20.7-10 shows John having difficulty incorporating disparate traditions (as, e.g., Bousset, *Offenbarung*, p. 439). There is no point in entertaining possible incoherent readings until the search for coherent ones comes up empty-handed.

2.   As held, e.g, by Rissi, *The Future of the World*, pp. 34-35; and similarly Metzger, 'Zwischenreich', pp. 114-15 (for the differences, see below); and Fiorenza, *Priester für Gott*, pp. 311-32. For her part, Fiorenza does not in fact seem

First, the idea of an eschatological attack in which ghosts and demons join forces will presumably have been a complete novelty to the Jewish and Christian eschatology of the day.[1] Thus if John had intended to convey such an unheard-of idea, he would have had to offer his readers clear indications that he had this particular idea in mind. But there is neither previous preparation in the text for the idea of a ghostly attack, nor a suggestion anywhere that it might be possible for the *spirits* of dead people to be released from the underworld without being resurrected.[2] As the text stands, it seems impossible that a contemporary reader could have reached this view, simply from a negative deduction based on verses such as Rev. 19.21.

The second problem is the more crucial because it is not based on silence, but from precisely what the text does say. The problem is that, on this view, the dead are to be destroyed by fire in a ghostly state (Rev. 20.9) before being resurrected and thrown into the lake of fire (20.15). But this obviously throws the whole context into confusion. That is, it both inexplicably doubles the fiery punishment of the dead,[3] and imports an unwanted third referent into the author's terminology about the 'second death'. If ordinary bodily death is presumably the 'first death' to which resurrected experience of the lake of fire corresponds as the 'second death' (v. 15), then what room is left for this third, supposedly intermediate ('ghostly death') experience?

On the basis of the foregoing discussion, it appears that none of the identifications commonly proposed for Gog and Magog creates a

---

entirely decided on this issue. On the one hand, she begins by saying (*Priester für Gott*, p. 311) that although it is 'imaginable' that the dead are in view, yet it is 'more imaginable' that the demons are to be understood. Yet she goes on to say, 'The meaning of Rev. 20.7-10 would therefore lie in showing that the eschatological church—the "beloved city"—will not be destroyed even by the direct attack of the demons and the powers of death'. For this point she cites Metzger and Rissi (pp. 311-12 n. 86), which would seem to indicate that she interprets 'Todeskräfte' as the dead (who according to her are ruled in the underworld by Satan). The same ambivalence can be found in her article, 'Die tausendjährige Herrschaft', pp. 113-15.

1.   Neither Rissi nor Fiorenza cites any parallels. *Jub.* 10.3-11 (*Priester für Gott*, p. 312 n. 86) deals only with wicked angelic spirits.

2.   On possible indications that Gog and Magog come from the underworld, see below.

3.   Worse, one will have to imagine that those who died by fire in the destruction of Babylon (Rev. 17.16; 18.8; etc.) will face *three* fiery ends.

really coherent reading. It will be appropriate therefore to return to the method put forward in this study, and to see if more positive results suggest themselves.

The key, of course, is tracing the *context* and the *preparation* that has been made earlier in the text. Compared with other pericopes discussed here, Rev. 20.7-9 will not be seen to have behind it an extensive system of references that build up progressively. Instead, almost all the context is close at hand, starting at the end of ch. 19.

In Rev. 19.21, as was discussed above, the 'kings of the earth' and their hosts were *slain*, and were by implication *imprisoned* along with the rest of rebellious humanity which had gone down to Hades before them. Also by implication, all of these together became the 'rest of the dead' who in 20.5 'did not come to life until the thousand years were completed'. In other words, all of wicked humanity were to be pictured as in subterranean prison for the 'many days' of the millennium just as Satan was (recalling Isa. 24.23).[1] But here is a fact which has gone by completely unnoticed in scholarly discussion: John has not only made a point of placing the slaying of the 'kings of the earth' and the imprisonment of Satan together at the parousia, but he has also pointedly placed the *release* of Satan and the *resurrection* of unrepentant humanity[2] precisely on top of one another in time.

One hears in Rev. 20.3 (cf. 20.7) that Satan is imprisoned '*in order that he might not deceive the nations any more, until the thousand years are completed*' (ἵνα μὴ πλανήσῃ ἔτι τὰ ἔθνη ἄχρι τελεσθῇ τὰ χίλια ἔτη). And then in 20.5 one hears also that the 'rest of the dead' did not come to life '*until the thousand years are completed*' (ἄχρι τελεσθῇ τὰ χίλια ἔτη). By conspicuously plotting the release of Satan from the underworld and the resurrection of the unrepentant at the same time, John is encouraging his readers to expect for the release of the unrepentant from the prison of Hades to issue in their resurrection and punishment with Satan, after the pattern of

---

1.   This of course remains true regardless of whether one accepts the exact equation of the abyss with Hades.

2.   That the 'rest of the dead' is not to be understood as including saints, is proven not only by such passages as Rev. 11.17-18 and 22.12, 14, but also by the whole tenor of the promises and warnings that conclude each of the letters to the seven churches (esp. 2.25-28; 3.3-5). Revelation never allows the reader to entertain the possibility that any later time than the parousia could be the occasion for reunion with Christ and reception of eternal life.

Isa. 24.21-22: 'They will be gathered together like prisoners in the dungeon, and will be confined in prison; and after many days they will be punished'.

In other words, just as Satan and the wicked were punished together at the parousia and imprisoned together for the duration of the millennium, so presumably they will be released and punished together 'after the thousand years are completed'. What this means is that any great crowd of people that appears in league with Satan at his release, and ends up being punished with him, will be recognizable as the 'rest of the dead'. They have also been released from the prison of the underworld, but in the manner which is proper to them, that is, by resurrection.[1] And Gog and Magog in Rev. 20.7-10 fit this description perfectly.[2]

---

1. In the case of human beings, to be sent to the underworld is to be stripped of bodily existence; conversely, to be released from the underworld is to be restored to bodily existence. (Cf. Farrer, *Revelation*, p. 201.) Commentators (with few exceptions, such as Charles, *Revelation*, II, pp. 193-98) give implicit assent to this conception when they assume from Rev. 20.13, 'the sea gave up the dead which were in it, and Death and Hades gave up the dead which were in them', that bodily resurrection is intended, even though neither the word resurrection, nor the word body appears in the passage. Charles's avoidance of the implication of bodily resurrection in Revelation motivated him to emend the text of 20.13 to read τὰ ταμεῖα (the storerooms, treasuries) in place of ἡ θάλασσα (the sea).

2. Smith (*Daniel and the Revelation*, pp. 747-48) is the only published commentator consulted who unambiguously takes this view. To indulge in a bit of speculation, it might be suggested that an element of serendipity could be involved in Smith's conclusion that resurrection was to be seen in Rev. 20.7-10. As a Seventh Day Adventist, he was committed to the rather tendentious project of disproving the idea that human beings might subsist as bodiless souls in 'the intermediate state'. As such, he could not admit the concept of a subterranean abyss such as Hades, where unresurrected souls might be imprisoned for the millennium. Thus, for example, he interprets the abyss in 9.2 as the desert of Arabia, and the abyss from which the beast comes (11.7, etc.) as the grave. What then is meant by the abyss in 20.1-3, considering the context of all humankind being slain in 19.21? Ingeniously, Smith sees it as the abyss of Gen. 1.2, as the earth itself turned back again to primaeval chaos, inhabited by nothing more than a multitude of corpses. As the interpretation falls out logically from this, the earth now enjoys a fallow sabbath age (as in *4 Ezra* 7.30), and the New Jerusalem hovers above the earth, ready to descend after the final judgment and the new creation (21.1). Meanwhile, Satan is bound and imprisoned not in a geographical sense (since he has already been on earth since ch. 12), but in the sense of being powerless any longer to deceive or harm the human race. And if Satan's *binding* at the beginning of the millennium is defined only in the precise

Given such an identification, the problems associated with the typical views begin to disappear. For example, if Gog and Magog are understood as the resurrected dead, there will be no contradiction with the fact that all of rebellious humanity was killed at the parousia, because Gog and Magog will not have come from the millennial earth, but from Hades. Furthermore, instead of conflict arising between the 'nations' of Rev. 20.3 and 20.7 (as in the view that sees the latter as demonic), the two verses will go hand in hand, since the two groups are explicitly the same.

But what then about the criticism of Rissi's view above? Will not a reading of Rev. 20.7-10 that is based on the present identification run into equally serious conflict with 20.11-15? The answer is that the question is premature. Having found a foothold for interpreting the passage in the clear preparation created by the foregoing text, the next step is to offer a reading of the whole of 20.7-10 on the same basis. Assuming that success attends this effort, then 20.7-10 will be added to 19.11–20.6 as the immediate contextual foundation for interpreting the next section, 20.11-15. It is only at that stage—in other words, in the course of attempting to interpret 20.11-15 in the context of the previous material, including 20.7-10—that the issue of paradoxes or contradictions can arise, and not before.

2. *Revelation 20.7-10: The Final Deception*

When one begins to examine Rev. 20.7-10 with a view to confirming the idea that Gog and Magog are to be recognized as the 'rest of the dead' who have been resurrected, supporting evidence starts to come to hand immediately. In fact, it will appear that John has managed to word his description of Gog and Magog in a way that points his readers continuously to the idea of resurrection or release from the realm of the dead. Attention may be drawn to each phrase in turn.

---

than that he has people to work on once more. As an incidental consequence of Smith's tendentious redefinition of the abyss, Satan's release from prison has become equivalent *by definition* to the resurrection of 'the rest of the dead'! There is not much to be said against this view here, except that the readers have no reason yet to picture the New Jerusalem in the sky, they have been given no reason to think that the earth might be left in a state of chaos during the millennium, and they do have reasons (Rev. 5.10 and Dan. 7 as background for Rev. 20.4-6) for expecting that the saints reign *on earth* during the millennium. The most substantial reasons for laying Smith's view aside will come to light in Chapter 9, on 21.1-8 (esp. §3.b).

a. *'To deceive the nations which are in the four corners of the earth'* *(Revelation 20.8)*

In the OT, as in apocalyptic literature, the outer edges of the earth are conceived of as the entrances to the underworld.[1] For example, in *1 Enoch* 18, Enoch sees the 'end of the great earth' (v. 10). Beyond that he sees an abyss where there are seven fallen stars burning. An angel says to him,

> This place is the end of heaven and earth: this has become a prison for the stars and the host of heaven... And Uriel said to me: 'Here shall stand the angels who have connected themselves with women [cf. Gen. 6.1-4; Jude 16; 2 Pet. 2.4]... here they shall stand, till the day of the great judgment, in which they shall be judged until they are made an end of' (*1 En.* 18.14; 19.1).[2]

In Revelation, the 'star from heaven which had fallen to earth' (9.1) creates an important conceptual link with this passage. For in *1 Enoch* 18, it is fallen angelic 'stars' (vv. 13-15) which are imprisoned in the fiery abyss that lies beyond the edges of the earth. In Rev. 9.1-2, the abyss is unlocked by a fallen 'star', and forthwith demonic 'locusts' come up out of the abyss and onto the earth, in order to attack all who have not been protectively sealed. As in *1 Enoch*, the abyss in Revelation is a place of fire, since the mouth of the abyss emits 'smoke like that of a great furnace' (9.2).

Of possible significance is the fact that angels had previously (Rev. 7.1) been seen stationed 'at the four corners of the earth' to hold back the winds (cf. *1 En.* 66.2). It was intimated that these angels

---

1. E.g. Ps. 61.3. Thus Rissi, *The Future of the World*, pp. 35-36; Beasley-Murray, *Revelation*, p. 160, in context of Rev. 9.1-4; joined tentatively by Sweet, *Revelation*, p. 291. In Revelation (cf. 7.1-3 and 8.7), it is clear that 'the four corners' of the earth constitute the boundaries of that cosmological realm. In 7.1, four angel sentries stand at its borders, and, depending on whether or not they allow or forbid forces (e.g. winds) to enter from outside, they have power either to protect or to harm the earth, sea and trees (cf. the same 'border guard' role in 9.14-15 and in *1 En.* 66.2). In chs. 8 and 9 (after the sealing), disasters come upon the human world from without: plagues strike the earth, sea, trees and then the earth's inhabitants, first from above the earth, and then from below.

2. Translation by R.H. Charles, in *idem* (ed.), *The Apocrypha and Pseudepigrapha of the Old Testament* (2 vols.; Oxford: Clarendon Press, 1913), II, pp. 200-201.

had the power to harm the earth, sea and trees. They were not to be allowed to do so until the servants of God were sealed. In the following chapter much harm does come to these elements (8.7-8), but it is only when the locusts come out of the abyss that the protective sealing is mentioned again (9.4), recalling once again the fact that the angels had been kept waiting until the servants of God were sealed. In other words, in retrospect the angel sentries, stationed at the four corners of the earth, seem to have been restraining the attack of the demonic locusts from the abyss, as well as the previous disasters from heaven.[1] Thus Kraft (although he sees Gog and Magog as demons) catches the image of 20.9 when he says,

> For the inhabitants of the underworld, the surface of the earth projects out over the ocean like a plateau. From all points of the compass, they clamber out (a daunting image!) and surround the saints in their stronghold. Such, according to Ezek. 38.12, is the ὀμφαλὸς τῆς γῆς, the middle point of the earth.[2]

It is instructive that Sweet, after suggesting the idea that the edges of the earth are conceived of as the entrances of the realms of the dead, finally retreats from making use of it in his interpretation of Rev. 20.8. This is because he thinks that in 20.1-10, 'the double reference to *deceiving the nations* (vv. 3, 8) suggests the residual turbulence of this earth even under the millennial kingdom'.[3]

But if it be granted that Rev. 20.1-3 (following Isa. 24.21-22) intentionally implies that Satan has been cast helpless into the same 'prison' as the nations whom he has been deceiving through the beast and false prophet, then the stated reason for his imprisonment (i.e. to keep him from deceiving them any longer) makes perfect sense. One may well ask what *better way* there could be of undeceiving the nations concerning the authority of the false god by whom they had been so overawed, than to throw him into the very same state of

---

1. In the *1 Enoch* passage above, there appears to be a three-way boundary at the ends of the earth between earth, heaven and the abyss. The same cosmology could well explain the fact that the angels standing at the four corners of the earth in Rev. 7.1 appear to hold off disasters from both other realms.

2. *Offenbarung*, p. 259. The bracketed aside is Kraft's.

3. Sweet, *Revelation*, p. 291, italics original. In agreement is, e.g., H. Stadelmann, 'Das Zeugnis der Johannesoffenbarung vom tausendjährige Königsreich Christi auf Erden', in *Zukunftserwartung in biblischen Sicht* (ed. G. Maier; Wuppertal: Brockhaus, 2nd edn, 1986 [1989]), p. 151.

helplessness as they.[1] For so long as Satan's former worshippers see him kept a prisoner no more potent than themselves, for just so long will his claim to godhood continue to be forcibly exposed for the lie that it is.

Bolstering this idea is the strong suspicion that it is not simply Isa. 24.22 that lies behind the binding of the Deceiver in Rev. 20.1-3, but also a particular reading of Isaiah 14, in which Satan is seen as the king of Babylon who is thrust down to Sheol in the ignominy of death:

> Sheol from beneath is excited over you to meet you when you come;
> It arouses for you the spirits of the dead,
> All the leaders of the earth;
> It raises all the kings of the nations from their thrones.
> They will respond and say to you,
> 'Even you have been made weak as we,
> You have become like us'.
> . . .
> How you have fallen from heaven,
> O star of the morning, son of the dawn![2]
> You have been cut down to the earth,
> You who have weakened the nations!
> But you said in your heart,
> 'I will ascend to heaven;
> I will raise my throne above the stars of God,
> And I will sit on the mount of assembly
> In the recesses of the north.
> I will ascend above the heights of the clouds;
> I will make myself like the Most High.'
> Nevertheless you will be thrust down to Sheol,
> To the recesses of the pit (Isa. 14.9-10, 12-15).

Even if John were unaware of this passage (which is highly unlikely in itself), it would nonetheless fittingly illustrate the point being made here. The description of the binding and imprisonment of Satan 'so that he should deceive the nations no longer', far from implying that

---

1.   Satan's implicit binding *within* the prison in Rev. 20.2 takes on special significance in this context: he has no power even over his fellow inmates. Cf. the refutation (Chapter 3, §6.c, above) of the notion that Satan rules in the abyss during the millennium.

2.   Cf. Rev. 12.3, 7-9, in which Satan's fellow rebellious angels are pictured as stars, and Rev. 9.1, where it is not impossible that Satan himself could be the fallen star (so Swete, *Apocalypse*, p. 112). Cf. *Apoc. Elij.* 3.28; Lk. 10.18.

the nations of vv. 3 and 8 must be living, instead suggests an ex-
quisitely just method of unmasking his deception and forcibly keeping
it unmasked. Satan cannot deceive the nations any more for the very
reason that he is imprisoned along with them in the underworld.[1]

The great irony (cf. Rev. 20.8) is thus that when the unrepentant
are released, they are immediately willing to forget the truth that they
have just been compelled to face for a thousand long years. Just as the
beast's subjects were still worshipping and following him after they
had watched him betray his own people and homeland to incineration,
so all the 'rest of the dead' are still blind enough to believe that Satan
can overcome God's people, even though he has been judged with
them and has been confined with them for a thousand years in the
abyss.

b. *'Gog and Magog' (Revelation 20.8)*[2]

In Ezekiel 38, Gog and his armies 'from the far north' arrive to attack
Israel, and are destroyed by fire from heaven. Many commentators
have noted the fact that the horde of Rev. 20.7-10 is described in
terms suggestive of universality. Thus Beasley-Murray notes,

> Whenever the theme of Ezekiel 38–39 is taken up in Jewish apocalyptic
> writers (e.g., *2 En.* 56.5ff., 2 Esd. 13.5ff., *Sib. Or.* 3.662ff.) it is the
> nations generally which combine in assault on Israel, and it is likely that
> John had a similarly undefined company in view.[3]

The epithets 'Gog and Magog', in other words, do not function as a
geographical or ethnographical reference, but rather as a literary one.
As opposed to pointing the reader's attention to nations from specific
parts of the world, they point to the parallel eschatological scenario in
Ezekiel 38. In other words, John indicates that, in what he is seeing,

1. Metzger ('Zwischenreich', p. 113 n. 32) emphasizes the fact that John will
have had ready precedent for the idea of *nations* inhabiting the underworld
(Ezek. 31–32; cf. Ps. 9.17).
2. The arguments put forward under this heading are indirect and inferential vis-
à-vis Revelation itself, since the phrase 'Gog and Magog' occurs here only. The
larger argument (point a above, together with points c, d, e below) stands on its own
without the conjectures proposed in this section.
3. *Revelation*, p. 297. Caird (*Revelation*, p. 256) notes that in the Talmud Gog
and Magog are identified as the nations referred to in Psalm 2 (e.g. *Ber.* 7b, 10a,
13a; *Šab.* 118a; *Pes.* 118a; *Meg.* 11a).

he recognizes (and he wants his readers to recognize with him) the eschatological event prophesied by Ezekiel. A look at the way John structures chs. 19–21 of Revelation will confirm that his prophecy is composed so as to evince close kinship with that of Ezekiel. J. Lust sets up a table of similarities in this way:

Revelation	*Ezekiel*
1. First resurrection (20.4) and Messianic millennial kingdom (20.4-6).	1. Revival of the dry bones (37.1-14). Reunited kingdom under Davidic Messiah (37.15-28).
2. The final battle against Gog and Magog (20.7-10).	2. The final battle against Gog and Magog (38–39).
2a. The 2nd resurrection (20.11-15).	2a. ———————————
3. The descent of heavenly Jerusalem (21–22).	3. Vision of the New Temple and New Jerusalem (40–48).[1]

What is usually not noted about Ezekiel 38–39, is that it contains not one oracle against Gog and Magog, but two oracles. The first (ch. 38) is set in the context of the messianic age of Ezekiel 37. This oracle pictures the attack as coming well into a long and peaceful era begun by the regathering and restoration of Israel from captivity, for during the whole of this era Israel has been dwelling in perfect security and prosperity. As Ezekiel says,

> After many days you will be summoned; in the latter years you will come into the land that is restored from the sword, whose inhabitants have been regathered from the nations to the mountains of Israel which had been a continual waste; but its people were brought out from the nations, and they are living securely, all of them (Ezek. 38.8; cf. 38.11-14).

The second oracle (Ezek. 39) recapitulates the first (cf. 38.1-4; 39.1-

---

1. Table modified slightly from J. Lust, 'The Order of the Final Events in Revelation and in Ezekiel', in J. Lambrecht (ed.), *L'Apocalypse johannique*, p. 179. Lust's conjectures about the possible relationship between Revelation and the unusual version of Ezekiel found in Greek OT Codex 967 (papyrus) are probably not helpful. In that manuscript, Ezekiel 37 comes between chs. 39 and 40. It is arguable that the order of eschatological events implied by the textual order in Codex 967 is *further* from that of Revelation than the conventional order for two reasons. The integral setting for the battle of Ezek. 38 is the peaceful age after the exile, and the dry bones and messianic kingdom section in Ezek. 37 does not properly parallel the judgment of the non-elect in Rev. 20.11-15, but rather the resurrection of the saints for the messianic age in 20.4-6. To cut and paste Ezekiel to match Revelation, one would want to see something like chs. 36–39–37–38–40.

2), but sets it in a different context, namely, the occasion of Israel's restoration and regathering from the nations:

> And I shall set My glory among the nations; and all the nations will see My judgment which I have executed, and My hand which I have laid on them. And the house of Israel will know that I am the LORD their God from that day onward. And the nations will know that the house of Israel went into exile for their iniquity because they acted treacherously against Me, and I hid My face from them; so I gave them into the hand of their adversaries, and all of them fell by the sword. According to their uncleanness and according to their transgressions I dealt with them, and I hid My face from them. Therefore thus says the Lord GOD.[1] Now I shall restore the fortunes of Jacob, and have mercy on the whole house of Israel; and I shall be jealous for My holy name. And they shall forget their disgrace and all their treachery which they perpetrated against Me, when they live securely on their own land with no one to make them afraid (Ezek. 39.21-26; cf. 27-29).

Taken as it stands, this set of statements places the defeat of Gog and his hosts *before* the age of peace assumed in the former passage.[2] Thus the defeat of all nations coincides here with the gathering of the exiles and the restoring of the fortunes, such that the victory of God sets the stage for the coming age of peace. But in Ezekiel 38, the battle occurs when the peaceful conditions of that age have been the norm for an indefinitely long period of time.

It is virtually undeniable that John sees these two entirely different contexts for the battles of Ezekiel 38 and 39. For he clearly sees the battle of Har-Magedon, which inaugurates the millennium, as fulfilling the latter (cf. Rev. 19.17-18; Ezek. 39.17-20), and the battle ending the millennium as fulfilling the former (cf. Rev. 20.7-10; Ezek. 38.1; 38.22).[3]

---

1. GOD = YHWH (an NASB convention).

2. To the modern scholar, the differences and similarities between these two passages may well suggest an involved source and redaction history (cf., for example, W. Eichrodt, *Ezekiel* [trans. C. Quinn; OTL; Philadelphia: Westminster Press, 1970 (1965–66)], pp. 519-21). But John will certainly have read this book as a unity (as also Isaiah), and so anyone wishing to understand his thinking must take this into account. In other words, there is little doubt that his interpretation will have grown out of the assumption that the final form makes sense as it stands.

3. So, e.g., Kiddle, *Revelation*, pp. 397-98, who agrees that John must have seen two distinct battles described in Ezekiel 38 and 39. Schlatter (*Alte Testament*, p. 93) shows that the Rabbis were united in the opinion that the days of Gog and

But there is another oddity in Ezekiel: Gog's main hosts, the armies of Meshech and Tubal, have already been found lying dead in Sheol (32.26).[1] How then do they manage to attack Israel? In other words, what did John do to resolve the puzzle of why Ezekiel pictured the same hosts appearing for battle long after they had been slain? Suppose one conjectures that he employed the very same strategy which he trains his readers to use: to look for an earlier prophetic context that will inform the passage at hand. How are such contexts identified? They are identified by an apparent equivalence of content, which is then confirmed by salient verbal parallels (as in the sixth and seventh seals).[2]

If one searches for an OT prophecy which, like Ezekiel's, features a fiery defeat of kings and armies, not at the catastrophic inauguration of the day of the Lord and the new age, but rather in the peaceful and secure setting of the new age inaugurated by that day, one has few options to choose from. There is one possibility however: it is highly probable that John saw parallels to Ezekiel 38 in Isaiah 26. As was demonstrated above, Rev. 19.11–20.10 parallels Isaiah 24–26 in some six significant points, among which is the fiery destruction of enemies in the context of an age of peace and security:

> In that day this song will be sung in the land of Judah:
> 'We have a strong city;
> He sets up walls and ramparts for security.
> Open the gates, that the righteous nation may enter,
> The one who remains faithful [cf. Rev. 22.14].
> The steadfast of mind Thou wilt keep in perfect peace,
> Because he trusts in Thee'. . .
> O LORD, Thy hand is lifted up yet they do not see it.
> They see thy zeal for Thy people and are put to shame;[3]

Magog were not the same as the messianic woes, but followed the age of the messiah: e.g. *Pes. K.* 28.

1. This is noted by Metzger, 'Zwischenreich', p. 113 n. 32; Rissi, *The Future of the World*, p. 99 n. 88; and Sweet, *Revelation*, p. 294.

2. In Revelation, John creates striking verbal resonances in order to signal a link between passages that do not always on the surface seem to be speaking of the same thing. For example, in the sixth seal (Rev. 6.13), John sees the stars falling to the earth (εἰς τὴν γῆν) like unripe figs which the fig tree casts (βάλλει), and in the seventh (8.5), he sees an angel fill a censer with coals of fire from the altar and cast it into the earth (ἔβαλεν εἰς τὴν γῆν). One confirms later that both passages are representations of the parousia.

3. NASB margin reads: 'Let them see Thy zeal for Thy people and be ashamed'.

> Indeed, fire will devour Thine enemies.[1]
> LORD, Thou wilt establish peace for us,
> Since Thou hast also performed for us all our works. . . .
> Come, my people, enter into your rooms,
> And close your doors behind you;
> Hide for a little while,[2]
> Until indignation runs its course.
> For behold, the LORD is about to come out from His place
> To punish the inhabitants of the earth for their iniquity;
> And the earth will reveal her bloodshed,
> And will no longer cover her slain.
> In that day the LORD will punish Leviathan the fleeing serpent,
> With His fierce and great and mighty sword,
> Even Leviathan the twisted serpent;
> And He will kill the dragon[3] who lives in the sea (Isa. 26.1-3, 11-12;
>   26.20–27.1).

Although the theme of the exile is present here (Isa. 26.13), the scenario of fiery judgment on enemies is apparently put in the context of an attack on a restored and peaceful Jerusalem, as in Rev. 20.7-10 (cf. v. 9: 'the beloved city'). Adding to this the fact that John puts the attack together with the final destruction of Satan (cf. Rev. 20.10 with Isa. 27.1), it is not at all fanciful to suggest that John saw Isa. 26.11, 21 as the resurrection and judgment of God's enemies, such that the words 'And the earth will no longer cover her slain' (Isa. 26.21) will have been understood by him both literally and figuratively.[4]

This appears all the more likely when one interprets Isaiah 26 in the context of Isa. 24.22. The latter passage, it will be recalled, leaves the door open for those judged at the inauguration of the kingdom of God[5] to appear for judgment a second time, as they apparently

---

1. Cf. Rev. 20.9: 'fire came down from heaven and devoured them'. John will have found a clear point of contact here between Isaiah and Ezekiel. Cf. Isa. 26.11 and Ezek. 38.18-19, which have the same key words in the same context of God's protectiveness over restored Israel: zeal, wrath, fire (Heb. קנא, אף, אש).

2. Cf. Rev. 20.3, μικρὸν χρόνον; Isa. 26.20, כמעט־רגע (LXX μικρὸν ὅσον ὅσον).

3. Isa. 27.1 LXX has δράκοντα ὄφιν (cf. τὸν δράκοντα ὁ ὄφις in Rev. 20.2).

4. For further detail on this, cf. below under §2.f.

5. Armies, an attack on God's people and fiery judgment are present in the background of Isa. 24.22 as well as in Ezek. 38–39 and Isa. 26: cf. Isa. 24.6, 17-18; 25.5.

do in Ezekiel 38. Can more striking verbal parallels be found?

> So it will happen in that day,
> That the LORD will punish the host of heaven on high,
> And the kings of the earth, on the earth.
> And they will be gathered together
> Like prisoners in the dungeon;
> And will be confined in prison;
> And after many days they will be punished
> (Hebrew of this last line: מרב ימים יפקד) (Isa. 24.21-22).

> After many days you will be summoned; in the latter years you will come
> into the land that is restored from the sword (Hebrew of first phrase: מימים
> רבים תפקד) (Ezek. 38.8).

In view of the contextual approach to interpretation that John encourages his readers to use internally in the book of Revelation, and which he consistently uses himself in relation to the whole OT,[1] the conclusion is beyond serious doubt: John understood Ezekiel 37–39 as telling the same eschatological story as Isaiah 24–26. And he not only discovered in each prophecies of the resurrection and judgment of the unrepentant, but he also left markers to aid his readers in making the same discovery.

c. *'The number of them is as the sand of the seashore' (Revelation 20.8)*
This is an entirely familiar OT expression for describing a huge army. But on the other hand, in the only other occurrence of the phrase in Revelation, 'the sand of the seashore' was also the exact phrase used to describe the place where Satan stood to meet the beast as he came up out of the sea (Rev. 12.18 [13.1]).[2] And the sea in that

---

1. Many have been impressed by John's ability to recognize connections between distinct OT contexts and traditions and to present them woven together within his own narrative to form a single coherent picture. See for example the fascinating comments of Farrer on Rev. 5.6 (*Revelation*, p. 95). To give another example that will be treated more fully below, Rev. 6.14 ('the sky was split apart like a scroll, when it is rolled up') manages to allude to, tie together, and treat as mutually interpretative no less than three separate passages in Isaiah, and one in the Psalms (i.e. Isa. 34.4; 51.6; 64.4; Ps. 102.26). C.J. Hemer (*The Letters to the Seven Churches of Asia in their Local Setting* [JSNTSup, 11; Sheffield: JSOT Press, 1986], p. 3) has this comment: 'Often our text seems to derive from a meditation combining two or three scriptural passages and applying mingled reminiscences of them all to the present need of a recipient church'.

2. Sweet (*Revelation*, p. 292) and Kraft (*Offenbarung*, p. 254) agree on the presence of a significant allusion here.

case clearly symbolized the beast's ascent from the abyss (cf. 11.7; also 20.13, where the sea is one of the realms that gives up its dead in the resurrection).

d. *'And they came up on the broad plain of the earth' (Revelation 20.9a)*
There are actually two separate allusions being made in this phrase. First, the words 'they came up' is a peculiar way of speaking about armies assembling for battle on a *plain*.[1] And when one looks for some significance to the fact that the Greek word ἀναβαίνω is used here, one discovers that it is used in only three other contexts in Revelation: for smoke rising;[2] for someone going up to heaven;[3] and (which accounts for the majority of cases) for the beast 'coming up' out of the sea, for the second beast 'coming up' out of the earth' (both of which are symbolic of return from the realm of the dead),[4] and for the beast coming up out of the abyss.[5]

Secondly, the phrase the 'broad plain of the earth' (πλάτος τῆς γῆς) is a rare one in the Greek OT, only occurring in three places. Of these three, by far the closest in overall context to Revelation 20 is the LXX of Dan. 12.2, which predicts that 'many of those who sleep in the *breadth of the earth* (πλάτει τῆς γῆς) will arise, these to everlasting life, and the others to disgrace and everlasting contempt'.[6]

1. Cf. the quotation from BAGD, p. 666, cited below.
2. E.g. Rev. 8.4; 9.3; 14.11; 19.3.
3. E.g. Rev. 4.1; 7.2; 11.12 (going up into heaven or the sky).
4. As has been shown, the sea is one of the realms of the dead mentioned in Rev. 20.13, and the beast's 'coming up out of the sea' parallels his 'coming up out of the abyss' (11.7; 13.11; 17.8); the second beast's 'coming up out of the earth' also suggests the idea of rising from the grave, or of coming up from the realm of the dead.
5. Cf. Rev. 11.7; 13.1; 13.11; 17.8. (Cf. also 9.3, where it is used of demonic locusts coming up out of the abyss.)
6. Cf. BAGD, pp. 666-67 (*s.v.* πλάτος). Bauer has a fascinating comment on the relationship between ἀναβαίνω and the phrase πλάτος τῆς γῆς: 'Rv 20:9 comes fr. the OT (Da 12:2 LXX. Cf. Hab 1:6; Sir 1:3). But the sense is not clear. *Breadth = the broad plain of the earth* is perh. meant to provide room for the count- less enemies of God vs. 8, but the "going up" is better suited to Satan (vs. 7) who has recently been freed, and who comes up again fr. the abyss (vs. 3)' (p. 666). One could well argue that the sense becomes clear on the view presented here.

e. *'And fire came down from heaven and devoured them'*
(Revelation 20.9b)

As was pointed out above, this phrase recalls Isa. 26.11: 'fire will devour Thine enemies'. But realistically, just how strong is the case that John saw (and wanted his readers to see) the resurrection of the unrepentant in Isaiah 26? Is it not begging the question to appeal to a supposed move on John's part linking the imprisonment of Isaiah 24.22 to the attack in Isa. 26.11? To be really confident in claiming this, one would need to identify something in Isaiah 26 that (for John at any rate) would establish a clear and well defined relationship between the two passages. In other words, according to John's scheme, Satan finds himself thrown, along with the 'kings of the earth' and their armies, into the prison of the underworld at the parousia, to await final judgment (cf. Isa. 24.22). What concrete reason will he have had to see, in the fiery punishment of enemies in Isaiah 26, the 'visitation' that was to be the sequel to this imprisonment?

> The dead will not live,
> The departed spirits will not rise;
> Therefore Thou hast punished (פקד) and destroyed them (Isa. 26.14).

> Come, my people, enter into your rooms,
> And close your doors behind you;
> Hide for a little while,
> Until indignation passes over you.[1]
> For behold, the LORD is about to come out from His place
> To punish (פקד) the inhabitants of the earth for their iniquity;
> And the earth will reveal her bloodshed,
> And will no longer cover her slain.
> In that day the LORD will punish (פקד) Leviathan the fleeing serpent. . .
> (Isa. 26.21–27.1).

John obviously understands Isaiah 24–26 as prophesying a very specific set of eschatological happenings, each of which has found a clear and analogous part in his own prophecy. Not only has he plotted together the under-earthly *imprisonment* of Satan and the slaying of the 'kings of the earth' at the advent of the glorious time of salvation (Rev. 19.19–20.6 // Isa. 24.22–26.3), but he has also plotted together the release and 'visitation' of those imprisoned.[2]

---

1. Preferring NASB's literal marginal reading to the misleading paraphrase 'until indignation runs its course'.

2. Cf. the comments above on the phrase 'until the thousand years are

But the importance of these references concerns far more than managing to find the commonplace verb פקד, and so claiming a magical link to Isa. 24.22. Rather, it is overall content which most strongly links Revelation with both passages. John follows these verses from Isaiah 26 very closely when he states in Rev. 20.5-6 that those who have a part in the first resurrection are invulnerable to the 'second death'. In other words, they are exempt from a second and final judgment that awaits the rest of mankind, the dead who 'did not live' when God's people *were* brought to life at the parousia (cf. Isa. 26.14, 19).[1]

Rev. 20.9 is to be seen in this context. Two groups of resurrected people, together making up the whole of humankind, stand together on the earth. In the middle stands 'the camp[2] of the [resurrected] saints', which is God's 'beloved city'. John's readers have every reason to assume that this city is the New Jerusalem, since a permanent place within it was promised to them in the context of the promise of their future eternal life, kingship and priesthood, and in the context of the parousia. As Jesus says in Rev. 3.12 (cf. 20.6),

> I am coming quickly; hold fast what you have, in order that no one take your crown.
> He who overcomes, I will make him a pillar in the temple of My God, and he will not go out from it any more; and I will write upon him the name of My God, and the name of the city of My God, the new Jerusalem, which comes down out of heaven from My God, and My new name.

In Rev. 19.11-16, the readers have seen Jesus coming from heaven to take up his reign on earth with the saints, and now in 20.9 they will

---

completed'. On John's reading of Isa. 24.22 and the above passages, Satan will be equally identifiable as member or leader of the 'hosts of heaven', and as Leviathan the ancient dragon (cf. Rev. 12.7-17). Although nothing hinges on the possibility, it is perhaps worth remarking that he *may* have seen, in the reference to the serpent's home 'in the sea', a veiled reference to imprisonment in the abyss (Isa. 27.1).

1.   It has been demonstrated above that John makes no room for people to come into eternal life at any other time than the parousia. Therefore, the strict choice seems to be either receive eternal life through resurrection at the parousia, or face the second death. Rissi's argument that one might come into eternal life *after* the second death (*The Future of the World*, pp. 77-78) will be treated below.

2.   παρεμβολή. For possible references to the city of Jerusalem as a 'camp', cf. 2 Chron. 22.1; Heb. 13.11-14.

infer that their home, the New Jerusalem, has come down with them.[1] For it will be recalled that, according to everything the readers have been told so far, the parousia is *the unique time* for all promised good things to be experienced.

Surrounding the New Jerusalem on all sides are the rest of the human race, as numerous as the sand of the seashore. They have been judged and punished for a life of hostility to God and his people; they have had to wait a thousand years to taste the freedom of resurrection. But even in resurrection they retain their hostility against God and his people, and they are unanimous in their intent to make *war* (v. 7). Even in resurrection they are willing to listen to Satan's *deception*, which proposes rebellion with the false assurance 'You surely shall not die!' (Gen. 3.4). But even in resurrection they are vulnerable to death: the *second* death which befalls the *resurrected* self. A ring of annihilating fire sweeps them away at a stroke, leaving those 'over whom the second death has no power' completely untouched.

f. *'And the devil...was cast into the lake of fire...'*
(Revelation 20.10)
To be compared with this statement is an earlier passage:

> And another angel, a third one, followed them, saying with a loud voice, 'If any one worships the beast and his image, and receives a mark on his forehead or upon his hand...he will be tormented with fire and brimstone in the presence of the holy angels and in the presence of the Lamb. And the smoke of their torment goes up forever and ever; and they have no rest day and night, those who worship the beast and his image, and whoever receives the mark of his name' (Rev. 14.10-11).

> And the devil who deceived them was thrown into the lake of fire and brimstone, where the beast and false prophet are also; and they will be tormented day and night forever and ever (Rev. 20.7-10).

The readers have been told in Rev. 20.4-6 of the blessings that attend the resurrection of those who refuse to worship the beast or to

---

1.   Zahn says that the very fact that John does not feel it necessary to refer to the 'beloved city' by name presupposes that his readers will be familiar with the term as meaning the New Jerusalem (*Offenbarung*, p. 596). Although it remains highly dubious that there is any evidence for making a distinction between the 'millennial' and the 'eternal' Jerusalem (see Chapter 9, §2.b, below), not much is taken away from the position maintained here by allowing it: the important point is that the eschatological Zion/Jerusalem is meant by the expression 'the beloved city' (cf. Pss. 78.68; 87.2; 122.6; Isa. 66.10; Zeph. 3.17).

receive his mark. Now in v. 10, they are reminded that the fate of Satan will be precisely that unending torment which is to be the fate not only of the 'resurrected' beast and his false prophet, but equally of those who have worshipped and received the mark of the beast. These are the very ones who most emphatically *do not* come to life (i.e. experience resurrection) 'until the thousand years were completed' (20.5). For human beings, the parallel words *tormented, day and night, forever and ever*,[1] suggest not a millennium-long stay in the abyss, but something entirely permanent, that is, resurrection. The *picture* of armies being destroyed by fire in Rev. 20.7-10 follows Isaiah 26 and Ezekiel 38, but the implication being *suggested* is that resurrection and unending punishment are in view.[2]

3. *Revelation 20.7-10: Conclusions*

It appears that John is giving his readers every possible hint that the scene of Rev. 20.7-10 pictures the resurrection and judgment of the 'rest of the dead'. The key elements of the argument are the following. (1) John closes off entirely the possibility of unresurrected people taking part in the millennium, so that consistency restricts the possible identity of 'Gog and Magog' to the rest of the dead. (2) He places Satan's release from the prison of the abyss in precise juxtaposition to the resurrection of the 'rest of the dead'. (3) He implies that the 'rest of the dead' are destined as such to the 'second death'. (4) He describes 'Gog and Magog' (a) with the phrase 'the sand of the seashore', which alludes to the beast's ascent from the sea/abyss in 13.1, (b) with the phrase 'the four corners of the earth', which (at least indirectly) alludes to the demonic hordes coming up from the abyss in 9.4 (cf. 7.1), and (c) with the word ἀνέβησαν, which alludes to the resurrection of the beast from the abyss. (5) He describes their fate in a way that gives a cogent sense and an appropriate fulfilment to the expression 'the second death'. (6) He describes the fate of their leader Satan in a way that both alludes to the fiery punishment of the resurrected beast, and recalls that the same fate awaits all who worship him.

---

1. βασανίζω, ἡμέρας καὶ νυκτός, εἰς [τοὺς] αἰῶνας [τῶν] αἰώνων.

2. When the lake of fire comes into the picture explicitly for 'the rest of the dead' in Rev. 20.15, comments will be offered on the paradox of two different models for final punishment: annihilation by fire from heaven versus unending torment in the lake of fire.

All appeal to the OT has been left out of the points summarized here. This is in order to demonstrate that the readers are offered clear and sufficient grounds for coming to the proposed interpretation of Rev. 20.7-10, even given the strict contextual boundaries of the book of Revelation. It should be obvious nonetheless that the OT has played an intimate part in the composition of Revelation, and that it is intended to play an intimate part in its interpretation. But the difference between a reading of Revelation 20 without the OT and a reading with the OT is not so much analogous to the difference between an encoded message without and with a code book, as it is analogous to the difference between a picture in black and white, and the same picture in colour and in a 3-D stereoscope.

One may anticipate here a rather obvious complication that looms for the present interpretation, namely, that the resurrection and judgment of the 'rest of the dead' are about to be described explicitly in imagery and circumstances that on the surface are quite different from those set out in Rev. 20.7-10. In Rev. 20.11-15, the dead are apparently raised not to a battle, but to a trial. But if Rev. 20.7-10 is truly intended to describe the resurrection of the dead, then it must be possible to detect indications that, in spite of first appearances, the two scenes are actually to be interpreted as describing the same event. And it will be demonstrated in due course that such indications indeed exist.

For the present, however, a brief summary of conclusions is in order before proceeding to the exegesis of Rev. 20.11-15. It has been shown on a number of different grounds that the battle of 20.7-10 is prepared for and described in such a way that the reader is both encouraged and forced to reach a particular conclusion: Gog and Magog and their hosts are the 'rest of the dead' (conceivably joined by the fallen angels) who have been released by resurrection from the prison of Hades. In striking thematic parallelism to 19.11-21, judgment is being pictured as a battle scene as opposed to a courtroom scene. But the reader will not conclude from this that the battle of Rev. 20.7-10 is identical with that of Rev. 19.11-21, since the contexts are entirely different, and the flow of the narrative has added up to a consistent progression of events. Instead, the reader will see the battle of Rev. 20.7-10 as working out the final stage of an ever increasing irony of deception: the unrepentant keep following their false god and fighting against the people of the true God right to the bitter end, even to the resurrection itself. Beasley-Murray's reflection is thought-provoking in this context:

> It is likely that Genesis will have taught John as truly as Ezekiel, since its
> pictures of the first paradise are used by John to depict the last paradise.
> Genesis will have suggested that as Satan was allowed to enter the first
> paradise to expose the nature of man's heart, so in the restoration of
> paradise he will be permitted to do so again.[1]

It has been argued that John intends Rev. 20.7-10 to be interpreted
equally by Isaiah 24–26 and Ezekiel 38, and that he almost surely saw
the pair of OT prophecies as interpreting one another. Sweet's comment, cited in Chapter 4, §2, bears repeating in more detail:

> [John] had an astonishing grasp of the Jewish Scriptures, which he used
> with creative freedom. He never quotes a passage verbatim, but para-
> phrases, alludes and weaves together motifs in such a way that to follow
> up each allusion usually brings out further dimensions of meaning. . . In
> fact Revelation can be seen as a Christian re-reading of the whole Jewish
> scriptural heritage, from the stories of the Beginning to the visions of the
> End.[2]

Finally, what expectations will the readers be entertaining as they
stand on the threshold of Rev. 20.11-15? The answer, perhaps surprisingly, is 'none'. As John has set up the story, all loose ends have
been tied up. The Satanic trio are burning in the lake of fire, the unrepentant have been resurrected and destroyed, and the saints have all
been resurrected and will now (one supposes) live on undisturbed for
eternity in the 'beloved city', as kings and priests to God. Anything
that is related from now on will presumably have the purpose of fleshing out one or another story element that has not yet been fully revealed. To take a glimpse ahead, the visions of the New Creation and
the New Jerusalem are going to be examples of this. It is thus in the
context of a story already finished that one encounters Rev. 20.11-15.

---

1. *Revelation*, p. 291. More reflections on this theme will be offered in later
chapters of the study.
2. *Revelation*, p. 40.

Chapter 8

REVELATION 20.11-15: THE FINAL JUDGMENT

John's vision of the Enthroned One both opens this scene and becomes the presupposition of all that happens in it. Everything he sees will presumably happen 'before the throne' (Rev. 20.12). The first step towards a satisfactory exegesis of the present passage is therefore to go back to the beginning of Revelation, and, by tracing forward all the major references to God's throne, to become aware of the sorts of ideas and images the readers will be intended to have brought with them as they encounter it here in 20.11. It will be discovered in this process that by the twentieth chapter of the book of Revelation one has been as frequently confronted with visions of the Almighty on his throne, as with any other single image or subject.[1]

1. Revelation 20.11: The Throne (and the Heavenly Temple)

Reference to God's throne occurs for the first time in the epistolary address (Rev. 1.7), and it is immediately (if indirectly) tied to the imagery of the 'heavenly temple'[2] by the way in which the throne is related spatially to the sevenfold Spirit:

---

1.   'The first thing John sees in heaven is a throne [Rev. 4.2]. From first to last John's vision is dominated by this symbol of divine sovereignty' (Caird, *Revelation,* p. 62).

2.   John clearly shares with the writer to the Hebrews (Heb. 8.4-5), and with early Judaism, the idea that the earthly temple is a model for heavenly realities. Thus, for example, one will find the phrase 'the temple of God which is in heaven' in Rev. 11.19. For some rabbinic citations, cf. P. Billerbeck (and H. Strack), *Kommentar zum Neuen Testament aus Talmud und Midrasch.* III. *Die Briefe des Neuen Testaments und die Offenbarung Johannis* (Munich: Beck, 1926), pp. 702-704 (on Heb. 8.5).

After the Thousand Years

> Grace to you and peace, from Him who is and who was and who is to come; and from the seven Spirits who are before His throne; and from Jesus Christ, the faithful witness. . . (Rev. 1.4-5).

This is apparently a trinitarian formula.[1] The Spirit's designation as 'the seven Spirits' will gradually be made understandable on the basis of its place in a whole system of temple imagery. First, in the inaugural vision, Christ is seen walking among seven golden lampstands as a kind of heavenly priest (Rev. 1.12-20; cf. Exod. 25.37). He later promises that the overcomer will be made 'a pillar in the temple of My God, and he will not go out from it any more' (3.12). Finally, when John is caught up to heaven in ch. 4, he sees that

> a throne was standing in heaven, and One sitting on the throne . . . And from the throne proceed flashes of lightning and sounds and peals of thunder. And there were seven lamps of fire burning before the throne, which are the seven Spirits of God; and before the throne there was, as it were, a sea of glass like crystal; and in the center (ἐν μέσῳ, 'in the presence of') and around the throne, four living creatures full of eyes in front and behind (Rev. 4.2, 5, 6).

The throne here, with its cherubim, corresponds to the earthly ark of the covenant. One is reminded not only of the divine throne-visions of Ezekiel (1.4-28; 10.1-22), but also of the appellation 'Thou who art enthroned above [or between] the cherubim' (Pss. 80.1; 99.1; Isa. 37.16; cf. Exod. 25.22).[2] The seven lamps of fire correspond to the flames of the seven-branched lampstand that stood before the veil of the holy of holies. This is the lampstand about which Zechariah was told, 'Not by might, nor by power, but by My Spirit, says the Lord of hosts' (Zech. 4.2-6).[3] The glassy sea appears to be the heavenly coun-

---

1.   However unlikely the phrase 'seven Spirits' may sound at first as a reference to the one Holy Spirit, a relatively satisfying explanation for the terminology is nonetheless available (cf. Farrer, *Revelation*, p. 95). Angelic beings are probably not meant, since this would put created beings on equal footing with God and Christ as sources of divine blessing. Cf. Beasley-Murray, *Revelation*, pp. 54-56.

2.   Schlatter (*Alte Testament*, p. 26) notes that in the 'Palestinian school' heaven is at once pictured as God's throne and God's temple.

3.   If there was any uncertainty as to John's reference to Zechariah here, it is taken away by his interpretation of the seven eyes of the Lamb: they are 'the seven Spirits of God, sent out into all the earth' (Rev. 5.6), which paraphrases Zechariah's angel, who interprets the seven flames of the lampstand as 'the eyes of the LORD which range to and fro throughout the earth'. Cf. Farrer, *Revelation*, p. 95, for illuminating comments.

terpart of the water in the bronze 'sea' of the laver (Exod. 30.17-21; 1 Kgs 7.23-26; 2 Chron. 4.2-5). Later the reader will encounter the altar of sacrifice (Rev. 6.9; cf. Exod. 29.12[1]), the golden incense altar (Rev. 8.3-5; cf. Exod. 30.1-8), the ark of the covenant (Rev. 11.19; see below), and the 'sanctuary of the tabernacle of testimony' (i.e. the tent of witness: cf. Rev. 15.5-8; Exod. 38.21).

The point to be gained from these observations is not that John necessarily wanted his readers to have specific images of the 'heavenly furniture'. Nor is it that he intended for them to envisage the realities referred to in temple terminology and imagery in any exact spatial relationship to one another. The point is rather that he is experiencing as visual metaphors the heavenly realities to which the earthly tabernacle/temple and its furniture correspond. If on some occasions the 'temple metaphor' is sustained in his descriptions of heavenly things, on other occasions it is exposed as metaphorical and indirectly interpreted by the addition of elements that break its conceptual limits. On still other occasions, it is exposed by simple interpretation. In other words, the three possibilities for the use of temple metaphors are: (a) to sustain the metaphor uninterpreted, (b) to point to its interpretation by transcending or breaking it, (c) to interpret the metaphor. The following are examples of each.

(a) And the temple of God which is in heaven was opened; and the ark of His covenant appeared in His temple, and there were flashes of lightning and sounds and peals of thunder and an earthquake and a great hailstorm (Rev. 11.19).

(a) I looked, and the temple of the tabernacle of testimony in heaven was opened, and the seven angels who had the seven plagues came out of the temple, clothed in linen. . . And the temple was filled with smoke from the glory of God and from His power; and no one was able to enter the temple until the seven plagues of the seven angels were finished (Rev. 15.5-8).

(b) I saw underneath the altar [of sacrifice] the souls of those who had been slain. . . (Rev. 6.9).

(b) And another angel came and stood at the altar [of incense], and much incense was given to him, that he might add it to the prayers of all the saints upon the golden altar which was before the throne. And the smoke

1. Cf. the comments on Rev. 5.9 in Chapter 4, §3, above.

of the incense, with the prayers of the saints,[1] went up before God out of the angel's hand (Rev. 8.3-4).

(c) As for the mystery of the. . . seven golden lampstands. . . the seven lampstands are the seven churches (Rev. 1.20).

(c) the four living creatures and the twenty-four elders fell down before the Lamb, having each one a harp, and golden bowls full of incense, which are the prayers of the saints (Rev. 5.8).

(c) And he [the beast] opened his mouth in blasphemies against God, to blaspheme His name and His tabernacle, that is, those who dwell in heaven (Rev. 13.6).

These examples show that John is anything but naïve in his understanding of heaven as the 'temple' of God. He makes it clear that he not only interprets the earthly temple and its accoutrements as metaphorical for heavenly realities, but more radically, *he carefully trains his readers to interpret metaphorically his descriptions of what he sees in heaven* (e.g. Rev. 5.8). It will later appear as significant that with the exception of the throne, ark and the glassy sea, all of the temple imagery employed prior to ch. 19 is used to symbolize the relationship between God and his people.

For the present, however, this digression will have served to establish support for the idea that the imagery of the throne of God both arises from and belongs to the context of the 'heavenly temple'. In terms of their ultimate reference, therefore, both the Ezekiel-style throne of Revelation 5 and the 'ark of the covenant' of ch. 11 are a unity. The ark is metaphorical for the throne of God; the throne of God is metaphorical for that 'place' where God's holiness and power stand openly revealed. Thus it is no wonder that the quasi-natural phenomena attending the throne in ch. 4 are those most strongly evocative of awe and mystery: 'from the throne proceed flashes of lightning and sounds and peals of thunder' (4.5).

Upon reflection, it is also no wonder that these same elements appear after the opening of the seventh seal in Rev. 8.5, along with the earthquake, which ties the seventh seal to the sixth as representations of the parousia. For the readers learned from the sixth seal

---

1.   In the Greek, there is no preposition 'with' here: the phrase 'the prayers of the saints' is simply in the dative case. But cf. the quotation of Rev. 5.8 below in the main text under (c), for the meaning: the angel is adding much more incense (metaphorically, *prayers*) to the prayers that are already on the altar.

(6.16-17) that the parousia of Christ is equally the parousia of the Enthroned One, and the seventh seal has underlined this. The readers are thus being trained to think 'God is revealing himself on his throne', when they meet with lightning, thunder, sounds and earthquake.[1]

Therefore, when they encounter the seventh trumpet, and the ark of the covenant is revealed along with the very same elements (cf. the quotation of Rev. 11.19 above), the readers should be able to recognize yet another reference to the parousia of the Enthroned One.[2] Once this has been grasped, it becomes manifestly clear that everything that has happened following the seventh trumpet (cf. 11.15-18) has prepared for just such a revelation.

Finally, as if to remove any doubt, the same pattern appears yet again after the seventh bowl:

> And the seventh angel poured out his bowl upon the air; and a loud voice came out of the temple from the throne, saying, 'It is done'. And there were flashes of lightning and sounds and peals of thunder; and there was a great earthquake, such as there had not been since man came to be upon the earth, so great an earthquake was it, and so mighty (Rev. 16.17-18).[3]

What conclusion is to be drawn from this theme and imagery of the 'heavenly temple' as the highly developed context for the throne of

---

1. Sweet comments on Rev. 11.29: 'Each septet ends with these manifestations of the sovereignty of the divine throne (4.5)' (*Revelation*, p. 193).

2. This contention stands in spite of the fact that, among the commentators I consulted on the subject, no one made the equation: Ark (Rev. 11.29) = Throne (4.2). Farrer, for instance, begins by splitting the throne from the ark, and so misses the most obvious point to be inferred from his own following remarks:

> St John ought not to be taken to mean that the temple of God, hitherto closed to his eyes, now opens its doors, and that what the opening supremely reveals is the Ark. The temple of heaven, which is the presence-chamber of God's glory, opened its doors to St John at iv. 1. The Ark cannot be the central manifestation of divine presence there; to enter the temple is to see God on his throne (*Revelation*, p. 139).

Ironically, Farrer has already shown why the throne should be described here precisely under the figure of the ark, by pointing out that the reference to the ark is one in a series of elements clearly evoking the fall of Jericho. Cf. the central importance of the ark in Josh. 6.4-11; the blowing of seven trumpets in Josh. 6.15; the 'shout' which followed the blowing of the seven trumpets in Josh. 6.16, paralleled by the 'loud voices' of Rev. 11.15 (Farrer, *Revelation*, p. 137).

3. Both the seventh trumpet and the seventh bowl are further linked by the feature of a great hailstorm (cf. Rev. 11.19; 16.21).

God? Simply this: the 'throne' finds its place in a complex scheme of what might be called 'visual metaphors'. In a text where seven lamp-stands 'are' seven churches, where the seven flames upon them 'are' the distributions of the Holy Spirit's power to each church, and where bowls of incense 'are' the prayers of the saints, and so on, what is *the throne of God*? It is the locus of God's complete self-manifestation, where his full majesty is revealed.[1]

Before the parousia, the full glory and holiness of God have only been manifest in 'heaven'—in other words, beyond the glassy sea. What will happen if Isaiah's prayer is answered, and God decides to 'rend the heavens and come down' (Isa. 64.1)? Isaiah expects that neither humankind nor creation will be able to stand:

> O that Thou wouldst rend the heavens and come down,
> That the mountains might quake at Thy presence—
> As fire kindles the brushwood, as fire causes water to boil—
> To make Thy name known to Thine adversaries,
> That the nations may tremble at Thy presence (Isa. 64.1-3).

In an earlier part of Isaiah the same thought is expressed:

> For the LORD of hosts will have a day of reckoning
> Against everyone who is proud and lofty,
> And against everyone who is lifted up,
> That he may be abased
> . . .
> And men will go into caves of the rocks,
> And into holes of the ground
> Before the terror of the LORD,
> And before the splendor of His majesty,
> When He arises to make the earth tremble (Isa. 2.12, 19).

John undoubtedly read these prophecies, and he must have under-stood clearly from them that the day of God's visitation was going to be a shattering experience for his whole creation. That John's expec-tation is akin to that of Isaiah is obvious when one reads Rev. 6.12-17, which describes the collapse of all the 'permanent' features of the created world: sun, moon and stars; the expanse of the sky; all moun-tains and islands. Finally the cause of this global catastrophe is revealed, and the implication is that creation itself has been unable to stand in 'the presence of Him who sits on the throne' and before the

---

1.   As Minear says, 'The throne-heaven is the realm where the unlimited power and love of God are fully known and fully operative' (*I Saw a New Earth*, p. 274).

'wrath of the Lamb', who is co-enthroned with him (cf. Rev. 3.21). This idea of the dissolution of the created order will have been a familiar one to John through his reading of prophetic passages such as the following, which comes from Jeremiah:

> I looked on the earth, and behold, it was formless and void;
> And to the heavens, and they had no light.
> I looked on the mountains, and behold, they were quaking,
> And all the hills moved to and fro.
> I looked, and behold there was no man,
> And all the birds of the heavens had fled.
> I looked, and behold, the fruitful land was a wilderness,
> Before the LORD, before His fierce anger (Jer. 4.23-26).

Jeremiah's phrases, literally translated from the Hebrew, would read: 'from the face of (מפני) the LORD, from the face of the heat of His anger'. John's words in Rev. 6.16 display an unmistakable parallelism: 'hide us from the face (ἀπὸ προσώπου) of Him who sits on the throne, and from the wrath of the Lamb'. Clearly John is both aware of and in tune with the idea behind these passages.

His statement that 'the sky was split apart like a scroll when it is rolled up', along with his comparison between falling stars and figs shaken off the tree in a high wind, suggests yet another passage from Isaiah:

> And all the host of heaven shall be dissolved, and the heavens shall be rolled together as a scroll: and all their host shall fall down, as the leaf falleth off from the vine, and as a falling fig from the fig tree (Isa. 34.2-4).[1]

As usual, John interprets the above passages from Isaiah and Jeremiah synoptically. For him, in other words, each reveals something important about the parousia, but something which only comes out when one *puts them together*. And that is what he is training his readers to do, both with OT prophecies, and with his own multiple visions of the parousia.

---

1. John differs from the LXX (cf. RSV, NASB) in his interpretation of the last phrase here (but agrees, e.g., with KJV [here quoted], NEB and NIV), in that he assumes figs, rather than leaves, to be the implicit subject of the participle וכנבלת (and like that which falls). The assumption that figs are meant comes from the fact that the immediately preceding word for a leaf (עלה) is masculine, and seems out of accord with the (abstract?) feminine participle, whereas fig (תאנה) agrees, being feminine, and fits nicely into the imagery of falling.

One element in his description of the events following the opening of the sixth seal will bring this out strikingly. The relationship between these passages illustrates this:

> Of old Thou didst found the earth;
> And the heavens are the works of Thy hands.
> Even they will perish,[1] but Thou dost endure;
> And all of them will wear out[2] like a garment;
> Like clothing Thou wilt change them, and they will be changed
> (Ps. 102.25-26).

> Lift up your eyes to the sky,
> Then look to the earth beneath;
> For the sky will vanish[3] like smoke,
> And the earth will wear out like a garment,
> And its inhabitants will die in like manner (Isa. 51.6).

All these passages share the idea that the present creation is imperfect, and that it is destined to collapse in the day of Yahweh's visitation. But whereas Isaiah and the psalmist compared that collapse to a worn-out garment falling into shreds, John compared it to a scroll wearing out (Rev. 6.14). Mounce rightly catches the imagery when he comments,

> The heavens are removed like an unrolled papyrus scroll which, should it break in the middle, would roll quickly back on either side.[4]

In the context of the parousia (Rev. 6.15), this description is equivalent to saying that the throne of God and of the Lamb will appear as through a widening tear in the expanse of the sky. In other words, the sky is being pictured as rushing away on both sides from the theophany of the Enthroned One and his messiah. What is amazing about this imagery and its expression is not only that it manages to allude to

---

1. אבד, literally 'to wander off, run away, be lost'.
2. בלה, literally 'to fall, or to fall away (like clothing which has become torn from long wear)'.
3. מלח (niph.), literally 'to slip away, to flee'; hence, 'to vanish'.
4. *Revelation*, p. 162. It is perhaps worth noting Lattimore's translation of Rev. 6.14: 'and the sky shrank upon itself like a scroll curling. . .' (*Four Gospels and Revelation*, p. 262). Although it is hard to understand how he decided to render ἀπεχωρίσθη (normally 'was split, separated, parted') as 'shrank upon itself', his rendering of the participle ἑλισσόμενον as a middle, as opposed to a passive ('curling', not 'was rolled up'), goes well with Mounce's way of interpreting the imagery.

and tie together three separate passages in Isaiah (and one in the Psalms), but that it also comprehends the distinctive imagery of each, and further suggests an image which encompasses them all at once. When God reveals himself at the parousia, he will indeed 'rend the heavens and come down' (Isa. 64.1), and the heavens will be 'rolled up like a scroll' (Isa. 34.4); they will indeed 'flee away like smoke' (Isa. 51.6) and 'run away... and fall (into shreds) like a garment' (Ps. 102.26). Rev. 6.14, in other words, supplies a clear example of John's 'synoptic' reading of the OT.

It is evident from examples such as these that John's way of expressing himself has grown out of long and intensely imaginative meditation on the eschatological meaning of OT passages. And he obviously feels no obligation to limit his own prophecy by making only those references which a person might be expected to catch on a first reading. Instead, he leaves a trail of verbal clues to the connections he sees, evidently hoping that at least some of his readers will later learn to follow his footsteps through the careful study of his work.[1]

After coming to Rev. 20.11 and having been introduced to 'Him who sits on the throne', the present method of interpretation dictated that major references to the theme of God as the Enthroned One should be traced forward from the beginning of Revelation, right up to ch. 20. In this way, a sense could be gained as to the ways in which the reader would have been prepared to hear the words of 20.11. By the end of ch. 6, what themes, images and OT backgrounds have attached themselves to the 'throne'?

First encountered is the set of themes and images connected to the 'heavenly temple' (the system of metaphors expressing both God's transcendence from the world, and his intimate relationship with his people; cf. Rev. 14.6). Second is the idea, steeped in the images of

---

1. Admittedly, claims about intention are always less than certain. D. Cain ('Artistic Contrivance and Religious Communication', *RelS* 8 [1972], p. 42) asks to be excused from discussing intention, speaking instead about the textual phenomena of Revelation. He concludes that Revelation exemplifies a kind of religious communication

> which is not capable of being exhausted immediately (or ever, for that matter)—a form of communication which retreats as far as possible from the communication of a straight 'what' that can be understood immediately apart from any qualification of the person receiving it. That there is a kind of religious communication to which artistic contrivance gives a form, a depth and a richness which needs to be lived with and brooded on and grown into is evidenced by the Book of Revelation.

Isaiah and other OT writers, that there will come a time when the Enthroned One will come, and that when he does, neither wicked humanity nor the creation itself will be able to bear his anger; all creation will disintegrate before him. In Revelation 6, however, the coming of the Enthroned One and the coming of the Lamb are pictured as a single event. A reader will therefore tend to look for references to the dissolution of the created order when presented with further passages dealing with the parousia of the Enthroned One with his Christ.[1]

Going on to look at Revelation 7, it has already been pointed out that vv. 9-17 picture the parousia as the fulfilment of a promise made to the martyrs in ch. 6: namely, that their time of waiting for vindication was to last only until the full number of their 'brethren and fellow-servants' should be reached. The martyrs had prayed that justice be done to the 'earth-dwellers' (6.10), and this prayer was clearly answered in the sixth seal (6.16-17). Therefore in 7.9, when the uncountable multitude appear before the very same 'throne and before the Lamb', but exult in praises instead of cowering in disgrace, it is clear that this is the same parousia, but that it is a day of rejoicing for the saints.[2]

When John asks the meaning of the saints worshipping before the throne and before the Lamb (Rev. 7.9-12), the scene is interpreted to him as follows:

> [Because they have washed their robes in the blood of the Lamb] they are before the throne of God; and they serve Him day and night in His temple; and He who sits on the throne shall spread His tabernacle over them. They shall hunger no more, neither thirst any more; neither shall the sun beat down on them, nor any heat; for the Lamb in the center of the throne shall be their shepherd, and shall guide them to springs of the water of life; and God shall wipe every tear from their eyes (Rev. 7.15-17).

Focus may be placed on just a few items here: first, the phrase 'He who sits on the throne shall spread His tabernacle over them' recalls

---

1.   For some, the question will arise as to whether and to what extent John will follow Isaiah in predicting a re-creation in the wake of the dissolution that accompanies Yahweh's visitation (cf. Isa. 66.22). But since it is only in the first verses of Revelation 21 that John will offer any clear indication of whether he will follow Isaiah in this, the question of a renewal will have to remain in the background during treatment of the present chapter (on 20.11-15).

2.   For proof of this contention, cf. Chapter 9, §2, below.

Isa. 4.2-6, whose subject is the coming of the glorious 'Branch of Yahweh':

> then the LORD will create over the whole area of Mount Zion and over her assemblies a cloud by day, even smoke, and the brightness of a flaming fire by night; for over all the glory will be a canopy. And there will be a shelter to give shade from the heat by day, and refuge and protection from the storm and the rain (Isa. 4.5-6).

The idea of protection from 'heat' is not only common to this passage and Rev. 7.16, but also to another passage in Isaiah that speaks of a restoration after the exile:

> Along the roads they will feed,
> And their pasture will be on all the bare heights.[1]
> They will not hunger or thirst,
> Neither will the scorching heat or sun strike them down;
> For He who has compassion on them will lead them,
> And will guide them to springs of water (Isa. 49.9-10).

John's angel is clearly paraphrasing this promise to the returning exiles. Mention of the 'great tribulation' in Rev. 7.14 also shows that deliverance from severe injustice is the common context of both passages (cf. Isa. 49.4-9).

There is no hint from John that Rev. 7.9-17 is a scene of judgment: for these redeemed, to be 'before the throne of God' is to be saved from the false judgment of persecuting humanity and to have been conducted with joy into the intimate and life-giving presence of the Almighty.[2] The prospect of full communion with God is also central to yet a third passage in Isaiah, which is recalled by the reference to the wiping away of tears (Isa. 25.6-8).[3]

Between this passage and the one from Revelation 6, one has

---

1. Note the imagery of sheep and the leading shepherd here, which in Rev. 7.17 becomes applied to Jesus as the divine messiah who is paradoxically both Lamb and Shepherd (cf. Isa. 53; Ezek. 34.23; Jn 10.14-16).

2. John probably intends (and would have approved in any case) a reference to Jer. 2.13 and 17.13 (so, e.g., Caird, *Revelation*, p. 102; Lohmeyer, *Offenbarung*, p. 73). In these passages the LORD claims the title 'the fountain of living waters', i.e. (literally) the fountain of the waters of life. In Rev. 22.1, the 'water of life' is to appear once again, and its significance obviously includes both the visual idea of an artesian spring, and the spiritual idea of the source of eternal life. Well in line with Jeremiah, John notes that its fount is precisely the throne of God and of the Lamb.

3. Fuller treatment of this passage awaits the discussion on Rev. 21.1-8.

received entirely opposite impressions. To be before God's throne (or, to do without the metonymy, to be in God's full presence) connotes judgment, terror and death to the 'earth-dwellers', but to those who 'wash their robes', it is deliverance, joy and life. Each passage gives exclusive attention either to the one or to the other set of connotations (negative or positive)—a fact that will be relevant in the discussion of how a consecutive reader will be inclined, based on the patterns previously encountered, to interpret Rev. 20.11-15.

Moving forward to Revelation 11, the sounding of the seventh trumpet brings another liturgy of praise before the throne of God, but in this case specific mention of the throne itself is noticeably absent (cf. 11.15-17). In line with a point argued above, one suspects that this is so that there will be no interference between the 'throne' and the 'ark of the covenant' when it appears in 11.19, for the two are not to be separated, but rather equated. From what has gone before in chs. 6 and 7, it is obvious that 11.18 is summarizing the two sides of the parousia, and underlining the paradox that the same event means opposite things, depending on one's relationship to God. The following verse deserves particular attention:

> And the temple of God which is in heaven was opened; and the ark of His covenant appeared in His temple, and there were flashes of lightning and sounds and peals of thunder and an earthquake and a great hailstorm (Rev. 11.19).

The revelation of the Enthroned One here in Rev. 11.19 happens when 'the temple of God which is in heaven' is 'opened'. Its imagery harkens back first to John's statement in 4.1 that he saw 'a door standing open in heaven', and to the fact that, when invited to 'come up here', he immediately saw God's throne. It also recalls the events following the opening of the sixth seal, when John saw the skies separate like a splitting scroll. Judging from people's reactions in that situation, it was clear that it was none other than the throne of God and his messiah that they saw through the tear in the sky. To open the door to heaven (4.1), in other words, is to see the inside of God's temple. To tear away completely the vault of the sky (6.14-17) is to achieve the same thing, only in a radical way. Thus John's wording of 11.19 expresses the same idea (heaven opening to reveal the parousia of the Enthroned One) in the same context (a final confrontation with wicked humanity—11.18), except that here he describes the revelation of God's throne in terms of the system of temple metaphors, and refrains from explicit mention of Christ.[1]

In Revelation 16, after a hint that what is to follow is 'the war of the great day of God, the Almighty' (v. 14), John reports,

> And the seventh angel poured out his bowl upon the air; and a loud voice came out of the temple from the throne, saying, 'It is done'. And there were flashes of lightning and sounds and peals of thunder; and there was a great earthquake, such as there had not been since man came to be upon the earth, so great an earthquake was it, and so mighty. . . And every island fled away, and the mountains were not found (Rev. 16.17-21).

The first sentence here is somewhat cryptic. It may possibly be over-interpretation to call this an auditory revelation of the parousia corresponding to the visual revelation of Rev. 11.19, but that the parousia is being described is in no doubt. As Beasley-Murray comments, '"It is done". We are reminded of the observation in 15.1, that with these plagues the wrath of God is ended.'[2] John's readers should now be well familiar with the pattern: (1) final confrontation between God and wicked humanity (cf. 6.16-17; 11.18; 16.14, 19), (2) attention drawn to the throne (cf. 6.16; 11.19; 16.17), (3) a stock of elements denoting the awesome revelation of God upon his throne (cf. 4.5; 8.5; 11.19; 16.18), (4) earthquake (cf. 6.12; 8.5; 11.19; 16.18), (5) destruction of mountains and islands (cf. 6.14; 16.20), (6) hail (cf. [6.12; 8.5]; 11.19; 16.21).[3]

---

1. Not that he is absent! The reader knows from the immediate context that there is no separating the kingly parousia of God from the parousia of his vice-regent (Rev. 11.15). Jesus has a parallel 'solo appearance' when his parousia from heaven is described in 19.11: 'And I saw heaven opened; and behold a white horse, and He who sat upon it is called Faithful and True. . .' But again, this is balanced by a liturgy before the throne of God (19.1-7, see below).

2. *Revelation*, p. 246.

3. On this whole subject, cf. R. Bauckham, 'The Eschatological Earthquake in the Apocalypse of John', *NovT* 19 (1977), pp. 224-33. The first two references may merit inclusion in an indirect way, since in both there are numerous (more or less spherical?) objects falling out of the sky, and hail is the precise element within the larger recurring pattern that is left out in each case. Cf. Schlatter's observation that it was common in Jewish exegesis of the plague of hail in Exod. 9.24 to understand the words 'fire in the midst of (בתך) the hail' as indicating that there was fire in each hailstone (*Alte Testament*, p. 84). In this context, both the stars falling to earth in 6.12, and the bowl of coals from the incense altar being thrown into the earth in 8.5, may correspond to an Exodus-style plague of hail (also cf. the combination of fire and hail in Ezek. 38.22, and the combination of hail and coals of fire in Ps. 18.12-

In Revelation 19, preceding the revelation of Jesus on a white horse, John describes a triumphal liturgy before the throne of God, which has affinities both with the scene of 7.9-12 and with that of 11.15-17. Praises are offered to 'God who sits on the throne' because of the justice of his judgment in the overthrow of Babylon (19.1-3); and then, as in 16.17, 'A voice came from the throne', saying,

> 'Give praise to our God, all you His bond-servants, you who fear Him, the small and the great'. And I heard, as it were, the voice of a great multitude and as the sound of many waters and as the sound of mighty peals of thunder, saying, 'Hallelujah! For the Lord our God, the Almighty, reigns. Let us rejoice and be glad, and give the glory to Him, for the marriage of the Lamb has come and His bride has made herself ready' (Rev. 19.5-7).

The first sentence here clearly harks back to Rev. 11.18, where the parousia was predicted as the time for God's reward to be given to 'Thy bond-servants the prophets and to the saints and to those who fear Thy name, the small and the great'. Similarly, the giving of praise to God because he has taken up his eschatological reign (v. 6) points back to 11.15-17. The 'great multitude', the sound of whose response to the call for praise can only be compared with all the loudest and most awesome sounds of nature rolled into one, just as clearly harks back to the 'great multitude' of 7.9-10 that 'cried out with a loud voice, "Salvation to our God who sits on the throne, and to the Lamb"'.[1]

In Revelation 19, the throne of God is shown for the third time (cf. 7.9-17; 11.15-18) to denote the parousia not only as an occasion of wrath, but also as one of rejoicing. It all depends on what group of people is facing the throne. For God's saints, whom he has saved from the 'great tribulation', the parousia means triumph and vibrant celebration before the throne. But for God's enemies, and indeed for creation itself, the parousia means terrible exposure and destruction before the very same throne.

---

13). It is at least certain that John sees the hail-plague in Rev. 16.21 in Exodus terms, in the light of his whole way of constructing the context of the seven bowls. Cf. Rev. 15.3-4, and compare the phrase 'such as there had not been since man came to be on the earth' in Rev. 16.18 with Exod. 9.18; 10.6, 14; 11.6.

1.   Note the further parallel created by the words 'our God', which point back to Rev. 7.9-12 via 19.1—'After these things I heard, as it were, a *loud* voice of a *great multitude* in heaven, *saying*, "Hallelujah! *Salvation and glory and power* belong to *our God*..."' (words in italics paralleled in 7.10, 12).

2. *Revelation 20.11-15: Preparatory Remarks for Exegesis*

At this point, the major ideas and images connected with the throne of God have been traced to the threshold of Rev. 20.11. Now that an account has been given of the extensive contextual system behind the key concept in the verse, exegesis may proceed.

It will be worthwhile, however, to begin by recalling the immediate setting. In reading the previous verse (Rev. 20.10), one will have reached the apparent end of the eschatological drama, and a situation where no major 'unfinished business' remains in the story. In other words, by the tenth verse of Revelation 20, all the expectations created in the text have come to some kind of resolution. For example, in 20.3 it was said that Satan would have to be released from his prison, and so until one read of his release in 20.7 there was still a thread of the story left hanging. On a different but equally important level, there was an implicit question about Satan's ultimate fate, the answer to this unspoken question being given in a satisfying way in 20.10.

As the reader encounters Rev. 20.11, therefore, an interpretative decision will be called for. Is what John describes here something new and unprepared for, something which is to be understood as happening after the end of the (apparently completed) story of 4.1–20.10? Or does it function as an amplification of, or a new viewpoint upon, something in the story that has already been related? If the readers have learned well from what has gone before, they should be aware that the latter option (i.e. the possibility of encountering new viewpoints on matters previously revealed) remains wide open; in fact, it will be far more in character with the rest of Revelation than the former.

3. *Revelation 20.11: The Parousia of the Enthroned One*

> And I saw a great white throne, and Him who sat upon it, from whose presence earth and heaven fled away, and no place was found for them (Rev. 20.11).

John's readers obviously have been thoroughly prepared for this imagery by their previous encounters with the throne of God. Furthermore, they will have every reason to recognize in this verse a reference to the same 'parousia of the Enthroned One' which they have encountered in chs. 6, 11 and 16.

Nevertheless, there is a pair of elements here that is new, and deserves attention. The first is that the throne is described as great, and as white or shining (μέγας λευκός).[1]

a. *Revelation 20.11a: A Throne, Great and White*
The word 'great' is a favourite of John's. Yet, in spite of phrases such as 'the great day of His wrath' (Rev. 6.17), 'the great day of God the Almighty' (16.14), and 'the great supper of God' (19.14), the ascription of greatness to God's throne here in 20.11 does not seem to refer specifically to any earlier context in Revelation. Farrer understands the *whiteness* of the throne to symbolize victory,[2] and this seems defensible, in view of such passages as 6.1 and 19.11, 14 (where white horses connote victory). But the colour white also clearly symbolizes purity (cf. 3.4-5, 18; 7.9, 13-14; 15.6; 19.14).[3] Again, no particular earlier context in Revelation seems to be being recalled. Looking to the OT, one finds in Daniel a description of the Enthroned One, and although his clothing is white, his throne is fiery (Dan. 7.9). The next verse (Rev. 20.12) will show that John definitely had this passage from Daniel in mind, but it remains puzzling that neither *great* nor *white* seems to be pointing anywhere specific within Revelation. A satisfying explanation of this description will therefore have to wait until later passages in Revelation lend their assistance.

In the meanwhile, however, the rest of Rev. 20.11 is bristling with instructive verbal parallels:

> And I saw a great white throne, and Him who sat upon it . . . (20.11a).

> And I saw heaven opened, and behold, a white horse, and He who sat upon it. . . (19.11).[4]

Just as Christ has had his appearance as the judge of the living at his parousia in Revelation 19, now in 20.11-15 the Enthroned One will be pictured as he whose parousia signals the judgment of the dead (20.12). Nonetheless, the reader will have learned from chs. 6 and 11

---

1. For the connotation of λευκός as shining, cf. Mt. 17.2; Lk. 9.29, where light and lightning respectively count as λευκός.
2. *Revelation*, p. 209.
3. So, e.g., Swete, *Apocalypse*, p. 267.
4. In Greek the verbal parallels (disregarding case), are: καὶ εἶδον, οὐρανός, λευκός, καὶ ὁ καθήμενος ἐπ᾽ αὐτόν. In imagery, the opening of heaven (Rev. 19.11) is close to heaven fleeing God's presence.

that these two parousias and two judgments are inseparable (esp. 11.18). Vögtle aptly remarks,

> The picture of the Enthroned One does not exclude, but rather *includes* Christ, just as he has been recognizable right from the beginning (1.7)— and especially in his first eschatological judgment vision (16.16c-17). John has no more difficulty with such a conflict than does the apostle Paul, who can speak equally of the judgment seat of Christ (2 Cor. 15.10) and of the judgment seat of God (Rom. 14.10).[1]

b. *Revelation 20.11b: From whose Face Earth and Heaven Fled . . .*

> he from whose face the earth and the sky fled, and no place was found for them (Rev. 20.11b, Lattimore).

> the sky was split apart like a scroll when it is rolled up; and every mountain and island were moved out of their places. . . hide us from the presence [lit. face] of Him who sits on the throne. . . (Rev. 6.14, 16).[2]

> And every island fled away, and the mountains were not found (Rev. 16.20).[3]

An examination of these passages reveals that John is suggesting a synoptic reading of chs. 6 and 16, and that he is using the same exact method (of employing key words and phrases) that he uses in relation to the OT. By using the same techniques he uses to recall two or three OT passages in one sentence, he points here to the key antecedents within his own narrative. In fact, with the exception of the words *great* and *white*, virtually every aspect of the wording of Rev. 20.11 can be traced back to some striking parallel within the context of the parousia of the Enthroned One. Caird's comment on this verse is worth repeating because of its harmony with the spirit of Rev. 6.12-17 and its OT roots:

> Earth and heaven did not merely vanish like a puff of smoke, they *fled*; they *fled* in dismay before the moral grandeur of God, because they were

---

1. A. Vögtle, *Das Buch mit sieben Siegeln: Die Offenbarung des Johannes in Auswahl gedeutet* (Freiburg: Herder, 2nd edn, 1985 [1981]), pp. 159-60.

2. In Greek the verbal parallels with Rev. 20.11 are: οὐρανός, τόπος, θρόνον. . . καὶ τὸν καθήμενον ἐπ' αὐτόν. . . Rev. 6.16 reads ἀπὸ προσώπου τοῦ καθημένου ἐπὶ τοῦ θρόνου.

3. In Greek the verbal parallels with Rev. 20.11b are: ἔφυγεν, οὐχ εὑρέθησαν.

unfit for his continued presence, because they were contaminated beyond the possibility of cleansing.[1]

c. *Revelation 20.11b: Dissolution or Disappearance?*

What response can be made to the (common) notion that whereas Revelation 6 saw the radical *disturbance* of the created order, 20.11 pictures the *annihilation* of it? For instance, Farrer says,

> Nothing can stand before him. Earth and heaven flee away; the things previously shaken (vi. 14, xvi. 20) are now removed.[2]

It may be argued that this comment, rather than stemming from any substantial difference in imagery between these passages, more likely reflects Farrer's expectation that things described in Rev. 20.11 will happen a thousand years after the parousia, since 20.11 comes in the text after the narration of the millennium and its close in 20.7-10. But John has narrated some five or more visions of the parousia before the 'principal' one in 19.11,[3] so why should he not be allowed to present yet another vision or visions of it *after* the 'principal' one? One can imagine the response of most interpreters: 'If one allows the kind of radical destruction of the created world pictured in 20.11 to be connected to the parousia, then the whole (living) human race would presumably be destroyed, and no one would be left to enter the millennium (and rebel at the end of it)'. But the mistakenness of this response has already been demonstrated in detail in the chapters above: John's insistent point, from ch. 6 on, has been that no one on earth survives the parousia. Moreover, every indication has been given that the hosts involved in the rebellion of 20.7-10 came from the underworld, not from supposed outlying societies who escaped judgment at the parousia. Taken at face value, the upheavals of chs. 6 and 16 are just as fatal as those of Rev. 20.11.

Perhaps someone will ask, 'But what about the fact that "no place was found" for earth and heaven in Rev. 20.11? Must not this point to a radical removal of the whole cosmos, as opposed to simply a removal of "mountains and islands" (6.14; 16.20)?' There are two

1. Caird, *Revelation*, pp. 258-59 (italics original).
2. *Revelation*, p. 209. Picturing things similarly, Lohmeyer says that after Rev. 20.11, 'God and the dead stand. . . in an awesome void' (*Offenbarung*, p. 164).
3. Cf. Rev. 6.12-17; 7.9-17; 11.15-19; 14.1-5; 14.14-20; 16.17-21 (not to mention 8.5).

reasons for a negative reply to these questions.

First, it is quite a different matter for an ancient to say 'the earth fled away' than it would be for a modern. Few ancients had the modern concept of the earth as the 'globe'; instead, the earth (γῆ) denoted the *land* (as opposed, for example, to the sea and the sky). The earth, in other words, is the dry land, with its fields, valleys and mountains. To say that the earth fled away, therefore, would presumably be to say that all the familiar features of the land rushed away like so many rucks being shaken out of a carpet. And this is precisely the kind of image evoked not only by the words of Rev. 16.20, but also by OT passages well known to John, such as Jer. 4.23-26, quoted above. Equally close in context, and even closer in imagery, however, is Ps. 97.1-5:

> The LORD reigns; let the earth rejoice;
> Let the many islands be glad.
> Clouds and thick darkness surround Him;
> Righteousness and justice are the foundation of His throne.
> Fire goes before Him,
> And burns up His adversaries round about.
> His lightnings lit up the world;
> The earth saw and trembled.
> The mountains melted like wax at the presence of the LORD,
> At the presence of the Lord of the whole earth.[1]

For Jeremiah, what results from this kind of encounter between creator and creation is not a cosmic vacuum, but rather an earth returned to its primaeval state of (uninhabitable) chaos (cf. Jer. 4.23; Gen. 1.2-3). If one notes that such a state of chaos in Genesis comes before the creation of the great vault of heaven, and before the establishment of the dry land above the waters of the abyss, then the fleeing away of earth and heaven in Rev. 20.11 will quickly be understood as indication of a return to primaeval conditions.

The second response is to note that the words 'no place was found for them' echo Dan. 2.35:

> a stone was cut out without hands, and it struck the statue on its feet of iron and clay, and crushed them. Then the iron, the clay, the bronze, the

---

1.   Literally, 'from before the face of (מלפני) the LORD'; LXX (96.5): τὰ ὄρη ἐτάκησαν . . . ἀπὸ προσώπου κυρίου. The image (closely related to that of Jer. 4) is that of wax melting away from a flame or very hot object (cf. Ps. 68.1-2; once again lit. *from before his face*: מפניו in v. 2 [ET v. 1], similarly v. 3 [ET v. 2]).

> silver and the gold were crushed all at the same time, and became like
> chaff from the summer threshing floors; and the wind carried them away
> so that not a trace of them was found.[1] But the stone that struck the statue
> became a great mountain and filled the earth (Dan. 2.34-35).

What is being pictured here is not the annihilation of the statue in a
technical sense, but its radical dismantling: its atomization and complete redistribution. In other words, 'no place was found' for the gold,
silver, bronze, iron and clay parts of the statue, not in the metaphysi-
cal sense that their components no longer existed anywhere in the
physical universe, but in the sense that they experienced such a complete loss of form, that they were no longer there to be perceived as
such. This is exactly the sort of 'disappearance' which is affirmed in
Rev. 16.20 with the words 'fled away' and 'were not found'.[2]

In conclusion, although the annihilation of the world may have been
conceivable for John and his contemporaries, there is nothing in his
wording of Rev. 20.11 which either demands or even particularly
suggests such a conception. On the contrary, his imagery coheres best
with the notion that at God's visitation, the earth will dissolve into its
primaeval state of uninhabitable chaos (as in Jer. 4.23-26).

4. *Revelation 20.11-15: Setting the Time Frame for the Judgment*

Given the above discussion in this chapter of the throne, the dissolution of the creation, and the parousia, the reader of the present essay
could be forgiven for expecting an interpretation of Rev. 20.11-15
that immediately puts the scene in the context of the parousia. There

---

1.   The words τόπος οὐχ εὑρέθη (Rev. 20.11c) are exactly paralleled in
Theodotion. Commentators also point to the same expression in Zech. 10.10 (Heb.),
where the context is eschatological over-crowding in the promised land. If the clause
'and no place was found for them' thus reflects the Hebrew idiom for lack of room,
then the picture being painted is one in which the elements crush and trample one
another in their frenzied rush to escape the presence of the Enthroned One. It would
be very much in character for John to have both contexts in view.

2.   The interpretation of Daniel's vision follows: 'And in the days of those [last]
kings the God of heaven will set up a kingdom which will never be destroyed, and
that kingdom will not be left for another people; it will crush and put an end to all
these kingdoms, but it will itself endure forever' (Dan. 2.44). If John is indeed
evoking Dan. 2.35 by the words 'no place was found for them' in Rev. 20.11, then,
as a reader, one will have yet another reason to understand that the parousia is being
evoked, as opposed to something after the millennium (cf. Rev. 11.15-17).

remains, however, a very significant gap between what has been shown above, and the idea that 20.11-15 invites interpretation as a scene that happens at the parousia. For it must be taken into account that, *if* a scene is finally to be recognized as a new viewpoint on something previously revealed, it will then be possible to show at what point, or in response to what specific prompting(s), such a realization is likely to happen. One does not, for example, *begin* reading Rev. 20.4 on the assumption that it will offer a new viewpoint on the parousia already described in 19.11-21 and elsewhere. Instead, this fact suggests itself as the terms, pictures and promises from earlier in the text converge so as to indicate that the same reality is being referred to in each instance. In other words, the strategy that readers first bring to a narrative is to try a chronological approach:

> Our first impulse with any tale when the order of telling is clear is to take the order of occurrence to be the same as the order of telling; we then make any needed corrections in accord with temporal indications given in the narrative and with our antecedent knowledge both of what happened and of causal processes in general.[1]

What is implied by this comment is that even though the parousia has been involved virtually every time the throne of God has appeared previously in Revelation, the reader will still instinctively begin interpreting Rev. 20.11 in a chronological way—in other words, by taking the appearance of the throne as introducing a vision of something that happens next after the destruction of Gog and Magog in 20.10. Thus answers must be given to the following questions. How will the section be read following from such a first reaction? At what point, and in what way (if any), will the reader be given reason to conclude that he or she is being given a new narration of something which has already been described?[2]

---

1.   N. Goodman, 'Twisted Tales', *Critical Inquiry* 7 (1980), pp. 103-19 (104). Goodman goes on: 'But discrepancy between order of telling and order of occurrence cannot always be discovered instantaneously—or at all'.

2.   It has already been conceded in the introduction that the majority interpretation is able to make reasonably good sense of the text of Rev. 20.1-15, *given the proviso that the chapter is taken in isolation.* Similarly here, it may be granted that if one has read through 20.7-10 without picking up the indications of resurrection, then one's interpretation of 20.11-15 will require no time adjustments. For one will assume that one is seeing the resurrection of the 'rest of the dead', joined by 'Gog and Magog' who have just been killed (as mortals) at the end of the millennium. In

After the Thousand Years

To begin with, I assume that the reader is a Koine Greek speaker, has come more or less automatically to associate the revelation of the Enthroned One and the attendant dissolution of creation with the parousia, and has recognized the picture of resurrection in Rev. 20.7-10.

It is arguable that for such a person Rev. 20.11 will be susceptible of two distinct interpretations. Which of these interpretations is chosen will depend on whether one assumes that something long after the parousia is in view, or whether, as was discussed above, one concludes that something revealed earlier is being narrated from a different perspective. In the former case, the words οὗ ἀπὸ τοῦ προσώπου ἔφυγεν ἡ γῆ καὶ ὁ οὐρανός (lit. he from whose face fled the earth and the heaven) will not suggest that John has seen a great white throne and One sitting on it, and that he then sees the fleeing of earth and heaven before that One.[1] Rather, one will hear that John saw the throne and the One who sat there, and that this is He from whose face earth and heaven fled *at the parousia a thousand years ago.* Thus Richmond Lattimore renders the verse this way:

> And I saw a throne, great, white, and sitting upon it was he from whose face the earth and sky fled, and no place was found for them.[2]

It is clear from this translation that Lattimore did not think John intended to narrate the fleeing of earth and heaven from the presence of the Enthroned One. He took John to mean that he recognized the One sitting on the great white throne as the same One from whose enthroned presence he had seen heaven and earth flee in Revelation 6.[3]

other words, the text might have a whole level of information that can be ignored while still producing a distinct and reasonably coherent reading. This double (or multiple) potentiality is clearly designed into the text, and a possible rationale for such a design will call for discussion at a later point.

1.   This is the standard way of understanding and translating the verse. Thus the NEB rendering: 'and the One who sat upon it; from his presence earth and heaven vanished away, and no place was left for them' (similarly NIV: 'Then I saw a great white throne and him who was seated on it. Earth and sky fled from his presence, and there was no place for them').

2.   Lattimore, *Four Gospels and Revelation*, p. 284.

3.   I wrote to Lattimore in 1981 (shortly before he died) and asked him to explain his translation for me. Having myself come to the same rendering, I wanted to find out for certain whether his version reflected a specific interpretation of the relative pronoun οὗ, or whether it had simply resulted from a philosophy of following the word order as closely as possible. I argued at some length in that letter (cf. below)

There are a number of reasons for preferring Lattimore's translation to the standard rendering. First, in terms of grammar it is only by overlooking the fact that the relative pronoun stands in syntactical relationship with the following clause as a whole, rather than strictly with προσώπου, that most translations arrive at results like the following: 'and the One who sat upon it; from his presence earth and heaven vanished away, and no place was left for them' (NEB), and 'from whose presence earth and heaven fled away' (NASB). In Greek, the word for face (πρόσωπον) needs no possessive pronoun as it would in English, so the relative should not be translated as though it simply filled that function. Weight needs to be given to the fact that the relative pronoun *precedes* the prepositional phrase (cf. Lattimore's translation), but this is entirely lost in modern translations.[1]

Secondly, in terms of style, John simply does not use relative clauses to convey action in his narrative. Instead he uses them for description: e.g. τὸ θηρίον τὸ πρῶτον οὗ ἐθεραπεύθη ἡ πληγὴ τοῦ

that, of the 80 or so relative pronouns in the narrative portion of Revelation, not one carried an action in the narrative: all rather pointed backward (or forward) to salient actions or features encountered elsewhere in the text (e.g. 4.1; 12.5; 13.12). Nowhere, in other words, does John make a relative pronoun the subject or object of a clause in which action is being narrated—his relatives are all used to introduce adjectival, descriptive clauses, rather than narrative action clauses. Lattimore's written response to my argument follows in its entirety: 'I have read your letter with some care, two or three times over, and find myself in complete agreement. My translation was made originally some twenty years ago, and reprinted, with only a few corrections, to accompany the Four Gospels, so that I am unable to retrace the process of thought gone through at the time, but rereading now, I still think that the relative, like your other cases, is descriptive rather than narrative.'

1. As far as I am aware, among modern Western translations in English, German, French, Spanish and modern Greek, Lattimore's alone avoids this pitfall. Ancient versions do much better: Syriac (Peshitta, Harclean and Philoxenian), Coptic (Sahidic and Bohairic), Armenian and Old Latin (Irenaeus) all leave the relative outside the prepositional phrase (Ethiopic, Vulgate, codex Gigas dissent). The crux, of course, is whether the former versions are being 'word-order literal' at the expense of smooth grammar, or whether they appreciate the stylistic and other factors referred to below. No ability is claimed to make a judgment on this issue, but one thing is clear: in general the oldest versions lend consistent support to the point made here, at least to the extent that it is *possible for them to do so*. Incidentally, the pleonastic addition of αὐτοῦ in some MSS does not affect the argument, since it probably reflects an unconscious assimilation of one of John's Semitic habits (cf. M. Zerwick, *Biblical Greek* [trans. J. Smith; Rome: Pontifical Biblical Institute, 1963], p. 65).

θανάτου αὐτοῦ (Rev. 13.12). Aside from 1.2, which is outside the vision narrative proper, John never once (in over 80 examples) uses a relative in the way NEB translates 20.11.[1]

Thirdly, in terms of John's general habits of narration, it merits notice that in Rev. 20.11 as well as many other passages in Revelation, interpreters expect far more action narrative from John than he actually offers.[2] The expectation of action seems to be so great here that translators cannot see the simple grammar of description. What one in fact encounters in 20.11, is *the re-introduction of a character into the narrative*. One of John's favourite techniques for doing this is to describe the character by means of a relative clause referring back to salient actions or features encountered previously in the text.[3] Perhaps the closest example to 20.11 in this regard (along with 13.12, quoted above) is 12.5, where John is describing the heavenly sign of the woman and child. The child is described as ἄρσεν, ὃς μέλλει ποιμαίνειν πάντα τὰ ἔθνη ἐν ῥάβδῳ σιδηρᾷ, which recalls 2.26-27 and prefigures 19.15. If here Jesus is introduced with dynamic characteristics encountered earlier, so similarly 'he who sits on the throne' is introduced in 20.11 as the same One whose presence had earlier

---

1. The only passage that even appears close to being an exception to this rule is Rev. 16.14. There John identifies as follows the three 'frogs' which he has seen coming out of the mouth of the beast and the false prophet: εἰσὶν γὰρ πνεύματα δαιμονίων ποιοῦντα σημεῖα, ἃ ἐκπορεύεται κτλ. G. Mussies, in his detailed grammar of Revelation (*The Morphology of Koine Greek as Used in the Apocalypse of St John* [NovTSup, 27; Leiden: Brill, 1971], p. 334), seems to have treated ἐκπορεύεται as a historical present, which would give the relative, ἃ, close to demonstrative force (For they are demons performing signs. *These* went out. . .). But John is not narrating that the spirits of demons go out to gather the kings of the whole world for the battle of the great day: he is explaining that the three frogs that he saw in his vision *represent* demons that go out and do particular things. In other words, the relative clause is a true adjectival clause and it is not the locus of the narrative action, which has already been expressed by John's statement that he saw the three frogs going out of the mouths of the beast and false prophet. Once more: John is not saying that in his vision demons went out to gather the kings of the earth. What he is saying is that in his vision he saw three frogs go out, and that he understands these frogs to represent demons that perform particular functions.

2. If Mussies intended to classify ἐκπορεύεται as a historical present (although it is not entirely certain that he did), then he did so because he so expected action that he missed the fact that he had before him a dynamic description.

3. Some examples of this may be found in Rev. 4.1; 10.5, 8; 12.5; 13.2; 17.2, 8b; 19.2, 20.

caused earth and heaven to flee (cf. 6.14-17, and 16.18-20).

What this means is that the fleeing of earth and heaven does not function as part of the scene in Rev. 20.11-15, but rather stands in the past relative to it. In other words, it is an event which is recalled as having happened earlier, before the scene opens. The question of *how much earlier*, however, is not addressed by v. 11. It could equally have happened more or less immediately before, or a thousand years before (or anywhere in between, for that matter). But (1) at this point the reader knows the dissolution of the world in the presence of the Enthroned One happened at the parousia, and (2) the story has already been narrated through to the end of the millennium. Therefore, on one's first reaction, 20.11 will presumably suggest that the appearance of God on his throne after the millennium has naturally evoked John's earlier visions of the parousia in which the throne played a major role. By the end of 20.11, in other words, a sensitive reader will not yet have found any reason to 'switch gears' chronologically.

5. *Revelation 20.12: The Judgment of the Dead*

> And I saw the dead, the great and the small, standing before the throne, and books were opened; and another book was opened, which is the book of life; and the dead were judged from the things which were written in the books, according to their deeds (Rev. 20.12).

In encountering these words, the readers will for the first time have good reason to wonder if the parousia, rather than the end of the millennium, should be understood as the time frame for the vision. For the dead are being 'judged' here, and the readers will have learned already from Rev. 11.15-18 and from 20.4-6 that the parousia is the occasion for the judgment of the dead.[1]

Once this possibility has been allowed, the words 'I saw the dead standing before the throne' suddenly suggest a very clear and plausible scenario. For if the parousia has seen the land and sky ripped away before the throne of the Almighty, then, by implication, creation will have had its two uppermost layers stripped off, uncovering the great caverns of the earth and their subterranean waters.[2] In other words,

---

1. The phrase 'the great and the small' also conceivably helps recall Rev. 11.18.

2. For this cosmology, which sees the heavens as a kind of solid expanse above the earth, and the earth as a lid over the abyss (תהום) of subterranean waters, cf. Gen.

the great underworld of Hades and all its inhabitants will have been left standing exposed before him who sits on the throne. Sickenberger catches the image when he comments,

> Now there unfolds before the eye of the seer a picture apparently similar to Genesis 1.2: God's throne hovers 'above the waters'. Since the sea has not yet disappeared (20.13; cf. 21.1), the earth has apparently flooded over. Thus John sees the dead (i.e. people who have died) rising out of the sea. . . [1]

The phrase 'the books were opened' further ties the scene to the parousia, by recalling Daniel 7, which relates a similar judgment scene:

> I kept looking
> Until thrones were set up,
> And the Ancient of Days took His seat;
> His vesture was like white snow,
> And the hair of His head like pure wool.
> His throne was ablaze with flames,
> Its wheels were a burning fire.
> A river of fire was flowing
> And coming out from before Him;
> Thousands upon thousands were attending Him,
> And myriads upon myriads were standing before Him;
> The court sat,
> And the books were opened (Dan. 7.9-10).

As has already been shown, it is clear from a comparison between the next verse, Dan. 7.11, and Rev. 19.20, that John saw this scene from Daniel as a revelation of the parousia of Christ and of the beast's fiery end. The scene as it stands in Daniel, however, is not obviously

1.1-10; 7.11; 8.2; Job 38.16; Pss. 104.6; 135.6; Prov. 3.20; 8.24, 27-28; Ezek. 26.19; 31.15. The Gen. 7, 8 passages (along with various others) show that rain is conceived of as coming down through holes in the heavenly expanse, whereas springs are conceived of as coming up out of the abyss through holes in the earth. The writer of *1 Enoch* says that the subterranean waters were mixed with fire after the flood, for the punishment of rebellious angels (*1 En.* 67.1-13). This could be taken as an attempt to overcome a clash between the OT concept of an underworld which is watery, and the newer (whether Persian, Greek, NT or apocalyptic) idea of a fiery abyss. This paradox, however, is one that John shows no inclination to reconcile. It is characteristic of his writing that the same realities can be pictured by means of entirely different images.

1.   *Erklärung*, pp. 185-86.

one in which the dead are being judged, but one in which 'the saints take possession of the kingdom' (Dan. 7.18, 27). But John has already shown that he understands these words to refer to the martyred saints:

> And I saw thrones, and they sat upon them, and judgment was given to [or by] them. And I saw the souls of those who had been beheaded because of the testimony of Jesus and because of the word of God, and those who had not worshiped the beast. . . ; and they came to life and reigned with Christ for a thousand years (Rev. 20.4).

As has been observed above about Revelation 6 and 7, John's individual visions about the parousia may focus entirely either on its salvific or on its condemnatory side. With this in mind, it seems that it would be natural for the reader to conclude that Rev. 20.4-6 and 20.11-12 deal respectively with the positive and negative sides of the parousia as the judgment of those who have died. That is, 20.4-6 sees the judgment of Daniel 7 as the *vindication* of the *lives* (ψυχαί) of those who have been martyred (through their resurrection and reception of the kingdom), whereas Rev. 20.11-12 sees the same scene as the *conviction* of the *dead*.[1]

The 'book of life', which has no counterpart in Daniel 7, will also draw the scene into association with the parousia. This book lies open along with the other 'books' in v. 12. Whereas the words 'judged from the things written in the books, according to their deeds' indicate that the books contain the records of what people have done during

---

1. Kraft says the emphasis is on the *deadness* of the dead to separate them from the living of Rev. 20.4-6 (*Offenbarung*, p. 261). Likewise, Prigent rightly interprets John's refusal to use the term *resurrection* in 20.11-15 as pointing to the same distinction (*L'Apocalypse*, p. 317). Many other commentators note that the whole scene of Rev. 20.11-15 lacks any hint of a positive outcome, and so seems to correspond to 20.4-6 as the negative converse: e.g. Sweet, *Revelation*, p. 293; Rissi, *The Future of the World*, p. 36; D. Smith, 'The Millennial Reign of Jesus Christ: Some Observations on Rev. 20.1-10', *ResQ* 16 (1973), pp. 226-27; Kline, 'The First Resurrection', p. 371. Attempts to see a positive outcome in 20.11-15 generally evince an external theological agenda (e.g. Metzger, 'Zwischenreich', pp. 110, 114-15; Pohl, *Offenbarung*, p. 299). Adding further weight to this argument is the fact that 20.4 evokes 6.9-11, where the souls of people martyred for their faithfulness are in heaven, not in Hades. The discussion of 15.1-2 in Chapter 4 underlined this in a clearly cosmological way. John joins certain other NT writers in the understanding that it is only the unrepentant dead who are imprisoned in the subterranean abyss of Hades (*pace* Kiddle, *Revelation*, pp. 406-407). Cf. Rev. 11.7; 20.1-3; Mt. 11.23; 1 Pet. 3.18-20; 4.6.

their mortal lifetimes,[1] 'the book of life' is not obviously being consulted for information. Why then does it stand open, and what is it? Farrer answers,

> It had originally been conceived of as a muster-roll of God's living subjects; to have one's name expunged was simply to die (Exod. xxxii. 32-33, Ps. lxix. 28). But by St John's time it had come to be seen as a roll of those destined to receive the life of the world to come (Phil. iv. 3).[2]

John's readers will definitely have picked up this latter idea of predestination to eternal life through their encounters with the book of life earlier in Revelation:

> He who overcomes shall thus be clothed in white garments; and I will not *erase* his name from the book of life, and I will confess his name before My Father, and before His angels (3.5).

> And all who dwell on earth will worship him [the beast], every one whose name has not been written from the foundation of the world in the book of life of the Lamb who has been slain (13.8).

> whose name has not been written in the book of life from the foundation of the world (17.8).[3]

Swete calls the book of life 'the roll of the living citizens of the New Jerusalem',[4] and the soon to be encountered Rev. 21.27 will serve to confirm this. There should be some suspicion that this is the idea even for the reader who has not yet had access to 21.27, since Christ's promise to keep the overcomer's name in the book of life (3.5) parallels all the promises of eternal life in the epistles to the churches, and the next promise (3.12) is to have the name of the New Jerusalem written on one's forehead, and to be granted permanent residence in the eschatological temple of God.

It seems on this basis that the judgment from the books is to determine whether or not someone's name is worthy of being written in the

---

1. For the idea of record-books of deeds kept before God, cf. Dan. 7.10; Mal. 3.16; *1 En.* 90.20; *2 Bar.* 24.1; *4 Ezra* 6.20; *Jub.* 30.22.

2. *Revelation*, p. 209. Alongside the Philippians reference stands Dan. 12.1, which envisions people 'written in the book' being rescued from persecution to participate in the eschatological kingdom. Also cf. Isa. 4.3, where one finds the phrase 'those recorded for life in Jerusalem' in the same context.

3. Cf. also the later Rev. 21.27: 'nothing unclean. . . shall come into it [the New Jerusalem], but only those whose names are written in the Lamb's book of life'.

4. *Apocalypse*, p. 269.

book of life; that is, whether one deserves to be raised from death and granted citizenship in the eschatological community of God and Christ, the New Jerusalem. In other words, perhaps one's first impression will be that the book of life is opened to be written in, whereas the other books are open in order to be read from. At the same time, however, it may be possible to understand that something deeper and more paradoxical is going on: that the books of deeds are open not in order to make revisions in the book of life, but rather in order to put on public display the concrete and indisputable evidence ratifying the inclusion or exclusion of names from the book of life, which has always stood complete from eternity (13.8; 17.8).[1] But in any case, the reader will have good reason to assume that the issue to be decided is the same as in 20.4-6—that of who is, and who is not, worthy of being resurrected to eternal life at the parousia. And if, as has been suggested, the focus here is on the unrepentant, and one is to see here a negative judgment corresponding to the positive one in 20.4-6, then one will be equipped to know that the outcome will be no resurrection for them during the millennium, for

> The rest of the dead did not come to life until the thousand years were completed. This is the first resurrection. Blessed and holy is he who has a part in the first resurrection; over these the second death has no power. . . (20.6).

6. *Revelation 20.13-15: The Judgment of the Dead (Again?)*

But instead of some statement to the effect that the outcome was that these dead were judged unworthy of resurrection, the reader finds these words:

> And the sea gave up the dead which were in it,
> And death and Hades gave up the dead which were in them;
> And they were judged, every one of them according to their deeds.
> And death and Hades were cast into the lake of fire.
> This is the second death, the lake of fire.
> And if anyone's name [lit. anyone] was not found written in the book of
>   life,
> He was thrown into the lake of fire (Rev. 20.13-15).

This ending to the scene poses problems for the (consecutive) reader.

---

1. Cf. Kiddle, *Revelation*, p. 404, and Beasley-Murray, *Revelation*, pp. 301-302, for helpful comments.

Two different interpretative strategies suggest themselves, but neither makes enough sense in itself to be completely satisfying.

The *first* way of reading is to follow the scene through according to the original visual–cosmological setting. Following the removal of the earth and the heavens, the shades of the dead in the abyss (*the sea, death, Hades*) are left standing face to face with the Enthroned One.[1] Each is tried in the court of God according to the evidence contained in the books, in other words, according to deeds. That is, each is put to the proof on the basis of an exhaustive and accurate record of all his or her doings, from birth to death. This judgment completed, the dead are seen being drawn out of the abyss, which is to say, they are resurrected.[2] They are now tried a second time individually according to their deeds (Rev. 20.13).[3] Death and Hades (personified respectively as recruitment officer and housing manager of the realm of the dead—cf. 6.8), now bereft of their jobs, come into final punishment (v. 14). Interpretation of the lake of fire as the second death specifically recalls what was implied in 20.6, namely, that those condemned in the judgment of the dead at the parousia would be vulnerable *in resurrection* to the second death.[4]

1.   As Rissi says, 'It is quite wrong to perceive the second resurrection in the event of world judgment: mankind stands before the throne in their death condition, as *nekroi* (20.12)' (*Time and History*, pp. 121-22 [italics original]). This comment is accurate of Rev. 20.12, but not of v. 13, where the dead are to be brought *out* of their 'death condition' (cf. below). Rissi's denial of physical resurrection in the whole scene of 20.11-15 serves an indefensible larger agenda that I will discuss below (cf. Chapter 9, §3).

2.   Believing that the concept behind the beast's rising from the abyss/sea is resurrection (Rev. 11.7; 13.1; etc.), Roloff (*Offenbarung*, p. 196) thinks that the absence of the term *resurrection* implies that the dead stand bodiless before the throne. But the point John is far more likely to have intended by his silence is that the unrepentant are not really alive, even if endowed temporarily with functioning bodies (cf. the comments of Kraft and Prigent, above). To be at enmity with one's creator is to be dead in a deeper sense than the biological one.

3.   For the odd expression 'They were tried each (sg.) according to their (pl.) deeds', cf. Rev. 2.23. The phrasing in 22.12 seems in better grammatical accord: 'to render to each as his work deserves' (literally, *is*). The focus in all three passages is on the fact that judgment will hold each person accountable as an individual, and not just as part of a group.

4.   Once more (cf. Chapter 4, §4, above), this also fits in with the fact that the 'resurrected' beast and false prophet experienced the lake of fire at the parousia (Rev. 19.20).

It is clear that the overall pattern here has the *potential* to parallel that found in the first part of the chapter (Rev. 20.1-10): first, judgment at the parousia on the basis of one's conduct in former life (20.4-5 // 20.11-12), then, resurrection and judgment on the basis of conduct in resurrection (20.7-10 // 20.13-15). But two important questions suggest themselves. Why is there no mention either of the denial of resurrection, or of a gap of a thousand years between v. 12 and v. 13? Why does the whole scenario of final judgment (20.11-15) appear to be in conflict with that which precedes? For in 20.7-10, the resurrection of the unrepentant issues not in a final court appearance, but in a final 'war'. In itself, the scene of 20.11-15 does not seem to offer any immediate answer to these questions.[1]

It therefore makes sense to hold this interpretation in abeyance and to experiment with a different approach. Thus a *second* way of reading Rev. 20.11-15 is to 'shift gears' from expecting v. 13 to proceed directly to the outcome of the judgment in v. 12, to seeing the two verses in parallel:

> I saw the dead. . . standing before the throne (Rev. 20.12),
> And they were judged. . . according to their deeds (20.12),
>
> And the sea. . . and death and Hades gave up the dead which were in
>   them (20.13),
> And they were judged, every one of them according to their deeds
>   (20.13).

What is evoked in a parallel reading is a single judgment stated twice for emphasis.[2] Taking this tack, one will be left with the impression of a single resurrection and judgment of the unrepentant, which is connected either with the parousia or with the end of the millennium.

Yet regardless of whether the judgment is assumed to transpire at

---

1.   Admittedly, those receptive to indications that the millennium might ultimately resolve into a non-temporal viewpoint on the parousia (e.g. Fiorenza, Pohl) may well find it attractive to conclude that the resurrection and judgment of the unrepentant are simply being pictured as happening at the parousia, contradicting the previous verses (Rev. 20.1-10), which had posited a thousand-year delay in their resurrection. But for the moment, the ideal consecutive reader only faces an unanswered question, not a contradiction. To reach an a-temporal model from this point, one must proceed to show exactly *where* and *how* the reader is subsequently encouraged to find that particular solution to the difficulties encountered on a first reading.

2.   Sweet has a related and equally plausible way of taking Rev. 20.13-15: 'These verses elaborate what was summarily stated in v. 12' (*Revelation*, p. 295).

the parousia or at the end of the millennium, problems crop up with what has gone immediately before. For example, if the whole scene is interpreted in the context of the parousia, then what has happened to the delay in the resurrection of the 'rest of the dead' (Rev. 20.5)? Similarly, if it is seen as after the millennium, then how does it relate to the picture of a post-millennial resurrection, rebellion and judgment in 20.7-10?

The answer to these questions is that the text *offers no immediate answer*. By the end of Revelation 20, the reader is left with a set of questions to which no satisfying reply yet suggests itself, and with a puzzle whose pieces do not seem to fit together completely. But one has no reason as yet to conclude that the puzzle is unsolvable or defective; instead, one begins to look for the missing piece, which, together with those already in one's possession, is able to make a complete and satisfying picture. The puzzle here does not look like an accident. To the contrary, it appears as though it has been intentionally designed into the text. Through it, the reader encounters a challenge to read more actively, to *study* the text. One is encouraged to read what follows with an eye to finding clues that might clear up the enigma. Moreover, one is indeed to encounter something which has the potential, in retrospect, to shed a whole new light on the pictures in ch. 20. In particular, this statement should be considered:

> And he carried me away in spirit to a great high mountain, and showed me the Holy City, Jerusalem, coming down out of heaven from God, having the glory of God. Her light was like a very costly stone, like crystal-clear jasper (Rev. 21.10).

The word which has been translated as 'light' here is not the word for the light which shines *from* something (φῶς) but rather φωστήρ, which means *luminary,* or the light-source which shines *on* something.[1] How can it make sense that her light-source is being compared to a jasper stone? One must first realize that God himself is the light-source, for it is said here that she 'has the glory of God'. Later this idea will be filled in explicitly in the following words: 'the city has no need of the sun or of the moon to shine upon it, for the glory of God

---

1.   So, e.g., Swete, *Apocalypse,* p. 281. Commentators and translators alike consistently stumble over the phrase 'her luminary' (Rev. 21.11), but Farrer (*Revelation,* p. 216) is rightly adamant in his claim that φωστήρ means 'luminary', and not 'luminosity', and that it refers to God, rather than to the radiance of the city.

has illumined it, and its lamp is the Lamb' (Rev. 21.23).

But why is God compared to a jasper stone in connection with the New Jerusalem? Precisely in order to recall the vision of God on his throne in Revelation 4, where 'he who was sitting on the throne was like a jasper' (v. 3).[1] The reader seems to be prompted, in other words, to picture the New Jerusalem not only as God's throne, but also as θρόνος μέγας λευκός!

Looking at the OT background confirms that this is what John intends:

'And I will bring you to Zion. . . And it shall be in those days. . . ', declares the LORD, 'They shall say no more, "The ark of the covenant of the LORD". And it shall not come to mind, nor shall they remember it, nor shall they miss it, nor shall it be made again. At that time they shall call Jerusalem "The Throne of the LORD", and all the nations will be gathered to it, for the name of the LORD in Jerusalem' (Jer. 3.14-17).

A glorious throne on high from the beginning
Is the place of our sanctuary.
O LORD, the hope of Israel,
All who forsake Thee will be put to shame.
Those who turn away on earth will be written down,
Because they have forsaken the fountain of living water, even the LORD
(Jer. 17.12-13; cf. Rev. 22.1; 7.16).[2]

John is certainly aware of these passages, and his description of the New Jerusalem reflects that awareness, since he affirms not only that 'the throne of God and of the Lamb shall be in it' (Rev. 22.3), but that 'I saw no temple in it, for the Lord God the Almighty and the Lamb are its temple' (21.22). In other words, he understands that the whole New Jerusalem, and not just one localized part of it, has become the throne of God and the Lamb, the place of their eschatological dwelling.[3] John's readers are thus being encouraged to discover in

---

1. So, e.g., Beasley-Murray, *Revelation*, p. 319; Ford, *Revelation*, p. 340; Farrer, *Revelation*, p. 216; and Morris, *Revelation*, p. 249, who rightly infer from this that God is the luminary. Ford nicely illustrates the train of thought John is inviting here: 'the holy city, therefore, appears to resemble the throne of the deity' (p. 340).

2. The relationship between these three passages indicates that Rev. 7.16, 'the Lamb in the center of the throne shall be their shepherd, and shall guide them to the springs of the water of life', is a veiled promise that Jesus will lead the overcomers to himself and to God the Father (as similarly 2.17, etc.): see Chapter 4, §3, above.

3. Cf. Chapter 9 (below), on Rev. 21.2-5.

Revelation 21–22 that the New Jerusalem is God's glorious throne/ temple in its entirety.[1]

If this were not completely satisfying, one also finds striking confirmation in *1 Enoch*, a book apparently well known and revered by many first-century Christians:

> I saw at the end of the earth the firmament of heaven above. And I proceeded and saw a place which burns day and night, where there are seven mountains of magnificent stones, three toward the east, and three towards the south. . . But the middle one [the seventh] reached to heaven like the throne of God, of alabaster,[2] and the summit of the throne was of sapphire (*1 En.* 18.6-9).

> And from thence I went to another place of the earth, and he showed me a mountain range of fire which burnt day and night. And I went from there and saw seven magnificent mountains all differing each from the other, and the stones thereof were magnificent and beautiful. . . three towards the east. . . and three towards the south. . . And the seventh mountain was in the midst of these, and it excelled them in height, resembling the seat of a throne: and fragrant trees encircled the throne. And amongst them was a tree such as I had never yet smelt . . . And he said unto me: 'This high mountain which thou hast seen, whose summit is like the throne of God, is His throne, where the Holy Great One, the Lord of Glory, the Eternal King, will sit, when He shall come down to visit the earth with goodness. And as for this fragrant tree, no mortal is permitted to touch it till the great judgment, when He shall take vengeance on all and bring everything to its consummation. It shall then be given to the righteous and holy. Its fruit shall be for food to the elect: it shall be transplanted to the holy place, to the temple of the Lord, the Eternal King (*1 En.* 24.1–25.5).[3]

One has only to compare the passages above from *1 Enoch* with Rev. 22.1-5 to confirm that the parallels are both significant and substantial:

---

1. So, e.g., O. Böcher, 'Bürger der Gottesstadt', in *idem*, *Kirche in Zeit und Endzeit*, pp. 158-59. Commentators (including Böcher) very frequently note that the cubical dimensions and gold material of the New Jerusalem signify that it is in its entirety the eschatological 'holy of holies', where God's full glory rests for eternity.

2. Alabaster is a translucent white stone from which fine vessels and ornaments of various sorts were carved. On sapphire, cf. Ezek. 1.26.

3. This translation from R.H. Charles, in *The Apocrypha and Pseudepigrapha of the Old Testament*, II. A number of commentators cite *1 En.* 18 as background for the idea of a 'great white throne' in Rev. 20.11 (e.g. Ford, *Revelation*, p. 358; Mounce, *Revelation*, p. 364 n. 32; Swete, *Apocalypse*, p. 267), although none of them goes on to consider the possibility of the equation between the eschatological throne/judgment-seat of God and the eschatological Zion/New Jerusalem.

And he showed me the river of the water of life, clear as crystal, coming from the throne of God and of the Lamb, in the middle of its street [i.e. the street of the New Jerusalem]. And on either side of the river was the tree of life, bearing twelve kinds of fruit every month; and the leaves of the tree were for the healing of the nations (Rev. 22.1-5).

7. Revelation 20.11-15: The Judgment of the Dead (Again!)

All of this opens the door to a paradoxical and surprisingly cogent re-reading of Rev. 20.11-15.[1] For if the New Jerusalem and the Great White Throne are to be understood as a unity, then there is the possibility that the resurrection and judgment before the 'great white throne' in 20.11-15 might be a new viewpoint on the resurrection and judgment before the 'beloved city' in Rev. 20.7-10. In the following sections, the merits of this idea will be weighed from the perspective of a reader going back to 'study' the passage (with unlimited access to the text and its OT references). Will this interpretative tack ultimately prove viable?

a. Judgment: A Battle and a Trial
To begin with, one will discover that John has already set the precedent for the idea that the same judgment event can be viewed first as a battle/confrontation, and then as a courtroom scene. For in Revelation 19, the parousia was pictured as a battle in which Christ as judge (with the overcomers) defeated the beast and his armies. But in 20.4-6, John saw the parousia as a courtroom scene in which it was decided who would and would not be resurrected to participate in the millennium as kings and priests with Christ. Moreover, as has been shown above, each of these passages pointed back clearly to Daniel 7, which exhibits the same dual character in its portrayal of the parousia of the Son of Man.[2]

In other words, just as there is no final interpretative difficulty with

1.   The identification of God/Christ's eschatological throne with the New Jerusalem opens the door to a playful re-reading of the promise in Rev. 3.21 about sitting down with Christ on his throne. All the citizens of the New Jerusalem paradoxically join Jesus and his father on their throne, which is eschatological Mount Zion.

2.   See the discussion of Dan. 7 in Chapter 6, §1, above. Rev. 11.15-18 also opens the possibility of such a dual perspective, in that divine judgment and recompense are expressed in terms of an angry confrontation between God and human beings.

a stereoscopic image of the resurrected dead standing before the Great White Throne on the one hand, and that of the resurrected dead standing before the New Jerusalem on the other, so there is no real incompatibility between the images of the last judgment as a battle and as a courtroom proceeding. In a similar way to Rev. 19.11-21 and 20.4-6, the two scenes of Rev. 20.11-15 can be taken as providing complementary perspectives on a single reality.

b. *Punishment: A Fiery Rain and a Fiery Lake*

Considering another difference in imagery between Rev. 20.7-10 and 11-15, one recalls that in the former, those who are judged are devoured by fire that comes down from heaven, but in the latter, they are cast into the lake of fire. Note first that the images are fundamentally similar to begin with, and that the lake of fire does indeed figure in the first scene, since in 20.10 Satan is said to be cast into the lake of fire along with the beast and false prophet. But this is not all that is to be observed. Zahn's comment below points to the specific OT background that will point John's readers to the link that resolves the two images together as one stereoscopic image. He says,

> The thrice repeated (19.20; 20.10; 21.8) assertion that those who persist in enmity with God and Christ will find their end in a sea of fire and sulphur, and the twice repeated explanation that this is the second death (20.14; 21.8), was for every reader of Revelation even slightly acquainted with the OT, as well as for John himself, an unmistakable reminiscence of the destruction of Sodom and Gomorrah in the Dead Sea under a rain of fire and sulphur (Gen 19.24-28. . .).[1]

The author of the Epistle of Jude also encourages Zahn's conception of the lake of fire, when he says that what happened to Sodom and Gomorrah is a foretaste of what will happen both to human beings and to angels on the 'judgment of the great day': namely, the 'punishment of eternal fire'. But to pick up where Zahn leaves off, it will be evident to the astute that the 'lake of fire and sulphur' in Rev. 20.10 (cf. 19.20; 21.8) has been designed to recall not only the fate of Sodom and Gomorrah, but, more importantly, that of Gog and his hosts in Ezek. 38.22:[2]

---

1. Zahn, *Offenbarung*, p. 605.
2. Swete (*Apocalypse*, p. 268) connects Rev. 20.9 with both Gen. 19 and Ezek. 38, as well as 2 Kgs 1.9-14 (LXX), which is very close to 20.9.

I shall rain on him, and on his troops, and on the many peoples with him,
a torrential [שָׁטַף, from the root שָׁטַף; literally, 'flooding, drowning'] rain,
with hailstones, fire and brimstone [i.e. sulphur].

In the context of this passage, the difference between the images in
Rev. 20.9 and 15 has the potential to resolve down to no more than
the distinction between the torrent of fire that falls from heaven on the
one hand, and the resulting flood that engulfs those upon whom it falls
on the other.[1] Being devoured by fire and being cast into a lake of fire
are simply alternative pictures for a single final fate: the second death
of the resurrected person.[2]

c. *Judging the Dead and Judging the Risen*
At this point, it begins to look very much as though the original
puzzle of Rev. 20.11-15 may have resolved itself. Responding to
John's hermeneutical clues, the reader appears to have discovered that
the scene of 20.11-15 invites understanding as a restatement, using
different imagery, of the final judgment just narrated in 20.7-10.[3]

---

1.   Does John mean by this ultimate equation that the lake of fire signifies annihilation as opposed to unending torment? Many commentators are willing to argue
strongly for this even without the equation: e.g. W. Hadorn, *Die Offenbarung des
Johannes* (THKNT, 17; Leipzig: A. Deichertsche Verlags-buchhandlung, 1928),
pp. 202-203, who says that annihilation is the only interpretation reconcilable with
the Christian idea of God. One might well contemplate with an intense sense of
injustice the idea of infinite punishment being prescribed for finite sin. But (if a theological aside can be permitted) the weight of the matter can be argued to rest on the
side not of infinite revenge, but of infinite tragedy. In the Christian view, human
beings are creatures inconceivably valuable to God (cf. John's picture of the New
Jerusalem in terms of all that is priceless in human experience). The concept of their
ultimate perdition is therefore something so appalling that the picture of annihilation
alone cannot evoke in them the revulsion that it deserves. John therefore feels called
to prophesy in terms of both images, and to allow the paradox (annihilation versus
endless torment) to stand unreconciled and uninterpreted.
2.   So Shea, 'Parallel Literary Structure', p. 49. For an OT passage that apparently combines the images of fire falling on the wicked, and the wicked being cast
into a fiery pool, cf. Ps. 140.10.
3.   This is the tack taken by Shea, 'Parallel Literary Structure', p. 49 (whose
analysis, if detectably over-mechanical, remains on the whole correct): '"The lake of
fire", which is mentioned in vss. 14-15. . . has already been referred to in vs.
10. . . These two references obviously have in view the same "lake of fire". Thus, to
put the Great-White-Throne scene in correct chronological order, one would have to
insert it between vs. 9a and vs. 9b, because the fire that goes to make up that lake

But though this reading is obviously on the right track, it is still not completely satisfying. For it leaves two elements unreconciled: (1) in Rev. 20.11-15 (reading the scene as a unity), the dead are apparently resurrected to trial and punishment according to deeds done in their mortal lives (according to the things recorded in the books), whereas (2) in 20.7-10, the hosts of Gog and Magog are being punished for attacking the New Jerusalem—in other words, *for deeds done in the state of resurrection*. As one meditates on this difference, the first attempted reading of 20.11-15 inevitably reasserts itself.

Surprisingly, the original sequential reading of the scene can now be revived to produce an unexpected, paradoxical, but nonetheless completely coherent picture. For if (as above) one allows the images of the throne and the New Jerusalem, the battle and the trial, the lake and the rain of fire to converge into one larger stereoscopic image, then one finds in Rev. 20.11-15 the following sequence.

1. At the parousia, God (or Christ) appears from heaven on his throne, which is the New Jerusalem.[1] His resurrected people are with him (cf. Rev. 17.14; 19.7-14). Before him the land and sky have been stripped away, leaving the underworld exposed (v. 11).

2. The shades of the dead stand before the throne to be judged as to whether they are worthy of a part in resurrection and the new age of Christ's kingdom (v. 12a // v. 4). Or, more accurately, the unrepentant are confronted with the full reasons for the fact that they have been left in Hades while those who are with Christ have received resurrection and citizenship in the glorious New Jerusalem. By the end of v. 12, the judgment is complete: the books have been displayed, the dead have each been confronted with the evidence contained in them, and the entries in and exclusions from the book of life have been certified (v. 12b).

3. The dead are drawn out of the underworld, that is, the [primaeval] sea, death, Hades: they are resurrected (v. 13a // v. 8).

4. The resurrected dead are now judged again before the Great White Throne according to their actions and are punished (vv. 13b, 15 // v. 9).

Given the suspicion that Rev. 20.4-10 and 11-15 might tell the same story, it becomes noticeable that in vv. 13, 15 John says neither that

---

comes down in that point in the narrative. . . To some extent, therefore, the final two scenes of this chapter go over the same ground twice.'

1. Chapter 9 will discuss the confirmation of this understanding which is to be encountered in Rev. 21.1-7.

people were judged according to the records of past deeds, nor that
people were judged according to whether their names were written in
'the book of life'. Instead, it is simply observed that they were judged
according to their deeds, and that all those who had been released from
Death and Hades, whose names were *not* written in the book of life,
were cast into the lake of fire. Such is a possible second nuance of 20.14,
'And death and Hades were cast into the lake of fire. This is the second
death, the lake of fire.' To put it differently, in v. 14, Death and Hades
stand metonymically for the sum of their contents (all the unrepentant
dead).[1] But to accept this nuance is to understand that there was a
complete correspondence among three groups: the denizens of Hades
who were drawn out by resurrection and who directly experienced the
second death, those judged a second time in resurrection on the basis
of deeds, and those whose names were not found in the book of life.

Once again, since the Great White Throne is the New Jerusalem,
and the book of life is the roll book of the *citizens* of the New
Jerusalem, Rev. 20.13-15 can be interpreted as saying that everyone
who was not a citizen of the New Jerusalem stood resurrected before
it, committed certain deeds, was judged according to these deeds, and
was forthwith inundated in the lake of fire. In a word, Rev. 20.4-10
parallels 20.11-15. Both turn out to be different ways of looking at
the very same double judgment.[2]

And I saw thrones, and they sat upon them, and judgment was given to them.	And I saw a great white throne, and Him who sat upon it. . .
And I saw the *souls* of those who had. . . [lived and died worthy of resurrection], and they came to life and reigned with Christ for a thousand years. The rest of the dead did not come to life until the thousand years were completed. This is the first resurrection (20.4-6).	And I saw the *dead*, the great and the small, standing before the throne, and books were opened; and another book was opened, which is the book of life; and the dead were judged from the things which were written in the books, according to their deeds (20.11-12).

1.   Thus Sweet, *Revelation*, p. 295.
2.   Fiorenza (*Priester für Gott*, p. 300) notes that Rev. 20.4 and 20.11 are
strongly tied together by the words 'I saw' and by the 'throne(s)'. What she fails to
notice is that the double 'I saw' makes the two visions of 20.4-10 (not 20.4-6) and
20.11-15 parallel, covering the same chronological ground: each begins with a vision
of judgment throne(s), and ends with persons being thrown into the lake of fire.

And when the thousand years are completed, Satan will be released from his prison, and will come out to deceive the nations which are in the four corners of the earth, Gog and Magog, to gather them together for the war; the number of them is like the sand of the seashore. And they came up on the broad plain of the earth and surrounded the beloved city, and fire came down from heaven and devoured them (20.7-9).

And the sea gave up the dead which were in it, and death and Hades gave up the dead which were in them; and they were judged, every one of them according to their deeds. And death and Hades were cast into the lake of fire. This is the second death, the lake of fire. And if anyone's name was not found written in the book of life, he was thrown into the lake of fire (20.13-15).

The scene of Rev. 20.11-15 could of course never sustain this paradoxical two-stage interpretation if taken in strict isolation. But by the same token, neither could Rev. 20.4 sustain the paradoxical interpretation it invites[1] without the influence of other texts, both from within and from without the book of Revelation.

Moreover, it is already agreed on the part of most commentators that the text of Rev. 20.11-15 will have been calculated to create a certain amount of resistance to being read as a unified scene. It is at least mildly surprising on any reading, for example, that one should encounter a judgment scene in which the dead are described as coming out of their habitations (v. 13) after already having been judged before the throne (v. 12).[2] To lift some phrases from Chapter 3, §2, it

1. Cf. the discussion in Chapter 6, §1, above.

2. Charles deserves the credit for alerting me to the difficulty of reading Rev. 20.11-15 as a unity. Charles proposed reversing the order of vv. 12 and 13 so that the habitations of the dead gave them up before the books were opened and they were judged according to the things written in them (*Revelation*, II, pp. 194-95). Subsequent commentators have generally discounted his observation of the fact that 20.13 (which describes the resurrection) follows disjointedly upon 20.12, because his own suggestion that the two verses should be transposed does little to clear up the discontinuity. But unless one of the verses is to be excised altogether, this double presentation needs to be accounted for. Following Charles in seeing the need for a conjectural reconstruction of mismatched texts here, see M.-E. Boismard, 'L'Apocalypse ou les apocalypses de Saint Jean', *RevistB* 56 (1949), p. 523; P. Gaechter, 'The Original Sequence of Apocalypse 20–22', *TS* 10 (1949), p. 491 n. 11; Ford, *Revelation*, p. 38. Few commentators have been persuaded by this 'scissors and paste' approach, however, and Charles's argument for the emendation of *sea* to *treasuries* (discussed above) not only ignores and disrupts the intentionally negative character of the scene, but shows that he misunderstands the cosmology of

is possible here to detect 'tensions in the text...which create dissatisfaction with a straightforward reading and push one to look afresh at the work as a whole in search of a different interpretative model'.

When one interprets the various parts of Revelation 20 according to their verbal, thematic and visual relationships not only with one another, but with related materials throughout the rest of the book, then a new and strikingly rich picture begins to emerge. The paradox of the relationship between Rev. 20.4-10 and 11-15 is thus that, behind the seeming differences in perspective, there lie lines of interpretation that finally converge to bring a single multi-dimensional picture into focus. Taken together, each of the two versions contributes a complementary perspective—each serves both to interpret and to enhance the significance of the other. This coheres with what has been continuously demonstrated throughout this study, namely, that the layering on of mutually enriching perspectives is a major compositional characteristic of Revelation.[1]

It is true that, when read sequentially, the two versions of the double judgment facing the unrepentant (Rev. 20.4-10, 11-15) create a reasonably plausible chain of events.[2] Yet when read according to the clues laced throughout them, they reveal themselves to be two versions of the same story, which, when combined, create one stereoscopic whole. As he has done numerous times with the parousia, so John has done with the final events in the story of God's dealings with the unrepentant: he has given his readers two versions of the same story of judgment.

In one version, the unrepentant face judgment twice by provoking a final conflict with God and his people (Rev. 19.11-21 [// 11.18]; 20.7-

---

v. 11: 'The context [20.11b] cannot admit of a resurrection of a physical body from the sea—seeing that the sea and everything pertaining to it had vanished' (*Revelation,* II, pp. 194-95). To the contrary, if earth and heaven are removed, what remains is precisely the sea and the abyss of Hades.

1.   Prigent (*L'Apocalypse,* p. 372) rightly argues that this compositional strategy is designed to force the readers to interpret the book as a whole, and to discourage them from interpreting it sequentially. I would pull back somewhat from Prigent's radical stance to say that John does encourage his readers to expect at least a general sequence of eschatological events, but that he most frequently offers chronological information to them only indirectly and by inference. Cf. also the comment of Bauckham: 'The juxtaposition of more than one image with a single referent is a characteristic of John's visions' ('The *Figurae* of John of Patmos', p. 111).

2.   I.e. according to a standard pre-millennial model.

10), and in the other, they face judgment twice as a trial (20.4-5 [// 20.11-12]; 20.13-15). In one, judgment is pictured as something that God brings on the unrepentant, and in the other, it is pictured as something they bring on themselves. By means of this paradoxical double presentation, two mysteries are affirmed: (1) human agency and divine sovereignty each play a crucial role in the ultimate judgment and disposition of human beings, and (2) divine judgment will be based equally on corporate (19.11-21; 20.7-10) and on individual (20.11-15) responsibility.

But the question that now arises is this: what is signified by the fact that no obvious hint of the thousand year imprisonment of the unrepentant dead appears in Rev. 20.11-15? There is little doubt that different starting points will dictate different answers to this question, but the starting point dictated by the results so far observed here is clear: new perspectives *add meaning to*, rather than *take meaning away from*, things already revealed. Thus, it would be unwarranted to jump to the conclusion that the last judgment scene of 20.11-15 was designed to subtract the period of the millennium from the larger story, leaving the reader with the idea that final judgment actually occurs at the parousia. Given the way new materials have usually been shown to function in Revelation, it is advisable to look for reasons why the temporal distance between the two judgments of 20.4-10 might have been *left unexpressed* in 20.11-15, before reaching for the conclusion that this distance is being denied. The following sections present some suggestions along these lines.

d. *Theological Point: Two Sides of a Single Coin*

It is plausible to see two possible *theological* reasons for the presentation of two temporally separate judgment events as a composite whole in Rev. 20.11-15. The first of these is this: in spite of the fact that the two judgments of the unrepentant stand at opposite ends of the millennium in 20.4-10, yet in an important sense they are inextricably related. The issue involved in the former judgment is the revelation and punishment of deeds done in mortal life. The outcome (the denial of resurrection) represents the taking away of human freedom as the just punishment for the destructive use of that freedom. In the latter judgment, the bestowal of resurrection represents a new beginning, and a restoration of that freedom. But it also represents the opportunity of making of a fresh choice on the part of those whom it concerns. In the final analysis, it is possible to present the two judgments of Rev. 20.4-10 and of 20.11-15 as a virtual unity because of the mystery that they are mutually ratifying. The judgment and recompense according to deeds at the beginning of the millennium (20.11-12 // 20.4-6) and the judgment and recompense according to deeds at its end (20.13-15 // 20.7-10) reveal themselves as two movements of a single overall judgment.

Nonetheless, this two-stage model for judgment clearly has an irreducible temporal element built into it, since the 're-trial' of Rev. 20.7-10 only makes sense when it is pictured as following a time during which resurrection has justly been denied. In other words, John presents the millennium as an age of just punishment. In their mortal lives human beings persisted in the destructive use of the bodies God gave them; now, therefore, they must pay the penalty of having the gift of resurrection bodies denied to them for an appropriate period. A thousand years may be seen as appropriate because it is that length of time which Jewish tradition set as the maximum span of a mortal human life.[1]

Reading Rev. 20.12 in the light of 20.4-5, the millennial punishment of the unrepentant can thus be seen to consist precisely in the fact that for a 'lifetime', they must face their own deadness, and the full reasons for it. For the thousand years, Satan will have no more power to deceive them about themselves. Both he and they will have no choice but to recognize not only *who* they are, but also *what* they are, and what they have thrown away. But when they are resurrected at last, they will have finished serving the sentence God has decreed for a lifetime of sin, and will, so to speak, have a clean record. The only judgment that can now occur is a test of *present* actions: what response will they make to God when they are granted the freedom of resurrection?

---

1.   The idea is that, since the fall of Adam and Eve, human beings can live no longer than one of God's 'days' (i.e. a thousand years): 'For a thousand years are as a day in your sight' (Ps. 90.3), and 'in the day that you eat from it you will certainly die' (Gen. 2.17). A. Wikenhauser ('Die Herkunft der Idee des tausendjährigen Reiches in der Johannes-Apokalypse', *RQ* 45 [1937], p. 2) points to this interpretation of Ps. 90.3 in *Jub.* 4.30: (when Adam died) 'he lacked seventy years of one thousand years; for one thousand years are as one day in the testimony of the heavens and therefore was it written concerning the tree of knowledge: "On the day that ye eat thereof ye shall die". For this reason he did not complete the years of this day; for he died during it.' Also in agreement with this interpretation are Justin, *Dial. Tryph.* 81.3; Irenaus, *Adv. Haer.* 5.23.2; and *Gen. R.* 22 (14c).

What will they *do* with this divine discipline of self-recognition when they are paroled at last, raised again by God's grace? After the millennium, and for all eternity, the Lamb is still the Lamb. Presumably they are as free now as ever to accept the gift of reconciliation which his death has purchased on behalf of all human beings. Or will the freedom of resurrection simply supply them and their former master the opportunity to turn back to the self-deception and self-destruction which had been their former choice?

The whole episode could be seen against the background of Ps. 90.3-6:

> Thou dost turn man back into dust,
> And dost say, 'Return, O children of men'.
> For a thousand years in Thy sight
> Are like yesterday when it passes by,
> Or as a watch in the night.
> Thou hast swept them away like a flood, they fall asleep;
> In the morning they are like grass which passes away.
> In the morning it flourishes, but it passes away;[1]
> Towards evening it fades, and withers away.

Is the age-long gap between the parousia and the final resurrection of the unrepentant (Rev. 20.1-10) *denied* in the movement from Rev. 20.12 to 20.13, or is it simply foreshortened, *telescoped*? Looked at from the point of view of God's transcendence and foreknowledge, a thousand years may well be an insignificant length of time. To him who sits on the Great White Throne, the gap between the judgment of the parousia (20.4 // 20.12) and the final end of rebellious humanity (20.7-10 // 20.13-15) may indeed hardly be any gap at all. But for all that, a thousand years remain a thousand years in the imagination of a human being.

Thus John is probably not to be taken as inviting his readers to understand that the thousand-year imprisonment of the unrepentant is a temporal picture of realities which are essentially a-temporal. He is much more likely to be intimating that those who have proved themselves unworthy of the gift of resurrection at the parousia will prove themselves equally unworthy of it, even when they are granted it a thousand years later. The implicit picture is of a second chance, *offered* out of divine justice, grace and mercy, but *not accepted*.

---

1.   NASB, preferring the marginal translation 'passes away' to 'sprouts anew'.

e. Compositional Point One:
Revelation 20.11-15 as Preparation for 21.1–22.5

It has been argued that the presence of a very subtly articulated double judgment scene in Rev. 20.11-15 serves a *theological* function as a new viewpoint on the double judgment of Rev. 20.4-10. It may also be argued, however, that the absence of an obvious gap between the two judgments in 20.11-15 takes on *compositional* significance when one compares Revelation 19–20 with the pattern of prophetic oracles found in Ezekiel 37–48. As has been demonstrated above, John's composition of Revelation 19–20 evinces an awareness on his part that *two* 'last judgments' of Israel's enemies were to be seen in Ezekiel 38–39, the one taking place at the inauguration of the messianic age, and the other taking place long after that peaceful age had been established (i.e. 'after many days'; Ezek. 38.8). Further, as a look at Lust's table of similarities will confirm (p. 131, above), John's major difference with Ezekiel lies in his inclusion (in Rev. 20.4-6, 11-15) of *trial scenes* harking back to the trial scene found in Daniel 7. By employing in Revelation 19 and 20 pictures of final judgment evocative both of Daniel 7 and Ezekiel 38–39, John's prophecy puts forward something new and significant: that each of these two eschatological judgments is to be seen *both as a battle and as a trial.*

Furthermore, it is clear that John found precedent in Ezekiel 38–39 for laminating together the two great eschatological judgments of God's enemies, and for making a presentation designed so that only the very attentive reader would recognize the necessity of supplying a major chronological gap between them. Read carefully, the oracles of Ezekiel 38–39 reveal the same peoples appearing in confrontations on two entirely separate occasions, in two entirely different contexts. The one confrontation takes place at the inauguration of the messianic age, and the other takes place long after that peaceful age has been established ('after many days'; Ezek. 38.8). The effect of this rather cryptic double presentation is to allow Ezekiel 40–48 to end the book with visions on a purely positive theme: the New Jerusalem with its new temple. That is, Ezekiel 38 pictures the last battle, in which God causes Gog and his hosts to judge themselves by attacking the peaceful, prosperous and secure land of Israel during the messianic age. This judgment/battle oracle has been placed in the final composition (1) so that it follows the short description of the 'resurrection' of Israel and the messianic age (Ezekiel 37), (2) so that it becomes almost invisibly linked to a judgment/battle oracle concerning the *inauguration* of that age (Ezekiel 39) and (3) so that chs. 40–48 become free to concentrate on the wonders of the new Jerusalem and its temple, without the distraction of wrapping up the narrative business concerning the latter judgment of enemies (Ezekiel 38).

It is arguable that the same organizational strategy and rationale is to be detected in the prophecies of Rev. 19.11–20.15 in their relationship to Rev. 21.1–22.5. As has been discussed above, however, John's prophecy has added to the idea of judgment as battle (as found in Ezekiel) the Danielic picture of judgment *as trial*. Thus each of the battle scenes cast in the style of Ezekiel 38–39 (Rev. 19.11-21; 20.7-10) finds a counterpart in a courtroom scene styled after Daniel 7 (Rev. 20.4-6, 11-15). Although Revelation differs from Ezekiel in that its version of the double judgment *as battle* has been clearly presented to the reader as two events separated by a generous length of messianic age (cf. Rev. 19.17–20.10), yet the *courtroom scene of Rev. 20.11-15* has been presented in a way that evokes the double judgment oracle of Ezekiel 38–39.

Like Ezekiel 38–39, Rev. 20.11-15 is to be recognized as a composite of two separate judgments that intentionally leaves the overall first impression of a setting at the inauguration of the messianic age (i.e. the parousia). The desirable effect achieved by this presentation is similar to that encountered in Ezekiel. After a relatively short description of the messianic age, a scene is depicted in which the two distinct judgments of the unrepentant enemies (the one at the parousia and the other at the end of the millennium) are presented together in 20.11-15, so as to pave the way for an ending in which extended and undistracted attention may be given to the good things of that age (Rev. 21.1–22.5 // Ezek. 40–48).

f. *Compositional Point Two:*
Anticipating Different Levels of Response to Textual Information
There is yet another compositional rationale to be considered for the way the judgment is presented in Rev. 20.11-15. For though this study has assumed a reader who successfully processes all the information offered by the text, John must have known that his readers could only grasp much of what he was saying through concerted study of his book. From this point of view, ch. 20 appears to be designed so as to communicate the above theological points about the persistence

of rebellion even to the reader who misses a great deal of the information on offer. In other words, if readers take the conventional view[1] that the millennium is for people spared at the parousia, and miss the signals of resurrection in 20.7-10, they still end up with the same basic impression: God's clemency is extended even to the unbelieving nations, and even if they are offered everything that the saints receive, they will still be willing to be seduced again into rebellion.

I submit that Rev. 20.11-15 was designed so that it could fulfil two functions at the same time. For those able to put it into context, it could show a new perspective on the twofold judgment according to works in 20.4-10; and it could supply a resurrection and judgment of the 'rest of the dead' (20.5) for those who had missed the picture of it in 20.7-10. On the one hand, John's prophecy looked forward to a messianic age that was radically different from the models for that age becoming popular in his time. But on the other, he does not seem to have felt called to indoctrinate his readers with the alternative view he was revealing. Instead, he crafted his text so that his readers would get the deeper theological message (the ultimate extension, and the ultimate rejection, of grace) even if they misunderstood the details.[2]

1.   Conventional not only in the sense that most modern commentators assume it, but also in the sense that it was the view espoused by most of John's Jewish contemporaries. The world rule of messiah was generally understood to have its setting in history (see, e.g., the survey in Bailey, 'The Temporary Messianic Reign').

2.   Has the present study come around full circle to parallel a central point proposed by Gry? It will be recalled that in Gry's opinion John meant to reinterpret radically the earthly messianic reign, while presenting it in more or less conventional language (*Millénarisme*, p. 61; see Chapter 3, §2, above). Remarks on this convergence will be reserved for the conclusion (Chapter 10).

Chapter 9

REVELATION 21.1-8: THE NEW CREATION AND THE NEW JERUSALEM

In Rev. 21.1, John speaks of the passing away of the old heaven and earth as though it has been the preparation for the appearance of a new heaven and earth. Or, more accurately, the re-creation is expressed as a *replacement* of old with new:

> And I saw a new heaven and a new earth; for the first heaven and the first earth had passed away, and there is no longer any sea (Rev. 21.1).

On a first reading at least, John appears to be treating the dissolution and re-creation as a complex, rather than as two separate events. Thus, all other things being equal, the readers will have reason to expect indications in the following material confirming that the re-creation is to be understood in the context of the parousia, for they already know that a radical *dissolution* of the present earth and heaven attends the parousia.[1] In and of itself, however, the new creation is not a theme to which the readers have yet been introduced in any clear

---

1. See above on Rev. 20.11. As has been discussed in Chapter 1, Smith's model sees the millennium as a cosmic sabbath, during which the earth remains formless and uninhabited, and the New Jerusalem remains in heaven (*Daniel and the Revelation*, pp. 739-40). But if such a view is to be sustained, then it must be possible to show exactly at what point, and in what manner, the text leads the reader to begin picturing things this way. In reading up to 21.1, in other words, the reader has not yet been given any indication of a gap between the parousia and the earthly reign of the saints, nor of a delay in the coming of the New Jerusalem (see above on 20.4-9). And if the reader has not been given reason to suspect that the earth is empty and silent for the long age of the millennium by Rev. 20.15, then where, between Rev. 21.1 and the end of the book, is one going to pick up this idea? Smith's view fails (on the present method) not so much because it comes into direct conflict with the explicit statements of Revelation, but because it cannot realistically be shown to arise from those statements. On 8.1 as an alleged hint of a world-sabbath, and on Smith's reasons for rejecting the view presented here, see Chapter 9, §3, below.

way.[1] Consequently, the rest of Rev. 21.1-8 will have to be considered in terms of its key words, themes and pictures, and the contexts earlier built up for each of them will have to be uncovered. Given that a clear and uniform context can be drawn from these enquiries, then the new creation of 21.1 will have to be seen as belonging in that context.

It should be noted at this point that the placement of the new creation scene after the last judgment scene *in the text* need by no means prejudice the question of their chronological relationship. It has already been demonstrated (1) that Rev. 20.11-12 is located in the context of a story which has come to its conclusion a thousand years beyond the parousia (20.10),[2] and (2) that the function of the descriptions in 20.11-15 is not to carry that story further chronologically, but rather to step back in time and to present both a new viewpoint on the parousia as judgment (paralleling 20.4-6), and a new viewpoint on the resurrection of the unrepentant (paralleling 20.7-10).[3] If these demonstrations are valid, then clearly ample room has been made for the possibility that John's visions will jump back yet a second time from the resurrection of the unrepentant and its outcome (20.7-10 // 20.13-15), to the presentation of still another viewpoint on the parousia (20.11 // 21.1). In other words, the argument put forth in the previous chapter regarding Rev. 20.11 applies to 21.1 with double force:

> John has narrated some five or more visions of the parousia before the 'principal' one in 19.11, so why should he not be allowed to present yet another vision or visions of it *after* the 'principal' one?[4]

This, of course, is by no means a positive argument for the idea that Rev. 21.1-8 refers to the parousia and not to the situation presupposed to hold only after the final judgment described in 20.13-15. What the argument does indicate, however, is that John's readers will have no reason to give less attention to aspects of 21.1-8 suggesting that the parousia is in view, than they would have if such aspects had been encountered previous to ch. 19. It thus requires no apology to consider without prior scepticism questions regarding whether and

1. Rev. 2.7 (which promises the overcomer the fruit of the tree of life in God's paradise) will only later be confirmed as referring to the new creation and relating it to the parousia (22.1-2; cf. *1 En.* 24.1–25.5).

2. Cf. the comments in Chapter 7, §3, above.

3. Cf. Chapter 8, §§4-7, above.

4. Cf. Chapter 8, §3.c, above.

with what weight the various aspects of 21.1-8 can be seen as pointing to the parousia.

1. *Revelation 21.1: The New Creation*

It has already been shown in connection with Rev. 20.11 that, for John, the dissolution of the existing heaven and earth is directly tied to the parousia, and that some of the central OT background for this dissolution imagery is to be found in passages from the book of Isaiah. Likewise, in the picture of a re-creation of the world (Rev. 21.1), John's vision clearly recalls the prophecies of Isaiah:[1]

> For behold, I create new heavens and a new earth; and the former things shall not be remembered or come to mind (Isa. 65.17).

> 'For just as the new heavens and the new earth which I make will endure before Me', declares the LORD, 'So your offspring and your name will endure' (Isa. 66.22).[2]

Associated with the theme of re-creation in the immediate context of each of these passages is the theme of the restoration of oppressed Jerusalem (cf. Isa. 55.18-23; 66.9-12). This association will tend to encourage one's expectation that the re-creation of the world in Revelation will be presented in the context of the parousia. For it appears clear from earlier passages in Revelation that the age of Jerusalem's oppression coincides with the career of the beast, and so ends with the parousia (cf. Rev. 11.2; 13.5). As was earlier demonstrated (in dealing with texts from both Isaiah and Ezekiel), John has trained his readers to be sensitive to the difference in context between events that signal the end of Israel's oppression on the one hand, and events set in the context of an age of eschatological peace on the other.[3] Similarly, the theme of the regathering of exiles, which forms the context for the appearance of the re-creation theme in Isa. 66.20-22, will also tend to tie that theme to the parousia, since the one

---

1. OT context is discussed here because no direct preparation has been made for the theme of new creation in the text of Revelation itself. For the sake of the argument, observations about OT parallels have not, and will not here, be given independent weight.

2. For extra-biblical parallels, see, e.g., *LAB* 3.10; 51.5.

3. Cf. the observations in Chapter 7, §2, above.

passage describing exile in Revelation (figurative though it may be) also implicitly puts an end to that exile at the parousia.[1]

But these are external considerations, and therefore of only indirect value according to the restraints of the present method. Far more significant is John's statement that 'there is no longer any sea'. In what way (or ways) will the readers of Revelation have been prepared for this statement by their reading of the text to this point?[2]

a. *Revelation 21.1c: There is No Longer Any (Heavenly) Sea*

Going back in Revelation to the first occurrence of the word θάλασσα, one finds that the first 'sea' to be encountered was the glassy floor of the heavenly throne room in Rev. 4.6. For the reader acquainted with the OT, the 'sea' of John's vision is identifiable as the structure that Ezekiel described as 'something like an expanse, like the awesome gleam of crystal' (Ezek. 1.22; cf. 10.1), and which is described in Exodus as what 'appeared to be a pavement of sapphire, and as clear as the sky itself' (Exod. 24.10). Each of these passages pictures the sky as a solid expanse, clear and bluish like ice. This expanse is conceived of as defining the uppermost boundary of the human world, and, so to speak, the floor of God's dwelling place.

In Revelation, as in Ezekiel (and other places in the OT, e.g., 1 Kgs 22.19, Ps. 11.4), God's throne is pictured as resting on this expanse, and the various personages in heaven either stand on it, or sit on thrones arranged on it. In the book of Job, Elihu says that God created this expanse: 'Can you, with Him, spread out the skies, strong as a molten [= die-cast] mirror?' (Job 37.18). And, as discussed above, Genesis 1 says that the creation of this structure was the first major stage in the architectural work that God performed to prepare the earth for human habitation. John clearly shares the idea of a solid heaven presupposed by these OT passages. For instance (as discussed

---

1. The woman's period of hiding in the wilderness (Rev. 12.14), interpreted along with other passages in Rev. 13 and elsewhere, reveals itself as lasting for the three and a half years of the beast's career (which is brought to an end by the parousia). For a parallel to the idea that some sort of exile attends the appearance of the Danielic antichrist, cf. Mk 13.14-19 par.

2. It will appear as a paradox of the present method that the meaning of 'sea' (= underworld) present in the immediate context (Rev. 20.13) will come into the discussion last. This is because it is the meaning that the readers acquire last in a consecutive reading. This is not to deny that use in the immediate context must play a primary role in the interpretation of words.

in Chapter 8, §1, above), a 'door' must be opened in order for John to cross the barrier of heaven and enter into God's throne room (Rev. 4.1). But it is also quite clear that John's imagery in 6.14 (19.11) and 20.11 pictures the stripping away of this expanse at the parousia. Strong links were established between John's imagery and that of Isa. 64.1: 'O that Thou wouldst rend the heavens and come down...' In other words, John would have his readers understand that the glassy sea of heaven, which has been the age-old barrier between God and humankind, will finally be removed when God and his Christ take up their reign at the parousia.

A close look at the verses following Rev. 21.1 will serve to confirm that the phrase, 'the sea is no more', refers to the removal of this heavenly sea. For example, the immediate introduction of the New Jerusalem serves to interpret John's statement about the sea being gone:

> And I saw the holy city, New Jerusalem, coming down out of heaven from God, made ready as a bride adorned for her husband (21.2).

John says that she 'comes down out of heaven from God'. This implies two things: that she has been in heaven up until now, and that God has been in heaven until now. Earlier in Revelation the readers will have been made aware of some kind of correlation between the New Jerusalem and the sanctuary of God (3.12). They will also be in a position to know that his present sanctuary is in heaven, and that it consists of those among God's people who have (by overcoming) become privileged to dwell with him there (13.6).[1] This will also have been linked up with the fact that in 19.7-8 the 'bride' (cf. 21.2) is clothed with 'the righteous acts of the saints', implying that the bride is a figure for the saints viewed collectively.

The bottom line to all of these observations is this: if God's people (corporately pictured both as his sanctuary in heaven, and as the Lamb's bride) should come down from heaven to dwell on earth, then either they will cease to be his sanctuary in the fullest sense, or God

---

1. As Sweet says, 'God's dwelling, like his temple (ll. 1f.) is people, not a place; cf. 18.20' (*Revelation*, p. 211). Cf. also Rev. 3.12, in which Jesus promises to make the overcomer a pillar in the temple of his God. Böcher ('Bürger der Gottesstadt', in *idem, Kirche in Zeit und Endzeit*, p. 161) gives a sizeable list of NT parallels for the idea that people make up the building materials of the New Jerusalem: 1 Cor. 3.16; 6.16; Eph. 2.21-22; Heb. 3.[3-]6; 1 Pet. 2.4-5 (cf. Mt. 16.18; Gal. 2.9).

will have to be conceived of as 'coming down' with them. But if he should do so, then the barrier of the glassy sea, which in the present age separates his dwelling from the earth, *will have to have been done away with*. And that, one might well argue, is what John has just finished telling his readers. It is thus that he can go on to say,

> And I heard a loud voice from the throne, saying, 'Behold, the tabernacle of God is among men, and He shall dwell among them, and they shall be His people, and God Himself shall be among them, and He shall wipe away every tear from their eyes; and there shall no longer be any death; there shall no longer be any mourning, or crying, or pain; the first things have passed away' (Rev. 21.3-5).

When the New Jerusalem comes down to earth, prophesies John, God's dwelling will no longer be in heaven, but on earth. Illustrative of this idea is Isa. 24.23 and 25.6-9:[1]

> For the LORD of hosts will reign on Mount Zion and in Jerusalem,
> And His glory will be before His elders. . . (Isa. 24.23).

> And the LORD of hosts will prepare a lavish banquet for all peoples on
>   this mountain [Zion]. . .
> And on this mountain He will swallow up the covering which is over all
>   the peoples,
> Even the veil which is stretched over all the nations.
> He will swallow up death for all time,
> And the Lord GOD will wipe tears from all faces,
> And He will remove the reproach of His people from all the earth;
> For the LORD has spoken.
> And it will be said on that day,
> 'Behold, this is our God for whom we have waited that He might save us.

1.   Two unmistakable echoes from this passage can be heard in the words of Rev. 21.3-5 above: one immediately recognizes the promises that death will be done away with, and that God will personally wipe the tears from his people's faces. But the relationship runs to a deeper level as well. Isa. 24.23, which introduces the prophecy of the feast described above, says that 'the LORD of hosts will reign on Mount Zion and in Jerusalem. . .' John clearly interprets this passage as referring to the parousia (see Chapter 5, §2, above), but the point to be noted here is that in Isaiah, the kingly reign of the LORD is presupposed as the context for the presentation of a lavish banquet on Mount Zion (Rev. 25.7, above). The banquet is a royal banquet, personally prepared by God the King for his subjects, and for the purpose of celebrating the inauguration of his reign on earth. The guests, says Isaiah, will rejoice that day because God has saved them at last: and he has accomplished their salvation precisely by coming personally to them (v. 9).

> This is the LORD for whom we have waited;
> Let us rejoice and be glad in His salvation' (Isa. 25.6-9).

This idea that God himself is coming to be with his people is clearly being taken up and developed in Rev. 21.3:

> Behold, the tabernacle of God is among men, and He shall dwell among them, and they shall be His people, and God Himself shall be among them...[1]

These close verbal and thematic parallels add up to an intimate relationship between Isa. 25.7-9 and Rev. 21.3-4. In view of this relationship, I venture to speculate that, in John's interpretation of Isa. 25.7, the 'covering' and 'veil' over all the peoples which is 'swallowed up' refers to the heavenly sea of separation, which is removed at the parousia. But whether correct or not, this line of thinking leads to a very important point: namely, that it is straightforward to discover *from the text of Revelation itself* that John intends his readers to picture the expanse of heaven as corresponding (depending on context) either to the veil which served as the door to the tent of witness, or to the veil which separated the holy place from the holy of holies.[2] Several examples make this clear:

1. In Rev. 4.1-3, John sees an open door in heaven, and is told to come up. Immediately he finds himself in the heavenly throne-room/temple. In order to enter God's sanctuary in heaven, in other words, one must cross the barrier of the sky, just as the priests had to pass beyond the veil that formed the door to the earthly tabernacle (for OT examples of the comparison of the vault of heaven to a tent, cf. Ps. 104.2; Isa. 40.22).

2. In Rev. 6.14-17, the sky was split apart and fell away on both sides, revealing the Enthroned One and the Lamb to those on earth.

3. Closely corresponding to both of these texts is Rev. 11.19, where 'the sanctuary of God which is in heaven was opened; and the ark of His covenant appeared in His temple...' As demonstrated, both 6.14-17 and 11.19 present the parousia as

---

1. Cf. also Lev. 26.11-12; Ezek. 37.27. The latter passage clearly ties these promises to the inauguration of the messianic age (cf. 37.23-28).

2. The groundwork for this idea has already been laid above (cf. esp. Chapter 8, §1), so a summary of illustrating points is offered here.

an event in which God and his messiah are seen revealed in heaven by the removal of the barrier of the sky. In each case, the event of God's self-revelation is being pictured as a drawing back or removing of the veil to the holy of holies, which has kept the heavenly throne/ark of God hidden from human vision.

4.   In Rev. 15.5, John says 'the sanctuary of the tabernacle of testimony in heaven was opened, and the seven angels who had the seven plagues came out of the sanctuary'. From 16.1 it is clear that they have come out to pour their plagues on the earth (and its environs, including the atmosphere); in other words, they have come out of the tent of witness in heaven and into the realm of human habitation by crossing through an opening in the vault of heaven. And in 16.1 and 17, God's voice is apparently able to be heard through that open doorway. Thus, by implication, the heavenly vault is to be understood as corresponding to the veil forming the door to the tent of witness.

If John's readers add these data together and bring them to their reading of Rev. 21.1-5, then they will be in little doubt about the meaning of the words 'Behold, the tabernacle of God is among men, and He shall tabernacle among them. . .' In the new creation, God's dwelling (or 'tent'[1]) will no longer be separated from his earthly people by the vault of heaven. Once and for all, God will dwell in his full glory among his resurrected people on earth.

Of course, the reader will find another expression of this idea later in Rev. 22.1-5, where the throne of God is no longer pictured as resting on the glassy sea of separation in heaven, but on (the top of) Mount Zion, in the midst of the New Jerusalem. Thus it is no coincidence that both the street of the City and its river are described in terms distinctly echoing those used to describe the glassy sea in heaven (cf. 21.21; 22.1; 4.6).[2]

Moreover, in contrast to Ezekiel (chs. 40–48), John will exclude the idea that even an earthly sanctuary will hide God's glory from his

---

1.   σκηνή, evoking the Hebrew verb שׁכן (dwell), which is used in the OT to express the idea of God's eschatological presence in Zion (e.g. Joel 3.17; Zech. 2.10-11).

2.   So, e.g., Sweet, *Revelation*, pp. 307, 311.

people. On the contrary, he will insist that the full glory of God and the Lamb will be as open, public and permanent as a sun that never sets (cf. Rev. 21.23, 25; 22.5). In fact, they themselves will be his sanctuary (cf. 3.12; 13.6; 21.16),[1] and he himself will be their sanctuary (cf. 7.15; 21.22). To conclude this part of the discussion of the phrase 'there is no more sea', one may summarize the points made in favour of seeing here a reference to the expanse of heaven, and for seeing the parousia as the context for the removal of this 'sea'.

1. The readers' first exposure to the word 'sea' (θάλασσα) was in Rev. 4.6, where it was used to describe a glass-like expanse before the throne of God in heaven. This was in effect to be pictured as the floor of the heavenly realm.[2] Clear background for this imagery was found in the cosmological model assumed in such OT books as Genesis, Exodus, Job and Ezekiel. This model understands the sky as a solid expanse that arches over the earth.

2. John's words in Rev. 6.12-14 (cf. 20.11) indicate that the stripping away of this expanse is part of a general dissolution of all those elements in creation normally held to be permanent. It has already been demonstrated above (cf. Chapter 8, §3) that the parousia is the unequivocal occasion for this dissolution.

3. The descent of the New Jerusalem to earth (Rev. 21.2), along with the following statement that his tabernacle is among his people, expresses the promise of God's full eschatological residence on earth. This in turn implies that the heavenly sea of separation has been abolished.

4. Rev. 21.3-4, which says that the tabernacle of God has come

---

1. Many commentators have noted that the cubical dimensions of the New Jerusalem (Rev. 21.16), together with the fact that it is described as 'pure gold' (21.18), recall 1 Kgs 6.20. In Solomon's temple, the holy of holies was a cubical room whose walls were 'overlaid with pure gold'. Paradoxically, the New Jerusalem of John's vision is at the same time God's innermost sanctuary, and the place of his *unrestricted* presence: 'The material of the wall was jasper; and the city was pure gold, like clear [pure, transparent] glass' (21.18). The walls of this holy of holies have the function of *displaying*, rather than hiding, God's glory.

2. Cf. Rev. 15.2 for the same conception, and the comments on that passage above in Chapter 4, §3. In Ezek. 1.22 (one of the primary OT backgrounds for Rev. 4), this expanse is seen from below.

to be among his people, must be understood in the context of its background in Revelation. Earlier in the text, heaven has been pictured as the present tabernacle of God's abode, and the expanse of the sky has been treated as corresponding sometimes to the veil that served as the door to the tent of witness, and sometimes to the veil that separated the holy of holies from the rest of the sanctuary, hiding the ark of God from human sight. Thus the parousia was described in terms of the parting or removal of that veil (6.14; 11.28), so that God's throne could be seen. Hand in hand with this conception of the removal of the former separation between God's tabernacle and the abode of human beings on earth went 21.3-4,[1] which posited the establishment of a new sanctuary on earth, which has no such separating veil—God's people will corporately dwell in his immediate presence.[2]

John puts the matter yet more strongly, by inviting his readers to see themselves (in the symbol of the New Jerusalem) as corporately constituting his sanctuary on earth, just as they had in the previous age constituted his sanctuary in heaven (cf. Rev. 3.12; 13.6; 21.16). In the new creation (which follows upon the dissolution of the former heaven and earth at the parousia), God's tabernacle will be among his people once and for all. His presence will never again be hidden behind the separating veil of the sky, for in the new heaven and the new earth 'there is no longer any sea'.[3]

As the above discussion has served to demonstrate, there are unmistakable indications that John wanted his readers to recognize the glassy sea of separation as the 'sea' that is to be no more in the new creation. To say this, however, is by no means to close the subject. For John is

1. Cf. C. Deutsch, 'Transformation of Symbols: The New Jerusalem in Rv. 21.1–22.5', *ZNW* 78 (1987), pp. 106-26: 'The Temple, as symbol of access to the divine presence, is replaced by the Presence itself' (p. 115).

2. See similarly Rev. 7.15; 21.16, 22; 22.4. Behm offers a pithy comment on 21.22: 'Kein Gotteshaus, in dem Gott zu hause wäre' (*Offenbarung*, p. 110).

3. As Vögtle says, on Rev. 21.1-5, '"Heaven and earth" stand in the biblical cosmology as two distinct realms that separate God and humankind from one another. Thus, could it not be that John simply wanted to express the concept that the separation between these two realms was abolished, and that "heaven" and "earth"— the dwelling of God and of humanity—were one?' (*Das Buch mit sieben Siegeln*, p. 172). Similarly Rissi, *The Future of the World*, p. 56.

quite able to say more than one thing at once, as can be attested from a multitude of passages, such as Rev. 15.2.[1] It is therefore prudent to discover whether there are other earlier occurrences of the word 'sea' that have the potential to suggest an additional meaning or additional meanings for the statement 'the sea is no more'.

b. *Revelation 21.1c: There is No Longer Any (Earthly) Sea*
Upon undertaking an investigation, one quickly finds that John focuses time and time again on the sea as one of the realms of a tripartite or quadripartite creation: heaven(s), earth, (abyss or springs and rivers), sea. This is highly significant, precisely because in Rev. 21.1 he mentions the passing away of the first heaven and earth, and immediately adds the remark about there being no more sea. It is therefore appropriate to survey the passages that use the word 'sea' in this connection. The first is Rev. 5.13:

> And every created thing which is in heaven and on the earth and under the earth and on the sea, and all things in them, I heard saying, 'To Him who sits on the throne, and to the Lamb, be blessing and honor and dominion. . .'

In Rev. 7.1-2, the sea is paired with the earth as a realm that is about to come under attack from damaging 'winds'. In ch. 8, one finds the following statement, which is framed by descriptions of disturbances to the earth, the springs and rivers, and the hosts of heaven, respectively (8.7, 10-12):

> And the second angel sounded [his trumpet], and something like a great mountain burning with fire was thrown into the sea; and a third of the sea became blood; and a third of the creatures, which were in the sea and had life, died; and a third of the ships were destroyed (8.8-9).

In Rev. 10.2, the sea and the land function as surfaces for an angel to place his feet on, and later a tripartite creation formula (heaven, earth, sea) is used:

> And the angel whom I saw standing on the sea and on the land lifted up his right hand to heaven, and swore by Him who lives forever and ever, who created heaven and the things in it, and the earth and the things in it, and the sea and the things in it, that there shall be delay no longer (10.5-6).

In Rev. 11.6, the same three-realm creation appears to be presup-

---

1. On the double meaning of 'sea' in Rev. 15.2, cf. pp. 75-76, above.

posed in John's statement about the universal authority of God's two witnesses:

> These have the power to shut up the sky (τὸν οὐρανόν), in order that rain may not fall during the days of their prophesying; and they have power over the waters to turn them into blood, and to smite the earth with every plague, as often as they desire.

The same may be said of Rev. 12.12, for when the dragon is expelled from heaven, woe is immediately pronounced on the earth and sea, the remaining realms of creation to which he is now confined. In chs. 12 and 13, the dragon, beast and false prophet are pictured as coming from the three realms of creation: heaven, sea and earth, respectively (cf. 12.7-10; 13.1, 11). In 14.7, the creation is catalogued in quadripartite fashion by an angel:

> and he said with a loud voice, 'Fear God, and give Him glory, because the hour of His judgment has come; and worship Him who made the heaven and the earth and sea and springs of waters'.

It was said above that the quadripartite formula is comprised of heaven, earth, sea and abyss ('under the earth'; Rev. 5.13). According to OT usage, the angel's words in the passage above actually follow this division, for the springs of the earth were conceived of as coming up out of the abyss of waters that lay beneath the earth. Hence to pronounce blessing on the abyss was equivalent to blessing someone's land with abundant springs.[1]

In Revelation 16, the same fourfold formula is presupposed as in 8.7-12, where heavenly bodies (as opposed to heaven itself) come under attack. As in the former passage, the sea is attacked second in the list of four: earth, sea, springs and rivers, sun (16.2-9). Whereas in 8.9 a third of all the creatures of the sea were killed, in 16.3 the sea appears to have been completely poisoned: 'it became blood like that of a dead man; and every living thing in the sea died'.

This survey shows that a very strong context is developed in Revelation for viewing the sea as a third, or sometimes a fourth, part of the created order. Furthermore, John will not have wanted his readers to miss the fact that the sea (along with every other part of the former creation) was ruined and made uninhabitable in the events leading up to the parousia. The earthly sea could not remain as it was

---

1. Cf. Gen. 49.25; cf. also Deut. 8.7; 33.13; Ps. 135.6; Prov. 8.24, 27-29.

in the new creation; presumably, it would either have to be removed, or else it would have to be replaced with a new one. It is thus perhaps natural to begin by taking Rev. 21.1 as saying that the former sea was removed along with the former heaven and earth, but that, unlike them, it was not to be re-created.[1]

The following comment by Caird shows why one might be tempted to look upon the sea as an element incompatible with the new creation. It should also be noted how he relates the two senses of the word 'sea' that have come under discussion above:

> The sea that vanishes with the first heaven and the first earth is the cosmic sea out of which that heaven and earth were made, the primaeval ocean or abyss which is an alias for the dragon Leviathan,[2] a home for the monster, and a throne for the whore (iv. 6; xii. 3; xvii. 1). Notwithstanding God's initial conquest of it in creation, it has remained, both on earth and in heaven, as the symbol of an incomplete victory and an incomplete sovereignty. It has been the barrier between man and God, through which the martyrs have had to pass in their new Exodus, and it has been poured from the bowls of God's wrath to engulf the throne of the monster.[3] But in a world where all things are spontaneously obedient to the rule of God it has no place.[4]

---

1. Commentators often draw a parallel between Rev. 21.1 and *Ass. Mos.* 10.5-6, which says that in the day of God's visitation, various aspects of the present creation will be disturbed: '[The sun and moon will be darkened], and the sea will retire into the abyss, and the fountains of waters will fail, and the rivers shall dry up' (10.5-6). Also cf. *Sib. Or.* 5.158-59; *T. Levi* 4.1. Such parallels are probably not relevant, however, since they deal with the woes of the end, rather than with the supposed condition of things in the new creation.

2. Cf. Isa. 51.9-10.

3. This last identification is probably mistaken. As in Exod. 9.8-12, where it was *ashes* from a kiln which caused boils to break out on the Egyptians, so in Rev. 16.2, 10 the first and fifth golden bowls of wrath seem to be bowls of charcoal- and incense-ash (cf. 5.8). These cause the beast's followers to break out in painful sores (cf. also the related image in Rev. 8.1-5). In the context of verses such as Rev. 16.3-7, the bowls are more naturally pictured as libation bowls (cf. Exod. 25.29), which contain the blood of sacrificial victims (cf. Rev. 6.9-11). Such a fluctuation of imagery is of course perfectly natural in Revelation. If the heavenly sea does figure in Rev. 16, it will not be as the content of the bowls, but as the chunks of ice that fall to the earth. In other words, might another picture of destruction and removal of the (icy) vault of heaven be intended in the events following the outpouring of the last bowl (16.21)?

4. *Revelation*, p. 262. For a full explanation of his view, see his pp. 65-67.

Caird is here interpreting the 'sea' of Rev. 21.1 by linking it to a well known Near Eastern creation myth that finds expression in the OT (primarily) in the books of Job, Psalms and Isaiah. Passages in these books show clear acquaintance with this myth in that they picture God's activity of creation or redemption as a taming of the primaeval waters of chaos, or metonymically as the slaying of the sea monster Rahab/Leviathan.[1] Assumed in Caird's analysis is the idea that, within the general world-view of the OT and apocalyptic, the sea was viewed as essentially chaotic. Its wildness was not removed, but only *limited* in the creation of the world.[2] It is thus not difficult to agree with Caird at least this far: if John did look at the sea in this traditional way, then he will have had to consider its nature as entirely incompatible with, and indeed antithetical to, the perfect order and harmony of the new creation that he described.

But it appears that Caird has pushed the idea of the sea's evil character significantly further than is warranted by the text of Revelation itself. To begin with, there is nothing, either in Revelation or in its *direct* OT background materials, which justifies Caird's view that the heavenly sea of glass is a symbol of evil.[3] On the contrary, in the passages cited above, the sea appears to be described as a structure of awesome beauty that is naturally associated with the heavenly theophany as a symbol of God's holiness. Thus, in line with the results of the discussion in §1 of the present chapter, above, it seems much safer to assume that the obsoleteness of the sea of glass in the new creation is dictated by the separation that it creates between God and humanity, rather than by its supposed chaotic or evil character.

Similarly, Caird's point is overstretched somewhat even when it comes to the way the *earthly* sea is treated in Revelation. For with few exceptions, the sea is mentioned on completely equal terms with the two or three other realms of creation, rather than being singled out as particularly chaotic or evil. Looking at the 'exceptions' will in fact turn up a different reason for the words 'there is no longer any sea' from the one Caird proposes.

1. Caird, *Revelation*, p. 262. The following are the main OT texts that employ this myth: Job 26.12-13; Pss. 74.12-17; 89.9-11; Isa. 51.9-10 (in some of these passages, the creation myth is used as a vehicle for reminiscence about the Exodus).

2. The following passages may be cited as examples of this perspective: Job 38.8-11; Isa. 57.20; Jer. 5.22. Cf. also Ps. 104.5-9; Prov. 8.27-29.

3. Cf. *Revelation*, p. 65.

First, Caird claims that the sea is a 'home for the monster'. Indeed, the beast is seen rising from the sea in Rev. 13.2. But this does not support Caird's larger point, for, as has been mentioned, the beast's rising from the sea is not unique, but clearly parallels the Dragon's origin in heaven, and the second beast's origin in the earth. In other words, *each* of the three realms of creation contributes a member of the anti-trinity, and thus this passage cannot be used to argue that the sea represents an element of the natural sphere especially conducive to the presence of evil.

Secondly, Caird calls the sea 'a throne for the whore'. But the 'sea' is not mentioned by name in the passage he has in mind (Rev. 17.1), but rather, 'many waters'. This phrase echoes the prophecy of Jeremiah against the historical city of Babylon (Jer. 51.13), and refers in the original context to the agricultural riches afforded by the river Euphrates and its tributaries.[1] In Revelation, however, the reference becomes a metaphor for the vast number of people who suffer under the harlot's dominance: 'The waters which you saw where the harlot sits, are peoples and multitudes and nations and tongues' (Rev. 17.15).[2]

Admittedly, it is conceivable that by using this language John intends to evoke OT passages such as Isa. 57.20-21 and Dan. 7.2. In the first of these texts, the unruly sea functions as a simile, and in the second as a symbol, for the constant trouble stirred up by a humanity estranged from God (cf. also Ps. 65.7). And although John chooses to

---

1. It is true that expressions like 'many waters' often relate to the sea and 'the great deep' in the OT. For example, cf. Pss. 18.4-5, 16; 69.14-15; Ezek. 27.26; Jon. 1.2-5. But the symbolism in these places is that of death and the watery under-world, rather than of chaos and rebellion. For other OT passages related to the expression 'waters', cf. (1) 'waters' as the abode of the spirits of the dead: Job 26.5; Ezek. 26.19-20; 31.15-16; Jon. 2.3-5; (2) 'waters' conceived of as beneath the earth: Deut. 4.18; 5.8; Ps. 136.6; Jon. 2.3-6; (3) waters synonymous with 'the deep', 'the abyss': Job 38.30; Pss. 69.14-15; 104.6; Isa. 51.10; Jer. 26.19; Jon. 2.3-5; (4) 'waters' as a place of distress, drowning (metaphorical for death): 2 Sam. 22.5-6 (waves); Pss. 18.16; 69.1-2, 14-15; 88.3-7 (waves); 124.1-5; 144.7; Isa. 43.2; Lam. 3.54-55; Ezek. 26.19; 27.26-27, 34; Jon. 2.3-5.

2. It is possible that this is partially interpreted in Rev. 18.13 by the statement 'And the merchants of the earth weep and mourn over her, because no one buys their cargoes any more; cargoes of. . . slaves and human lives'. But it is also not out of the question that the multitudes exploited by the harlot are symbolized as waters because they have been slain by her (cf. the previous note, and Rev. 18.24).

make more explicit connections between the sea and *the realm of the dead* in Rev. 13.1, nonetheless Daniel's 'troubled history' meaning cannot be dismissed as a possible overtone. It is thus not an unfair comment on the words 'there is no longer any sea' in Rev. 21.1c to say that the agelong vicissitudes of human history have found their final end in the transition to the new creation.[1]

But none of this takes away from the fact that Revelation itself never encourages its readers to take a negative view of the ordinary, literal sea. On the contrary, the great majority of references place it on an equal footing with the other realms of the created order.

Why then should the earthly sea *not* be re-created? For one reads in Genesis 1 that when God created the sea he saw that it was good (1.10). Indeed, it is the hope of God's re-establishment (in the new age) of everything that he planned for the earth in the beginning that is the theological basis upon which the whole new-creation theme is developed in Revelation 21. In other words, John is called to prophesy that no aspect of the present creation—no matter how degraded or poisoned in the present age—will fail to be cleansed and renewed, as God himself is heard to insist in 21.5-6:

> And He who sits on the throne said, 'Behold, I am making all things new'. And He said, 'Write, for these things are faithful and true'. And He said to me, 'It is done. I am the Alpha and the Omega, the beginning and the end.'

One can gather from this passage that John looked for the end of the world as the time when God would restore the entire creation to the state of goodness and wholeness that characterized it in the beginning. It would thus count as a rather puzzling inconsistency for John to say that the sea was to have no place in the re-created world.

It is therefore at least worth investigating the idea that some kind of renewal of the sea is envisaged after all. For although John obviously is not shown an immediate re-creation of the sea, yet consistency would still push the reader to expect such a re-creation in some manner and at some point. Upon reconsideration, the fact that John sees no sea in his vision of the inauguration of the new creation does not in and of itself prove that he expected the sea to be permanently left out of the new creation. For if one takes into account the fact that in popular knowledge rivers serve as the source for the waters of the sea

---

1. Rev. 21.4 certainly resonates with this possible shade of meaning from v. 1.

(e.g. Eccl. 1.7), then a new possibility begins to appear: namely, that John foresaw a gradual re-creation of the sea from the river that flowed from God's throne:

> And he showed me a river of the water of life, clear as crystal, coming from the throne of God and of the Lamb, in the middle of its street. And on either side of the river was the tree of life, bearing twelve kinds of fruit, yielding its fruit every month; and the leaves of the tree were for the healing of the nations (Rev. 22.1-2).

John's words here unmistakably recall those of Ezekiel:

> Then he[1] brought me back to the door of the house; and behold, water was flowing from under the threshold of the house toward the east, for the house faced east. . . Then he said to me, 'These waters go out toward the eastern region and go down to the Arabah; then they go toward the sea, being made to flow into the sea, and the waters of the sea are healed.[2] And it will come about that every living creature which swarms in every place where the river goes, will live. And there will be very many fish, for these waters go there, and the others are healed;[3] so everything will live where the river goes. . . And by the river on its bank, on one side and on the other, will grow all kinds of trees for food. . . They will bear every month because their water flows from the sanctuary, and their fruit will be for food and their leaves for healing' (Ezek. 47.1, 8, 9, 12).

It has already been shown that John reinterprets the temple (the *house* referred to above—cf. Joel 3.18) as the unhidden presence of God himself and the Lamb (Rev. 21.22). In harmony with this, John sees the river of life not coming from beneath the threshold of the temple, as in Ezekiel, but coming directly from the throne of God and the Lamb. But otherwise the conception is remarkably similar. So also is that of Zech. 14.8:

> And it will come about in that day that living waters will flow out of Jerusalem, half of them toward the eastern sea and the other half toward the western sea. . .

In view of the close relationship between these two passages and Rev. 22.1, it is worth asking whether John might have wanted his readers to imagine the gradual filling of a new but empty seabed with

---

1. Both here and in Rev. 22.1, it is an angel with a measuring rod who shows the prophet the river (cf. Rev. 21.15).

2. Literal marginal reading. NASB text: 'become fresh'.

3. See previous note.

the 'water of life'. In other words, the poisoned and lifeless water of the former sea could be conceived of as being entirely removed at the parousia, in order that a new sea might be formed from the divine spring water of the new creation. If this were the case, then indeed John would not be able to say 'I saw a new sea' in his vision of the inauguration of the new creation, in which the throne of God was just then coming down from heaven. At that moment, clearly the most that could be said would be that 'the [former] sea is no more'.

In this light, John's refusal to speak of a new 'sea' could be understood as stemming from a motivation similar to that which forbade him to refer by name in Rev. 20.13-15 to the final resurrection and bringing to life of the unrepentant. Just as he 'retired' those words on a positive note in 20.6 to keep his readers from mixing their good connotations with the final negative experience of the unrepentant (and vice versa), so a similar strategy is conceivable in chs. 21 and 22.

If John retires the word 'sea' in Rev. 21.1, this is not necessarily because he intended to preclude the idea that the new creation might contain something corresponding to the former earthly sea just as a resurrected person corresponds to his or her former dying self. Rather, 'the sea' has become a negatively charged *term* in his text,[1] and he does not want his readers to associate their own largely negative connotations of the natural sea with the new creation.[2] In other words, if there is to be a 'sea' in the new creation, it will be something inconceivably safer and more hospitable to humans than any sea they have known.[3] The difference between the empirical and the eschatological sea is thus so great that to speak of the latter by the same name would automatically detract from the idea by creating the wrong associations. John therefore chooses to focus exclusively on the 'river of life' in Rev. 22.1-2 (cf. 7.17; 22.17), and to leave to the imagination of his readers what glorious body of water might lie beyond its deltas.

---

1. Cf. below on the sea as a name for the realm of the dead.

2. Swete (*Apocalypse*, p. 272) and others show that for the ancients the sea was inevitably thought of as a place of great danger to human beings.

3. Cf. the remark of A. Schlatter, *Die Briefe und die Offenbarung des Johannes* (Schlatters Erläuterungen zum NT, 10; Stuttgart: Calwer Verlag, 1928), p. 327, about the sea as off-limits to humans.

c. *Revelation 21.1c: There is No Longer Any (Underworldly) Sea*
Beyond the clear references to the glassy sea of heaven above, the earthly sea below, and the symbolic sea of troubled human history, there is an additional connotation attached to the word 'sea' in Revelation, that the readers will have brought to their reading of Rev. 21.1. This connotation is of the sea as a symbol of death or the underworld.

In Rev. 13.1, the beast is seen coming up out of the sea, and, as was mentioned in the previous section, this comes to symbolize his return from the abyss, the abode of the dead. One must say 'comes to symbolize', first of all, because the sea is not used to evoke the idea of death prior to ch. 13, and, secondly, because in ch. 13 itself it is not the beast's rising from the sea which is readily interpreted in terms of death and resurrection, but rather his slain and revived head (13.3). It is this picture that has a retroactive effect on the possible symbolic value of the sea in 13.1.

Underworld symbolism may be seen in Rev. 18.21, where an angel throws something 'like a large millstone' into the sea, saying, 'Thus will Babylon, the great city, be thrown down with violence, and will not be found any longer'.[1]

It is in Rev. 20.13 that the expression 'the sea' comes into explicit relationship with the underworld. Chapter 8 has shown that the sea as the underworld makes very good sense both of the cosmological imagery and of the sequence of events in 20.11-13. In this light, there must be some connection between the sea as the realm of the dead in 20.13, and the sea that no longer exists in 21.1, for the simple reason that the two occurrences of the word for 'sea' are so close to each other in the text.

It must be admitted, in other words, that the readers will perceive a strong hint of the 'sea of death' in the words 'the sea is no longer'. For a reader who has begun by taking Rev. 20.11-15 as a single

---

1. A comparison with Ezek. 26.19-21 brings the underworld connotation all the more into focus:

> 'When I shall make you a desolate city . . . when I shall bring up the deep over you, and the great waters will cover you, then I shall bring you down with those who go down to the pit, to the people of old, and I shall make you dwell in the lower parts of the earth . . . I shall bring terrors on you, and you will be no more; though you will be sought, you will never be found again', declares the LORD.

Lust lists no less than seven references to Ezekiel's oracle against Tyre (Ezek. 26–27) in Rev. 18 ('The Order of the Final Events', p. 180 n. 5).

resurrection and judgment of the unrepentant occurring at the parousia,[1] this will not present any problems.[2] Such a person will be aware that the dissolution of heaven and earth happens at the parousia, so the re-creation of these elements, along with the doing away of the sea, will fit into place perfectly after 20.11-15.

But what will happen when one comes to realize that the New Jerusalem is the Great White Throne? The disappearance of the sea of death must now find a place in a new sequence of events: (1) parousia of Christ = beginning of the millennium = new creation = coming to earth of the New Jerusalem as God's Throne; (2) end of the millennium = resurrection of the unrepentant = great final battle = great final judgment. The answer is that reference to the sea fits best at the beginning, but in a paradoxical way.

For example, John has carefully worded Rev. 21.1c so that it stops just short of saying that the watery abode of death has now been annihilated. It is notable that he goes on to use the same expression in relation to death, sorrow, crying, tears and cursed things. Of each of these things it is affirmed that 'it will be no longer' (οὐκ ἔσται ἔτι),[3] not because it will not 'exist' in the strictest sense, but because none of them has any part in the renewed world and the experience of those who inherit it.

According to the book of Revelation, these negative experiences certainly do still exist, and not only after the parousia, but equally after the last judgment. They are in fact pictured as the exclusive and permanent inheritance of those who buy the lake of fire for themselves.[4] The point is that *these former evils have no power to trouble the redeemed*. It is for the overcomers, and for the overcomers alone, that such evils 'are no longer'. Thus, in the new creation, the sea as the underworld *may or may not* exist in some sense of the word, but it in no way has the power to encroach upon the resurrected community.

1. Cf. Chapter 8, §6, above. This is not a consistent reading, but it is perhaps the best one available until the equation Great White Throne = New Jerusalem can be made.

2. Nor, incidentally, will it create problems for the person who takes Rev. 20.11 as narrating the fleeing of earth and heaven after the millennium.

3. Cf. Rev. 21.4; 22.3, 4. Rev. 21.25 says 'there will be no night there'. Perhaps there will be night for those 'outside', but not for those inside the New Jerusalem (cf. 22.15).

4. Cf. Rev. 14.11; 20.10, 14-15.

The provisional disappearance of the sea of death at the parousia is also reconcilable with the cosmological imagery of Rev. 20.11-15. For if in v. 11 earth and heaven fled, leaving (v. 12) the shades of the dead standing in the abyss for the judgment of the dead at the parousia, then 21.1 could be taken as saying that in the new heaven and earth that appear after this judgment (and before that of 20.13-15), the watery abyss of the sea is no longer to be seen: it is completely covered over by the newly constructed firmament of the earth. In other words, it needs to be considered that, according to the OT cosmological model from which John consistently draws, the earth (= the dry land) is constructed as a platform that rests above the abyss of subterranean waters (often on supports such as pillars).[1] In the new creation, the earth is no longer surrounded on all sides by the sea, the open door to the watery underworld.[2]

In other words, to the person who has come to understand

---

1. For this cosmology, cf. 1 Sam. 2.8; 2 Sam. 22.16-17; Job 9.5-6; 26.5-7; 38.4-6; Pss. 24.2; 75.3; 104.5-9; 136.6. H. Bietenhard says the earth was viewed as a circular disk surrounded by ocean (*Die himmlische Welt im Urchristentum und Spätjudentum* [WUNT, 2; Tübingen: Mohr, 1951], p. 37). Cf. for example the vision of Cenez in *LAB* 28, cited in *The Biblical Antiquities of Philo* (trans. M.R. James; London: SPCK, 1917), pp. 165-67. Cenez first sees the world without form and void, with no mountains and no heavens, but only invisible (and audible) 'springs of water' without a foundation (§7). Then he sees a foundation laid 'like a shield', and then, out of the waters of the springs, a second foundation is formed over the first like 'a boiling froth' (§8). Then in the middle, between the two foundations, he sees people walking around: 'And these shall be for a foundation for 7000 years. And the lower foundation was a pavement and the upper was of froth, and they that came forth. . . are those that shall dwell therein' (§§8-9). It appears that the vision of Cenez departs slightly from Gen. 1.2-10 by picturing the founding of the firmament of the earth before the founding of the heavens out of the waters of the abyss. That this vision concerns the creation of the world (as opposed to some kind of intermediate heaven for the spirits of the righteous departed) is proved both by the reference to the future sin and judgment of 'those who dwell therein' in §9, and by the fact that Cenez cannot remember anything about his vision (§10). His single comment before he dies thus reflects not on the meaning of his dream, but on the state of ecstatic sleep: 'if the rest of the righteous be such [i.e. like the rest I just had] after they are dead, it is better for them to die. . .'

2. For the writer of Jonah, to drown in the sea was to go down directly into the abyss beneath the earth (Jon. 2.3-6). The waters of the sea were thus effectively the gates of the underworld. No such gates are needed in the new creation, because there will be no more death for those who live there.

Rev. 21.1-8 as reverting to the setting of the parousia after 20.13-15, the sea (as a manifestation of the underworld) will be conceived of as 'gone' from the new creation in the millennium, but not necessarily non-existent. It will rather be gone in the senses of being gone from the landscape,[1] and of no longer being a threat to the redeemed.

There is one residual sense in which the sea will eventually be 'no longer', and this is the one that will have come out most strongly on a first reading of Rev. 20.11–21.1. There is a final sense in which the sea of death will no longer have application to any human being. For 'the sea...and death and Hades gave up the dead' (20.13). Death and Hades were then cast into the lake of fire (v. 14). These manifestations of the underworld were shown being done away with once for all at the resurrection after the end of the millennium. Therefore, the statement about the sea in 21.1 cannot help but function to signal the final end to the remaining member of this trio of underworld elements. There is, in other words, a single sense in which the sea must remain until after the very last judgment.

But to the reader sensitive to all the layers of meaning resting upon the word θάλασσα, this last sense (which alone refuses to fit into the context of the parousia) will not overturn all the signals indicating that the new creation of Rev. 21.1-8 belongs to the parousia. Neither will it necessarily raise again the question of whether the final resurrection must attend the parousia after all. It will instead come to stand as a paradoxical surplus to all the other meanings:

> When Christ comes again, there will be no more separation between heaven and earth, no more heavenly sea.
>
> When Christ comes again, there will be no more polluted ocean, no more dangerous and hostile earthly sea.
>
> When Christ comes again, there will be no more restless history, no more rebellious human sea.
>
> When Christ comes again, there will be no more drowning places, no more entrances to the underworld sea.
>
> And at the end of the millennium, when Death and Hades are destroyed, and death as a temporary parting from the body is past, then there will finally be no more underworld sea.

In the final analysis, Rev. 21.1c does not indicate that the new

---

1. As in *Ass. Mos.* 10.6: 'The sea will retreat into the abyss'.

creation comes after the final judgment. But it does appear calculated to leave the reader with that impression.[1] Why? I submit that it is because John wishes to teach his readers two truths that he knows they will instinctively find incompatible. The first is that the parousia will see the advent of a new world for the resurrected ones, a world utterly unthreatened by sin, sorrow, evil and death. The second is that even the unrepentant will finally be given resurrection, and a belated (and refused) opportunity to enjoy this new world. Neither in their imprisonment, nor in their release are they to possess the slightest power to rob others of peace or happiness.

But according to the world view of most readers (ancient or modern!), there would not be much joy in picturing oneself on a renewed earth built over an underworld populated by hostile and unrepentant nations. Such a picture might have the same unsavoury effect as imagining oneself living in a beautiful palace above a basement full of corpses, or of hungry crocodiles.

There is definitely a cosmological paradox to be accounted for in this interpretation of Rev. 21.1c. But this paradox is not intended to be converted into a temporal paradox. In other words, Revelation offers no clear indication here or elsewhere that the readers are intended to reinterpret the millennium retrospectively by factoring it out of the chronological equation. On the contrary, John quite definitely gives his readers the concept of the millennium as a just jail sentence for the unrepentant, and the last battle/judgment as a final chance offered out of God's grace and justice. Irrespective of whether a given reader or interpreter should ultimately find this picture of the last disposition of the cosmos *palatable*, there is no doubt that it is this picture that has been offered, and that it is both meaningful and coherent. Thus the burden of proof must rest on the those who wish to argue (perhaps beginning from 20.13 and 21.1) for an a-temporal interpretation of the millennium narrated in Rev. 20.1-10.[2]

---

1.   Cf. Chapter 6, §2, above, on the dynamics of Rev. 20.4. The verse played down the strictly literal truth that there are some who will win eternal life without facing martyrdom in order to leave the reader in a more fitting emotional position (i.e. resolved to face the inevitable). Similarly, cf. Chapter 4, §4, above, on the way Revelation intentionally leaves the impression that a universal martyrdom precedes the parousia.

2.   The burden is to provide a detailed, coherent and textually supported alternative to which the reader turns after having first embraced the former temporal model.

2. *Revelation 21.2: The New Jerusalem*

The appearance of the New Jerusalem has of course been discussed already in §1, above. It has been argued in the context of the phrase 'there is no longer any sea' (Rev. 21.1c) that the heavenly city is a picture of the corporate people of God, whose ultimate communion with him on the earth begins at the parousia of Christ. It now remains to look at the question again from the beginning, focusing on the New Jerusalem itself.

a. *The New Jerusalem and the Parousia*

Does the appearance of the descending New Jerusalem in Rev. 21.2 suggest an event that is to be understood in the context of the parousia? To answer this question, the present method dictates that one begin by recalling how it is that Revelation trains its readers to recognize a reference to the parousia. In other words, if it can be determined that this or that sort of thing always or usually has the function of alerting the reader to the fact that the parousia is in view, then it can be asked if this or that thing is present in the description of the New Jerusalem (21.2-7). The following section therefore consists of a review of certain key texts in Revelation, each of which offers some contribution to the reader's expertise in relating visions to the parousia.[1]

The first clear reference to the parousia in the letters is in Rev. 2.25-28:[2]

'Nevertheless, what you have, hold fast until I come.
'And he who overcomes, and he who keeps My deeds until the end, to

---

If, for example, John ultimately wished for his readers to turn from the idea that a resurrection and judgment of the unrepentant dead would take place significantly after the parousia, then what concept(s) did he wish to communicate to them by presenting them first with this temporal model? Why could these not have been communicated equally well by using the alternative model in the first place? My own studies have not uncovered (either in Rev. 20.11–21.1 or elsewhere in Revelation) textual phenomena that strike me as appropriate or sufficient fuel for such an a-temporal interpretative engine. What the text of 20.11–21.1 *is* clearly doing, in my opinion, is redeploying the cosmological idea of the underworld in such a way as to remove its emotional undertones regarding the threatening and spoiling power of sin and death.

1. For a fuller survey complete with critical notes, cf. Chapter 4, §3, above.
2. I pass over Rev. 1.7 for the sake of brevity.

> him I will give authority over the nations; and he shall rule them with a
> rod of iron, as the vessels of the potter are broken to pieces, just as I also
> have received authority from My Father. And I will give him the morning
> star.'

The overcomer is here promised, in the context of the coming of
Jesus, the reward of participation with him in his role as king and
judge of the nations. As the readers are shortly to have confirmed for
them, Jesus is to exercise this role *par excellence* at his parousia. And,
as one will confirm at the end of the book, there lies in the reference
to the morning star a promise that the overcomer will receive Jesus
himself at the parousia (Rev. 22.16).

In Revelation 3, one reads:

> 'If therefore you will not wake up, I will come like a thief, and you will
> not know at what hour I will come upon you.
>
> 'But you have a few people in Sardis who have not soiled their gar-
> ments; and they will walk with Me in white; for they are worthy.
>
> 'He who overcomes shall thus be clothed in white garments; and I will
> not erase his name from the book of life, and I will confess his name
> before My Father, and before His angels' (3.3b-5).

When Jesus comes, it will be the occasion for the overcomers to
appear with him in white clothing, and it will be the time for them to
be publicly acknowledged as true citizens of his realm. The 'book of
life', in other words, contains the membership rolls of the eschatological kingdom of God and Christ.[1]

The next letter contains promises that both underscore these ideas
and make them more specific:

> 'I am coming quickly; hold fast what you have, in order that no one take
> your crown.
>
> 'He who overcomes, I will make him a pillar in the temple of My God,
> and he will not go out from it any more; and I will write upon him the
> name of My God, and the name of the city of My God, the new
> Jerusalem, which comes down out of heaven from My God, and My new
> name' (Rev. 3.11-12).

Here the references to garments and citizenship are being drawn
into clearer focus. On the one hand, the metaphor of the pillar suggests that the white garments earlier mentioned will be *priestly*

---

1.   For discussion, cf. Chapter 8, §5, above.

garments,[1] with the priestly image perhaps further amplified by the promise of Jesus writing the name of God and his new name on the overcomer (cf. the name of God on Aaron's forehead—Exod. 28.36-38; cf. Lev. 8.9). On the other hand, the earlier promise of one's acceptance in Christ's kingdom is now sharpened by implication to include citizenship in the New Jerusalem, which, like Christ himself in Rev. 1.7, comes down from heaven. These two ideas will later be tied together and confirmed in Revelation 21, when the New Jerusalem will be continuously described in temple terms. In other words, the readers are progressively given to realize that to speak of a permanent eschatological assignment to priestly service in God's temple on the one hand, and to speak of citizenship in the New Jerusalem on the other, are to express two aspects of the same reward.

What is it that tells the readers that this reward is to be given at the parousia of Jesus? In the letters, the most important suggestion is the immediate context. Reference to Christ's coming, followed immediately by a promise of reward to the overcomer, essentially forms the first part of the closing refrain in the seven letters, and this is most clearly the case in the three from which quotations have been taken. Obvious as well is the fact that an intimate part of the reward is Jesus himself at his parousia.[2]

In hearing the seven letters, therefore, the reader will naturally find him- or herself being trained to associate promised rewards with the parousia. This association will receive yet more basis in passages such as 'the last trumpet' (Rev. 11.15-18), which announces the parousia together with the promise that it is the 'time to give their reward to Thy bond-servants the prophets and to the saints and to those who fear Thy name, the small and the great' (v. 18).[3]

What then do the readers know about the parousia by the time the opening vision and the seven letters have been read? They know that

---

1. As has been discussed above in different contexts, Rev. 7.9-15 and 15.2 confirm this idea.

2. As discussed in Chapter 4, §3.c, above, it is more than conceivable that along with the promise of the morning star, two other cryptic promises refer to Jesus as well, namely the promise of a white stone, and the promise of hidden manna (Rev. 2.17).

3. At the end of the book there is the explicit statement, 'Behold, I am coming quickly, and My reward is with Me, to render to every man according to what he has done' (Rev. 22.12; cf. Isa. 40.10; 62.11).

the parousia is the public revelation of Jesus from heaven as king and judge of all humankind. They also know that, if they remain true to him, it will be: the time of their reunion with him, the time of their participation with him in his kingly rule, the time of their confirmation as royal priests and citizens of his kingdom, and the time of their confirmation as people of the New Jerusalem, which comes down from heaven. Given these foundational concepts, many further passages will now be recognized immediately as making reference to the parousia.

One example is the song to the Lamb in Rev. 5.9-10:

> Worthy art Thou to take the book, and to break its seals; for Thou wast slain, and didst purchase for God with Thy blood men from every tribe and tongue and people and nation. And Thou hast made them to be a kingdom and priests to our God; and they will reign on the earth.

When will the royal priesthood reign on the earth? When Jesus comes to reign with them at his parousia, without a doubt.

How is one prepared to interpret Rev. 6.12-18? This vision, which recounts the events following the opening of the sixth seal, clearly harks back to and fills in the first announcement of the parousia, read in Rev. 1.7. The authority of Jesus to rule the nations with a rod of iron and to shatter them like pottery (2.27) will likewise not be far out of the reader's mind. Jesus and the Father are now revealed through the torn heavens to the whole human race, and the human race is not pleased about it.

There is, however, something new added in Rev. 6.12-18 that the readers will not yet have encountered. That new element is the disintegration of the created order. The stars fall down, all the earth's permanent features such as mountains and islands are dislocated, and even the sky itself rips in two and flees in shreds. The readers thus stand prepared from this point on to picture the physical world dissolving into complete ruin at the parousia.

Not long after encountering these negative aspects of the parousia, the readers will encounter this positive picture:

> After these things I looked, and behold, a great multitude, which no one could count, from every nation and all tribes and peoples and tongues, standing before the throne and before the Lamb, clothed in white robes, and palm branches were in their hands; and they cry out with a loud voice, saying,
>
> 'Salvation to our God who sits on the throne, and to the Lamb'.

And all the angels were standing around the throne and around the elders and the four living creatures; and they fell on their faces before the throne and worshiped God, saying,

'Amen, blessing and glory and wisdom and thanksgiving and honor and power and might, be to our God forever and ever. Amen.'

And one of the elders answered, saying to me, 'These who are clothed in the white robes, who are they, and from where have they come?'

And I said to him, 'My lord, you know'.

And he said to me, 'These are the ones who come out of the great tribulation, and they have washed their robes and made them white in the blood of the Lamb.

'For this reason, they are before the throne of God; and they serve Him day and night in His temple; and He who sits on the throne shall spread His tabernacle over them.

'They shall hunger no more, neither thirst any more; neither shall the sun beat down on them, nor any heat; for the Lamb in the center of the throne shall be their shepherd, and shall guide them to springs of the water of life; and God shall wipe every tear from their eyes' (Rev. 7.9-17).

Given what they already know from earlier passages, the readers of Revelation will have ample reasons for seeing this vision as a representation of the parousia. This for at least four reasons.

1. The palm branches (Rev. 7.9) denote the joyous greeting of a returning conqueror, and also recall the story of the triumphal entry of Jesus into Jerusalem. The picture is of a victory celebration, in which Jesus and the Father are being welcomed.[1] This passage thus represents the opposite side of the parousia to that encountered in 6.12-17, where the rest of humankind is utterly terrified at being confronted with the revelation of God and the Lamb on their throne.

2. The emphasis on white robes (Rev. 7.9, 13-14) recalls 3.3-5 and

---

1.   Note that this forms a link with Rev. 6.16, where the parousia is of both the Lamb and the Enthroned One. For palm branches as expressive of a victory celebration, cf. 1 Macc. 13.51; 2 Macc. 10.7; *Lev. R.* 30.2. J.A. Draper argues that the palm branches are *lulabs* (the festive wands associated with the Jewish Feast of Tabernacles), but he fails to provide convincing evidence. In general, however, his case for 7.9-17 being a picture of an eschatological Feast of Tabernacles (cf. Zech. 14) is convincing ('The Heavenly Feast of Tabernacles: Revelation 7.1-17', *JSNT* 19 [1983], pp. 133-37). Methodius teaches that the parousia inaugurates the millennial Feast of Tabernacles (*Banquets of the Ten Virgins* 9.1). H. Ulfgard offers illuminating background on the Feast of Tabernacles in NT times (*Feast and Future: Revelation 7.9-17 and the Feast of Tabernacles* [ConBNT, 22; Stockholm: Almqvist & Wiksell, 1989], pp. 108-47).

suggests the fulfilment of the promises there. Noteworthy are the statements 'They will walk with Me in white' (3.4), and 'The Lamb...shall lead them' (7.17). The washing of the robes in the blood of the Lamb also links this passage to 5.9-10, in which passage the Lamb is praised for redeeming, with his shed blood, people from 'every tribe and tongue and people and nation' (cf. 7.9) to reign as priests on the earth.[1]

3. The fact that the great multitude are said to have 'come out of the great tribulation' (Rev. 7.14) will strongly suggest the parousia as the context for the victory celebration pictured, since it is the parousia that brings that time of persecution to an end.[2] Rev. 6.9-11 is in the immediate background:

> 'How long, O Lord, holy and true, wilt thou refrain from judging and avenging our blood on those who dwell on the earth?' And there was given to each of them a white robe; and they were told that they should rest for a while longer, until the number of their fellow servants and their brethren who were to be killed even as they had been, should be completed also.

In contrast to this passage, Rev. 7.9-17 appears to picture the time when passive 'resting' is over. The picture of active celebration before the throne is interpreted as day-and-night priestly service before the throne (note the present tense in 7.15). This implies that the number of martyrs is now complete, and that their vindication is finally accomplished through the parousia. Corroboration will be noted later in Rev. 20.4-6, which pictures the parousia as the occasion on which the divine court sits to vindicate the martyrs by granting them resurrection and kingly priesthood with Christ.[3]

4. Many of the blessings that are said to be given to the numberless

---

1. White robes for the saints will also be directly connected with the parousia in Rev. 19.14 (cf. 19.7-8). For confirmation of the idea that the saints and not just angels are to be seen here 'with him' in conflict with the beast, see 17.14 (cf. the discussion in Chapter 4, §3.c, above).

2. Ulfgard (*Feast and Future*, p. 100 n. 432) correctly notes that the present tense of the participle ἐρχόμενοι does not in itself indicate that the process of coming out is presently going on, but rather ties the multitude's 'coming out of the great tribulation' to the following clause ('they washed their robes'), so as to make clear that their coming out of the tribulation is posterior to the washing of their robes.

3. The loud cry of the great multitude (Rev. 7.10) is to be closely echoed in 19.1 (a scene connected with the central parousia vision).

multitude in Rev. 7.15-17 are recognizable as distinct echoes of previous promises clearly connected to the parousia.[1]

a. 'They are before the throne of God, and they serve Him day and night in His temple' (Rev. 7.15) correlates with the promise of being a pillar in the temple of God (3.11-12).[2]

b. The promise that 'They shall hunger no more, neither thirst any more' (Rev. 7.16) correlates with 2.7, 'To him who overcomes, I will grant to eat of the tree of life, which is in the Paradise of God'; and with 2.17, 'To him who overcomes, I will give some of the hidden manna'. And the reference to the quenching of thirst will be taken up again and related to the parousia in 22.17:

> And the Spirit and the bride say, 'Come'. And let the one who hears say, 'Come'. And let the one who is thirsty come; let the one who wishes take the water of life without cost.

If one adds together the various connections just observed, it is easy to see a sum emerging: the passage describing the numberless multitude before the throne shows itself to be laced throughout with clues telling the readers, 'This too is a picture of the parousia'.[3] As in the passages discussed from the letters to the seven churches, the means by which the readers are supplied with interpretative information is

---

1. Promises that have already been introduced in some way as parousia themes will generally be confirmed as such later on in Revelation. For example, 'The Lamb in the center of the throne shall be their shepherd' (Rev. 7.17) will connect up later with 14.4 (cf. 14.1 for the setting of the parousia): 'These are the ones who follow the Lamb wherever He goes'. The statement in 22.12 adds indirectly (via Isa. 40.10-11) to this theme: 'Behold, I am coming quickly, and My reward is with Me. . .' 'The Lamb in the center of the throne shall guide them to the springs of the water of life' (7.17) correlates with 22.17.

2. Most of these statements will be echoed in later representations of or promises concerning the parousia, and this will give the reader further confirmation. For example, as has been seen, Rev. 20.6 takes up the same theme: 'They will be priests of God and of Christ, and will reign with Him for a thousand years' (cf. also 22.3-5).

3. *Pace* Ulfgard, *Feast and Future*, pp. 102-104, who claims that, in addition to its future aspect, Rev. 7.9-17 pictures the Christian's present mystical victory in heaven. As Ulfgard says, 'Christ, who "had to" suffer, triumphed through suffering, thereby setting a paradigm for his followers. . .' (p. 155). I submit that the paradigm is: endurance of earthly suffering through to victory (overcoming), *then* being united with Christ (as he was with his Father), and reigning with him in resurrection (2.10, 25-28; 3.11). Cf. Chapter 3, §3, above.

straightforward to describe. Themes, words and pictures already explicitly connected with the parousia are brought into association with new ones in such a way as to draw the new elements into the composite picture or vocabulary. For example, after reference to Jesus as the Lamb who is also the Shepherd in Rev. 7.17, every similar reference will have the potential to serve, context permitting, as a clue that the parousia is being invoked. This is exactly what is to happen in the scene of 14.1-4, where v. 4 reads: 'These are the ones who follow the Lamb wherever He goes'.[1]

Attention may now be drawn to Revelation 19, where the most universally recognized parousia scene is to be found. In the following introductory passage many echoes can be heard from the texts already surveyed. The procedure under discussion, by which the new text joins itself to previous references to the parousia, remains vigorous in its operation here:

> And a voice came from the throne, saying, 'Give praise to our God, all you His bond-servants, you who fear Him, the small and the great'.
> And I heard, as it were, the voice of a great multitude and as the sound of many waters and as the sound of mighty peals of thunder, saying,
> 'Hallelujah! For the Lord God, the Almighty, reigns. Let us rejoice and be glad and give the glory to Him, for the marriage of the Lamb has come and His bride has made herself ready.'
> And it was given to her to clothe herself in fine linen, bright and clean; for the fine linen is the righteous acts of the saints.
> And he said to me, 'Write, "Blessed are those who are invited to the marriage supper of the Lamb"'. And he said to me, 'These are the true words of God' (Rev. 19.5-9).

The first sentences of this passage clearly evoke the seventh trumpet vision in Rev. 11.17-18, where the revelation of the parousia is likewise greeted with praise to God for entering upon his eschatological reign. A further link between the two passages is formed by the reference to bond-servants small and great, since this echoes the phraseology of 11.18.[2]

---

1. So, e.g., Beasley-Murray, *Revelation*, p. 222.
2. As Rev. 11.18 states, 'the time to give their reward to *Thy bond-servants* the prophets and to the saints and to those who fear Thy name, *the small and the great*. . .' One may add that the 'voice of a great multitude and as the sound of many waters and as the sound of mighty peals of thunder' (19.6) serves, together with the preceding 'loud voice of a great multitude' (19.1), as a verbal pointer to the parousia scene of 7.9-17 ('behold, a great multitude. . . in white robes. . . and they cry out

A new and noteworthy element finds a place here in Revelation 19: the figure of the wedding of groom and bride is now introduced to express the final union that Christ and the company of his saints enjoy at his parousia. The theme of being granted pure garments, which in the letter to Sardis tended to suggest the context of priestly worship, now functions with equal appropriateness in the wedding context. In the case of the worshipping community, as in that of the worshipping individual, it is neither inner beliefs nor verbal confessions that promise to be singled out as the criteria of worthiness to appear publicly alongside Christ at his parousia, but rather concrete actions (cf. 3.5).

The next major section of Revelation 19 corresponds to the passage just read, in the same way that the sixth seal vision in ch. 6 relates to the vision of the numberless multitude in ch. 7. In ch. 19, in contrast to ch. 6, the positive side of the parousia has been revealed first, to be followed by the negative side. Of all places in Revelation this is the least in doubt as a representation of the parousia. A quick review of major connecting points will therefore suffice for the present purposes.[1]

1. The open heaven (Rev. 19.11) recalls the splitting of the heaven in 6.14 and results, as it did there, in the revelation of Christ as agent of God's judgment.
2. Christ's titles, 'Faithful and True' (Rev. 19.11) and 'King of kings and Lord of lords' (v. 16), along with the reference to making war (v. 11b), serve to recall the reference to the parousia in 17.14: 'These [the beast and his allies: cf. 19.19] will wage war with the Lamb, and the Lamb will overcome them, because He is Lord of lords and King of kings, and those who are with Him are called and chosen and faithful'.
3. The robe dipped in blood (Rev. 19.13) recalls 7.14, in which the robes of the saints attending Christ's parousia were described as washed and made white in the blood of the Lamb.
4. The immediately following reference to the heavenly armies following Christ in clean white garments (Rev. 19.14)

---

with a loud voice. . .'; 7.9). The context is the same: a victory celebration in honour of God and the Lamb.

1. For full discussion of the contextual build-up to Rev. 19.11-21, cf. Chapter 4, §3, above.

strengthens the connection of point 3, and serves at the same time as another link to the just quoted 17.14.

5. The sharp sword (Rev. 19.15) correlates with the warning to the church at Pergamum in 2.16: 'Repent therefore; or else I am coming to you quickly, and I will make war against them with the sword of My mouth'.

6. The reference to Christ ruling the nations with a rod of iron (Rev. 19.15) closely echoes the words of 2.26-27, in which Christ promises the church in Thyatira that the overcomer will participate with him in his role as ruler and judge at the parousia.[1]

7. Mention of the winepress of God's wrath (Rev. 19.15) is a cross-reference back to the muted parousia figure of 14.19: 'And the angel swung his sickle to the earth, and gathered the clusters from the vine of the earth, and threw them into the great winepress of the wrath of God'.

To take note of these seven points of connection is to stand in a position to see Revelation 19 fitting squarely into the pattern repeatedly observed in this study. The meaning of almost every statement grows out of verbal or imagistic relationships with one or more previous passages. It would in fact be demonstrable of ch. 19 as a whole that it gathers together and develops *most* of the key words, phrases and themes earlier associated with the parousia. The readers of Revelation, trained from the beginning to recognize particular elements as belonging to the overall picture of the parousia, will thus naturally see in Rev. 19.11-21 the fullest and most explicit revelation of the judgmental side of the parousia yet offered.

At the same time, however, they have had introduced to them in the text of Rev. 19.1-10 an element that is new and belongs to the positive side of the parousia's conceptual orbit. Given the consistent pattern that has been observed, in which statement or promise anticipates later visionary explication, they will not be unwise to expect more along the same lines. That is, to an astute reader, the presence of the wedding theme in *promise form* will strongly suggest the possibility of its

---

1. Points 2–6 here, when added together, make it reasonably certain that John intended his readers to see human saints and not just angels in the 'armies of heaven' of Rev. 9.14.

development further on in the text in the form of one or more visions. And this is exactly what occurs in Rev. 21.2-7:

> And I saw the holy city, new Jerusalem, coming down out of heaven from God, made ready as a bride adorned for her husband.
>
> And I heard a loud voice from the throne, saying, 'Behold, the tabernacle of God is among men, and He shall dwell among them, and they shall be His people,[1] and God Himself shall be among them, and He shall wipe away every tear from their eyes; and there shall no longer be any death; there shall no longer be any mourning, or crying, or pain; the first things have passed away'.
>
> And He who sits on the throne said, 'Behold, I am making all things new'. And He said, 'Write, for these things are faithful and true'.
>
> And He said to me, 'It is done. I am the Alpha and the Omega, the beginning and the end. I will give to the one who thirsts from the spring of the water of life without cost. He who overcomes shall inherit these things, and I will be his God, and he shall be My son.'

In view of its numerous and clear connections with earlier themes and visions of the parousia, it is not going to be difficult to prove that this passage fits the pattern being discussed. Six points may be noted.

1. As expected, the appearance of the New Jerusalem as a bride in Rev. 21.2 takes up in visionary form the wedding announcement given in 19.7a. Further, the reference to the completeness of her adornment for her husband harks back both to 19.7b and 19.8, verses that introduced the concept of

---

1. NASB is perhaps justified in preferring the reading *people* (λαός) over *peoples* (λαοί). Although the second of these is arguably better attested (א A, against P and the preponderance of early versions), the first stands as the reading slightly more likely to have caused the other, given an inattentive copyist: the plural verb 'they shall be' presents the temptation to supply a predicate nominative in the plural. This is against most commentators (e.g. Deutsch, 'Transformation of Symbols', p. 110 n. 32), who prefer *peoples* because it is the harder reading. If anything it is slightly harder to imagine John writing λαοί than it is to imagine a scribe doing so. John says that the one kingdom of Christ is made up not of many peoples, but of individuals *from* (ἐκ, 'out of') all peoples (cf. Rev. 5.9-10; 7.9; 18.4, 'come out of her, my people' [singular]). The criterion of *lectio difficilior* should be applied from the point of view of the careless scribe (but, if possible, *not* from the point of view of the original author!). All this said, the *idea* conveyed by the reading 'peoples' (that God's community is made up of men and women from all ethnic groups, not just from Israel) stands in harmony with Revelation as a whole. From the point of view of ideological consistency within Revelation, in other words, the two readings stand on equal footing.

the bride's being in readiness for her marriage to the Lamb. The fact that the New Jerusalem is now *seen* coming down out of heaven from God refers back to the promise of citizenship given to the overcomer in 2.12. And if in 2.12 the overcomer can be referred to as a temple pillar, and in 13.6 the saints in heaven may be referred to corporately under the metaphor of the temple of God, then it will not be difficult here to take over from 19.7 the idea that the bride represents the saints in their corporate relationship with God and Christ.[1] The fact that she is seen coming down out of heaven from God will thus coincide on one hand with the fact that Christ appears from heaven at his parousia, and on the other hand with the fact that he has all the saints with him when he comes (17.14).[2]

2. The announcement in Rev. 21.3 that the tabernacle is 'among men', along with the reference to the drying of tears, specifically underlines the same promises given in the parousia vision of 7.15-17.

3. The promise in Rev. 21.4 that there will be no more death harks back to the promise to the overcomer in 2.10-11 that he or she will be given the crown of life, and will by no means be vulnerable to the second death.

4. The divine self-description, 'the Alpha and Omega', in Rev. 21.6a parallels two other occurrences in 1.8 and 22.13, both of which serve to give weight to promises of the parousia.[3]

---

1. Cf. Gundry, 'The New Jerusalem', pp. 254-64.

2. In some places such as Rev. 7.9-17, the concept is that Christ's parousia is the time of his union with the faithful. The paradox of the faithful being with Christ, and yet anticipating union with him, may conceivably help to explain the dual appellation bride–wife in 21.9.

3. Cf. Rev. 1.7-8: 'Behold, He is coming with the clouds, and every eye will see Him, even those who pierced Him; and all the tribes of the earth will mourn over Him. Even so. Amen. "I am the Alpha and the Omega", says the Lord God, "who is and who was and who is to come, the Almighty".' Also 22.12-14: 'Behold, I am coming quickly, and My reward is with Me, to render to every man according to what he has done. "I am the Alpha and the Omega, the first and the last, the beginning and the end." Blessed are those who wash their robes, that they may have the right to the tree of life, and may enter by the gates into the city.' The right to enter the New Jerusalem ('the city') is here connected with the parousia, which further attests

5. The wording of Rev. 21.6b evokes the parousia in the same manner as did the previous mention of the tabernacle and the drying of tears, namely, by recalling the parousia vision of ch. 7. Thus the promise that the thirsty may drink freely from the spring of the water of life in 21.6b links closely with the prediction in 7.16-17 that the faithful will thirst no more because the Lamb will lead them to the springs of the water of life.[1]

6. In Rev. 21.6, the Enthroned One announces that 'It is done' (literally, 'They are done' [γέγοναν]). This echoes the equivalent phrase that was heard from the throne upon the outpouring of the seventh and final bowl of God's wrath in 16.17 (γέγονεν). If the significance of the cry 'It is done' in the context of the seventh bowl was to signal the fulfilment of the parousia as the judgment of the world, then perhaps the positive 'They are done' here refers to the completion of both sides of the eschatological transition to God's kingdom, both negative and positive. As 21.4 affirms, 'The first things have passed away'. Yet not only has the old been judged and removed, but the new has been established in its place.[2]

More connections between Rev. 21.1-7 and other announcements or representations of the parousia could be added,[3] but these six should be sufficient to make the point. The scene that presents the descent of the New Jerusalem is described in such a way as to place it every bit as firmly within the conceptual orbit of the parousia *as any previous passage*. If Revelation had no ch. 20, there would not be the slightest

the close relationship between it and one's inheritance of the New Jerusalem.

1. As mentioned above, the same formula is to be repeated yet again in context of the parousia in Rev. 22.17. Mention of 'the bride' in that verse retrospectively ties 21.2, 9 to the parousia as well.

2. Sickenberger (*Erklärung*, p. 189) observantly connects the phrases 'I make all things new' and 'They are done' with the repeated phrases 'Let there be' and 'it was so' in Gen. 1, exposing a parallel between the first and the last acts of creation. The immediately following sentence, 'I am the Alpha and the Omega, the Beginning and the End', may well confirm this.

3. For example, compare the command to write in Rev. 21.5 with that in 19.9; 'Faithful and true' (21.5b) with 19.11; the promise to the overcomer in 21.7 with the promises in the letters to the seven churches. These connections are not as direct and indisputable as the others, and so need not be insisted upon.

question of separating the new creation or the appearance of the New Jerusalem from the parousia of Christ.

Given this state of affairs, it is easy to see why various commentators end up having difficulties with Rev. 21.1-8. For example, Zahn assumes that the new creation of 21.2 comes about after the millennium, but he senses very strongly that the wedding of the New Jerusalem belongs at the parousia.[1] So what happens to the Holy City, when 'earth and heaven flee away' (20.11)? Zahn justly rejects as 'unthinkable' the idea of Jerusalem going back to heaven at the end of the millennium.[2] But this leaves him with a chronological anomaly that he only succeeds in ironing out at the expense of Greek grammar.[3]

b. *Two New Jerusalems?*

Another expedient that is sometimes tried is to see two New Jerusalems, one of which appears during the millennium, and one which comes

---

1. Cf. *Offenbarung*, II, pp. 611-13. Cf. also Beasley-Murray, who argues cogently for the idea that the marriage and earthing of the New Jerusalem must come at the parousia (*Revelation*, pp. 315-16). The question left unanswered by Beasley-Murray's approach, of course, is how the New Jerusalem gets back to heaven so as to be seen descending (a second time?) in Rev. 21.1.

2. Cf. *Offenbarung*, II, p. 599. Nothing in the text supports the idea of Charles (*Revelation*, II, p. 189) that the New Jerusalem of the millennium is to be lifted up off the earth before the dissolution–re-creation. The necessity for such eisegesis should have alerted Charles to the presence of a radical flaw in his model for the millennium.

3. Zahn's rather desperate solution is to take the participle καταβαίνουσαν ('coming down') in Rev. 21.2 as adjectival (cf. 3.12) rather than adverbial. In other words, Zahn argues that in 21.2 John sees not the New Jerusalem coming down from heaven, but the New Jerusalem, *that city which comes down from heaven* (cf. the arguments made above about the adjectival versus verbal force of the relative clause in Rev. 20.11). It has been on earth since the parousia, says Zahn, and it is only logical to understand that it is still situated on the earth in the new creation. In other words, he seems to see things similarly to Commodianus, who pictures the destruction of the former creation going on all about the New Jerusalem, but leaving the holy city unscathed (cf. *In Favour of Christian Discipline against the Gods of the Heathens* [trans. R.E. Wallis; ANCL, 18; Edinburgh: T. & T. Clark, 1895], chs. 44–45). The difficulty is that the participle simply cannot do what Zahn wants it to do without the article, for, in the Greek of Revelation, anarthrous participles always have adverbial force. The new creation and the descent of the New Jerusalem must therefore go together.

down in the new creation.[1] There is something highly dubious in the fact that exponents of this approach usually end up appealing to the idea of textual displacements or to less than harmonious sources.[2] Were there not a ch. 20 of Revelation, there would be no question of splitting any one part of 21.1–22.5 off from another. On the contrary, it is entirely natural to see in 21.9–22.5 the visionary exposition of a theme that has been introduced very briefly (21.1-2) and backed up by announcements, promises and warnings (21.3-8).[3]

What is it, therefore, that makes it so difficult to see the appearance of the New Creation and the New Jerusalem in Rev. 21.1–22.5 as a picture of the parousia? It is rather obvious that the answer lies in Rev. 20.7-15. As discussed above, most readers must inevitably sense a deep conflict between the idea of the new creation on the one hand, and the unfinished business of the judgment of the unrepentant on the other. Granted, it seems tempting to feel that the beauty and perfection of the new creation would be deeply marred, both by the idea of hostile people under punishment (20.5, 13-15), and by the idea of an attack on the New Jerusalem by the same hostile people (20.7-10). John, however, has given his readers clear pointers to how this sense of incongruity is to be resolved.[4]

3. *Residual Issues*

A few issues have not been properly addressed above, because they have never been strictly relevant to the discussion as framed under the present method. Yet, although their treatment would have been a distraction to the flow of the argument elsewhere, they are nonetheless of enough importance to deserve proper acknowledgment and discussion. Such issues are therefore dealt with in the present section.

---

1. E.g. Rissi, *The Future of the World*, p. 56; Charles, *Revelation*, II, pp. 144-54; also Boismard, 'L'Apocalypse ou les apocalypses', p. 525; Gaechter, 'The Original Sequence', pp. 491-501; Preston and Hanson, *Revelation*, pp. 129-45; Ford, *Revelation*, pp. 339-46, 364-70; M. Wilcox, 'Tradition and Redaction of Rev. 21,9–22,5', in J. Lambrecht (ed.), *L'Apocalypse johannique*, pp. 205-206.

2. Cf. all the references in the previous note except Rissi.

3. So similarly, e.g., Roloff, *Offenbarung*, p. 197; Schnackenburg, *God's Rule and Kingdom*, p. 346; Sweet, *Revelation*, p. 301.

4. Cf. the discussion which concludes §1, above, in the present chapter.

After the Thousand Years

a. *Universal Salvation in Revelation 21?*

Various scholars have found in Revelation 21 elements that they take to be indications that the whole of mankind will be saved in the end. From the viewpoint of the present method, the question to put to such suggestions is this: at what point and in what way are the readers made aware of such a hope? In other words, up to Rev. 20.15, the readers have been given every reason to think that a significant portion of humanity will perish in a way that is both total and irrevocable.[1] It must therefore be shown that, in any given place, the reader is given reason to see a reversal, so that the possibility of universal salvation opens up for the first time. Several passages are to be considered as possibilities.

It is sometimes suggested that the phrase in Rev. 21.3, 'the tabernacle of God is among men', might point toward universalism.[2] In a text that had already introduced such an idea, this would certainly be a possible reading. But not here, however. From all that has gone before, the reader knows that the only people left on earth from the parousia onwards are the resurrected saints. Consequently, it is they and they alone who constitute the new (redeemed and reconciled) human race. That is, the resurrected saints, the citizens of the New Jerusalem, are the 'men' (= 'humanity') among whom God chooses to make his final dwelling. Verses 7 and 8 each confirm this. As always in Revelation, it is not everyone, but rather the *overcomer*, the victor in the battle, who inherits this relationship with God (v. 7). The *cowards* on the other hand (= the deserters), together with the unbelievers and all varieties of sinners, have no part in it; their part is in the lake of fire (v. 8).[3]

---

1. The fate of the worldwide followers of Satan and his beast has been represented both as annihilation (Rev. 20.9) and as unending torment (14.9-11; 20.10, 15; 21.8). The single text that looked as though it might present an exception (15.4) was discussed above in Chapter 4, §3.b, above. Revelation goes so far as to assert that all human beings are destined to face God and to admit to the justice of his dealings with humankind. But there is no hint that such an involuntary recognition of the truth issues in salvation. Hope of salvation is explicitly restricted to the overcomer.

2. E.g. D. Georgi, 'Die Visionen vom himmlischen Jerusalem in Apk 21 und 22', in *Kirche* (Festschrift G. Bornkamm; ed. D. Lührmann and G. Strecker; Tübingen: Mohr, 1980), pp. 351-72 (358); and (tentatively) Prigent, *L'Apocalypse*, p. 327.

3. In the varieties of sinners listed here (particularly the first type, 'cowards'), a number of commentators rightly see reference to those who give in to the worship of

For some, Rev. 21.24-26 suggests a 'mixed' millennium. In this view, Jerusalem is seen as the capital of the world in a this-worldly messianic kingdom. Through its gates, a constant traffic of the world's kings and nations comes, bringing tribute and conducting business. Will they not be healed of their rebelliousness by the 'leaves of the tree' (22.2)?[1] But this is to get the matter totally confused, as is shown by the complicated textual rearrangement necessary to give the notion a semblance of plausibility.[2]

For others, Rev. 21.24-27 is a picture holding out the hope of eventual universal salvation.[3] But neither does this view stand up to scrutiny. As the present study has shown, John constantly teaches his readers how to interpret OT pictures of the end within the framework of his own prophecy. For example, he teaches them to recognize the destruction of Gog and Magog from Ezekiel 38 as a picture of the resurrection and judgment of the unrepentant. How then does John teach his readers to interpret prophecies such as Ps. 72.10-11, Isa. 49.23, and 60.3-5, which he clearly cites in Rev. 21.24-27? Kiddle gives this unimpeachable answer:

> It was impossible that the new Jerusalem should give 'light' to the pagan nations, as Isaiah and the psalmists seemed to hope; there were no pagan nations, for the glory of the new Jerusalem was reserved for those whose names were written in the Lamb's book of Life. . .[4] But who are *the nations*? Not the heathen, certainly. Not those who joined Antichrist in the slaughter of the witnesses. *The nations* are the redeemed, who belong spiritually but not racially to the twelve tribes. Did not Christ redeem 'men from every tribe and tongue and people and nation'? Very well, *that* is how Christians must read these old prophecies: *they* are *the nations*. Similarly, the *kings of the earth*. . . (so we must infer) are the martyr monarchs, who reigned as the successors of the heathen rulers (cf. xx. 4-6); or perhaps all loyal Christians, of whom the heavenly hosts cried out: *they shall reign on earth* (v. 10).[5]

the beast. E.g. Caird, *Revelation*, pp. 167-68; Beasley-Murray, *Revelation*, p. 314.

1. So, e.g., Charles, *Revelation*, II, pp. 148-50.

2. Charles, *Revelation*, II, pp. 144-54; also, e.g., Gaechter, 'The Original Sequence', pp. 491-501; Preston and Hanson, *Revelation*, pp. 129-45.

3. E.g. Fiorenza, *Priester für Gott*, p. 359.

4. Cf. Rev. 21.27, and the comments in Chapter 8, §3, above, on the book of life as the citizen-rolls of the New Jerusalem.

5. *Revelation*, pp. 438-39 (emphasis original). This paragraph equally cuts across Rissi's unique proposal that the hostile 'kings of the earth' and their 'nations' will be saved from the lake of fire to enter the New Jerusalem (Rev. 21.24-27; cf.

Gundry's exposition is also astute:

> The meaning of 'bring into it' [21.24, 26] has to do with the glory and honor of the saintly nations of kings that make up the city, not with unsaintly traffic from countryside into the city. John immediately adds 21.27 to guard against a misunderstanding of the latter sort: 'and there will not enter into it anything unclean or anyone who practices abomination and lying, but only those who are written in the Lamb's book of life'. To enter the city is to help make it up—and there is nothing about leaving it once the glory and honor have been brought in. To the contrary, see 3.12. . . : the overcomer 'will not go outside any more'.[1]

b. *Millennium as a World-Sabbath?*

It will be recalled that the idea of a millennial world-sabbath was earlier touched upon. This view, propounded by the nineteenth-century expositor Uriah Smith, saw the millennium as an age during which the earth lay lifeless and inert. One of the arguments put forward against that conception had the following two-part form. First, it was asserted that the readers of Revelation would not have not found any positive indication of a dead-earth millennial age by the end of Revelation 20. Secondly, it was reasoned that (granted the correctness of the former assertion) they would certainly not find anything in the last two chapters of Revelation to make them *begin* thinking along those lines.

Although the second of these points seems irrefutable in combination with the first, the first still seems open to doubt at one specific

---

The Future of the World, pp. 77-78; *Time and History*, p. 124). Against Rissi, it is to be observed that in 21.27, no one can enter the city except its citizens, and those who experience the lake of fire are certainly not citizens (20.14-15). Secondly, Rissi only achieves his view by treating John's careful silence as evidence for a textually unsupportable doctrine of a redemptive 'second resurrection'. John refuses to mention the 'second resurrection' by name in 20.13, not because resurrection is not in view, but because he wishes to discourage the very idea that Rissi has in mind, that is, that the 'rest of the dead' will experience 'life' in the deepest sense when they finally 'stand again' in their bodies (see, e.g., Pohl, *Offenbarung*, II, p. 330 n. 986; and above, Chapter 8, §6). The second 'resurrection', that of the unrepentant, can hardly be called such because it issues not in everlasting life, but in the second death. According to the present view, Rissi is at least right this far: God's grace toward the unrepentant extends even to the point of inviting them belatedly into the life of the new creation and the New Jerusalem. If the present study represents him correctly, John's view differs from Rissi's in predicting that even this final gift will be rejected (Rev. 20.7-10; cf. Isa. 27.2-5).

1. 'The New Jerusalem', p. 264.

point. The specific point is this: certain interpreters have claimed to
see in Rev. 8.1 a reference to a period of world silence (as in *4 Ezra*
7.30).[1] If this suggestion should turn out to be defensible, then Smith's
model will appear to have a significant foothold in the conceptual
world of Revelation. Therefore, careful consideration must be given
to the merits of this view of 8.1. For otherwise, it will be difficult to
choose with undiluted confidence between Smith's model for the millennium and that proposed by the present study.[2]

It will probably be best to prepare for the discussion of Rev. 8.1
(-5) by quoting it alongside the supposed parallel which is to be found
in *4 Ezra* 7.30:

> Then [at the advent of messiah] shall the city that is now invisible appear,
> and the land which is now concealed be seen.
>
> And whosoever is delivered from the predicted evils, the same shall see
> my wonders. For my Son the Messiah shall be revealed, together with
> those who are with him, and the survivors shall rejoice four hundred
> years. And it shall be, after these years, that my Son the Messiah shall
> die, and all in whom there is human breath. Then shall the world be
> turned into the primaeval silence seven days, like at the first beginnings;
> so that no man is left.
>
> And it shall be after the seven days that the Age which is not yet awake
> shall be roused, and that which is corruptible shall perish [description of a
> general resurrection and judgment follows] (*4 Ezra* 7.26-31).[3]

Rev. 8.1-5 reads as follows:

> And when He broke the seventh seal, there was silence in heaven for
> about half an hour.
>
> And I saw the seven angels who stand before God; and seven trumpets
> were given to them.

---

1.   E.g. Rissi, *Time and History*, pp. 3-6, followed by Sweet, *Revelation*,
pp. 158-59.

2.   A fair amount of what has been demonstrated in the present study is capable
of being applied straight across to strengthen Smith's view. One thinks especially of
the arguments in favour of the total exclusivity of the millennium, and of those in
favour of seeing a dual picture of resurrection and judgment in Rev. 20.7-10 and
20.11-15. The latter point has been tentatively asserted by various scholars: e.g.
Shea, 'Parallel Literary Structure', p. 49, who follows Smith's view; and Metzger,
'Zwischenreich', p. 109, who comes closest to the view presented here. This view
has not been argued convincingly in the scholarly forum.

3.   Trans. G.H. Box, in R.H. Charles (ed.), *The Apocrypha and Pseudepigrapha*, II.

> And another angel came and stood at the altar, holding a golden censer; and much incense was given to him, that he might add it to the prayers of all the saints upon the golden altar which was before the throne.
>
> And the smoke of the incense, with the prayers of the saints, went up before God out of the angel's hand. And the angel took the censer; and he filled it with the fire of the altar and threw it to the earth; and there followed peals of thunder and sounds and flashes of lightning and an earthquake.

Certain obvious differences immediately appear between these two passages. To focus on just a few of these, in *4 Ezra* a seven day world-silence follows the earthly reign of messiah. In Rev. 8.1-8, however, it is the events leading up to the (second) advent of messiah which create the context (especially the seven seals and the seven trumpets). Nothing is said about the silence of the earth, but rather it is a question of a half hour of silence *in heaven*.

To the reader of Revelation 8 who either consciously or unconsciously pictures events as they are being narrated, this silence will not simply be an empty space in the story. To the contrary, the silent period will appear to be filled with symbolic activity. Without a sound, seven angels receive trumpets, which they will blow when the period of silence is over (cf. 8.6-7). Another angel attends the incense altar, adding a large quantity of fresh incense and burning it in a censer. No one in heaven says a word while this great incense offering burns, sending up clouds of smoke. But there is a paradox here: the silent cloud of incense speaks in countless voices, because it represents 'the prayers of the saints'. All heaven is silent not because the parousia has come, signalling the earth's rest (the parousia, one recalls, is a very noisy time in heaven![1]), but because God (and everyone else) is listening attentively to the pleas of the suffering saints on earth.[2] The silence is broken only when the offering of their prayers is complete; the censer, now filled with fresh coals from the altar, is cast into the earth, upon which follow loud sounds and thunder.

John's understanding of the symbolic nature of the temple activities that he sees[3] invokes a related image in Rev. 6.9-11, where the souls

---

1. Cf. Rev. 7.9-12; 11.15, 19; 14.2-3; 16.17-18; 19.1-7.

2. So correctly Beasley-Murray, *Revelation*, pp. 150-51. He (along with others, e.g., Charles, Lohmeyer, *in loc.*) cites a striking rabbinic parallel in *b. Ḥag.* 12b. There, the angels are said to praise God by night, but to be silent by day, so that God can pay attention to Israel and show them his lovingkindness.

3. Cf. the discussion in Chapter 8, §1, above.

[= the blood] of those slain for their witness to the truth cry out from the channel at the base of the altar of sacrifice. They are comforted with the assurance that they will only have to wait but 'a little while longer' until the time of their vindication. The 'little while' is the time that it takes for the rest of their faithful brothers and sisters to be sacrificed on earth, as they have been. At that point in the narrative, however, the martyrdom of the rest of the saints is not depicted, but rather there is an immediate jump to the parousia and their vindication (6.12-17). This means that the seventh and final seal has the potential to supply what was missing between the fifth and sixth seals, namely, the 'little while' during which the saints on earth gave their lives for the testimony of Jesus. In other words, the 'little while' and the 'half hour' fairly beg to be equated.

A re-reading of Rev. 8.1-5 with such a thought in mind serves to remove any doubts that the equation of the two periods of time is to be made. In typical style, John narrates the final act of the seventh seal (8.5) in such a way as to link it inextricably with the parousia vision of the sixth seal. Each symbolizes the same reality (the one in 'day of the LORD' imagery, and the other in heavenly temple imagery), namely, the inbreaking of the parousia as a divine response to the prayers of the saints. On the one hand, the picture of a censer full of burning coals thrown from heaven to earth represents the darkening of the sun and moon (i.e. from the smoke and ash; // 6.12), and the falling of the stars (the live coals; // 6.13). On the other, the earthquake stands for both the former earthquake and the fleeing of the mountains and islands (// 6.12, 14). The whole set of consequences (thunder, sounds, lightning, earthquake), if it does not do so already, will soon come to evoke the revelation of God on his throne (// 6.15-17).[1]

In conclusion, there is no particular connection between the 'half hour' of silence in Rev. 8.1 and the idea that a period of world-silence precedes the new creation. Instead, the idea of prayers being heard and answered in heaven makes perfect sense of the passage. Rev. 8.1-5 stands in fact as a clear paradigm of John's literary and prophetic style, in which a new passage weaves together images, themes and words from previous material in order to present a new viewpoint on a given reality.

---

1.   Cf. Chapter 8, §1, above, for discussion.

But if Rev. 8.1 does not open the door to the idea of a period of primordial conditions, then certainly neither does any other passage in Revelation. Correspondingly, this concept can never form the basis for an overall model of the millennium.[1]

To be fair, Smith's criticism of the view proposed here must be heard as well. He rejects the idea that the millennial reign takes place in the new earth and heavens, because

> it makes the wicked come up in their resurrection, and with the devil at their head, tread with their unhallowed feet upon the purified and holy earth, while the saints, who have held possession for a thousand years, are obliged to flee into the city. We cannot believe that the saints' inheritance will ever be thus marred, or that the fair plains of the earth made new will ever be soiled with the polluting tread of the resuscitated wicked. Besides outraging all ideas of propriety, there is no scripture from which even an inference can be drawn to support this position.[2]

Smith here voices the exact sort of antipathy towards mixing the resurrection of the unrepentant and the new creation that has been discussed above. Part of John's point, however, is that the 'wicked' *have no power* to mar, soil or pollute the new earth. Neither have they any more power to intimidate the saints. For in the new world, right is really and practically stronger than wrong. Instead, it is the unrepentant who are in a position of weakness and vulnerability, although they do not recognize it. As at the very beginning, Satan convinces them that they are invincible: 'You shall not die!' But both he and they are tragically mistaken (Rev. 20.9-10 // Isa. 26.10-12, 27.1).

In his last statement, Smith is overlooking a very significant passage:

> 'For just as the new heavens and the new earth
> Which I make will endure before Me', declares the LORD,
> 'So your offspring and your name shall endure.
> And it shall be from new moon to new moon
> And from sabbath to sabbath,

---

1. R.M. Johnston ('The Eschatological Sabbath in John's Apocalypse: A Reconsideration', *AUSS* 25 [1987], pp. 39-50) cites an interesting rabbinic discussion of the idea that the world would have a sabbath age corresponding to the fallow sabbath-year legislated in Lev. 25 (*b. Sanh.* 97a-b). He does not go on, however, to demonstrate any particular connection between this concept and the millennium of Revelation.

2. *Daniel and the Revelation*, p. 749.

All mankind will come to bow down before Me', says the LORD.
'Then they shall go forth and look
On the corpses of the men
Who have transgressed [margin, rebelled] against Me.
For their worm shall not die, And their fire shall not be quenched;
And they shall be an abhorrence to all mankind' (Isa. 66.22-24).

John read in these last verses of the prophet Isaiah (and others, such as Joel) that the final fiery judgment of the unrepentant was to take place right outside the Holy City (Isa. 66.20). But more than this, he read here that this judgment had as its setting the new creation of God. This reality John himself saw, and endeavoured to communicate to his readers. But he did so in such a way as to leave in their minds a last impression not of smoking Gehenna, but of the glory of the Lamb's bride.

Chapter 10

CONCLUSION

This study has been designed methodologically to cover an enormous amount of ground in Revelation. If this has turned out to be somewhat ungainly in terms of presentation, it has nonetheless been entirely appropriate in terms of the criteria proposed in Chapter 2 (§5) for an adequate alternative interpretation of the millennium:

1. It will be able to demonstrate that the literary function of the millennium (and its environs: Rev. 19.11–21.8) within the book of Revelation hinges on clear contextual ties with other parts of the book.
2. It will be able to give an account of these ties and their workings that is reasonably compelling from a literary standpoint.
3. It will be able to demonstrate that the contextual ties it has identified combine to *rule out* the received interpretation and suggest its replacement with a different one.
4. It will be able to provide an exegesis of the main section under consideration (Rev. 19.11–21.8) that not only interprets it plausibly in the context of its wider connections, but that also shows that a satisfactory (and ideally, *more* satisfactory) account can be given of the main section in and of itself.

It is for the reader to judge whether and to what extent the present essay has met its own criteria for success. It may however be useful to conclude by stepping back to review the cumulative exegetical argument of the central part. In the following summaries, the word 'context' will carry the special meaning required when discussing the book of Revelation, that is, background built up continuously from the beginning of the text.

1. *Exegetical Arguments and Results*

First, the context was established for Christ's appearance as Witness, Warrior and King in Rev. 19.11-21. It was established that these roles were intimately linked, and that Christ's way of expressing his authority to judge and rule was to *expose* the state of things. In other words, it was discovered that the process of divine judgment, given over into the hand of Christ, had consistently been presented not as the process of chastisement, but as the process of *revelation*. Christ was seen judging the world by revealing the true character of human beings, both individually and corporately. For example, in harmony with this, the 'sword of his mouth' (19.15) was interpreted as the revealing power of his true testimony against the human race's supreme self-deception in following the beast. From ch. 6 onwards in Revelation, the essential murderousness of the human race had been testified to, but no sign had been given that it would be willing to face the facts about its own character. In line both with crucial precedents in the book of Revelation itself and with the direct OT background of the passage (Ezekiel 39), the slaying of the kings of the earth and their armies in Rev. 19.17-21 was interpreted paradoxically as their own complete mutual destruction.

It was also discovered that John had clearly, repeatedly and emphatically prophesied to his readers that no one on earth would be exempt from this fatal judgment which was to attend the parousia of Christ. The picture in Revelation 19 was seen as entirely consistent with the expectation that had been steadily developed from ch. 6 onwards: to their peril, all the remaining inhabitants of the earth would be united in enmity towards Christ when he appeared (19.17-21).

This analysis led to the question of Christ's faithful: what role if any were they to be imagined as playing in this scene? A study of the theme of the cost and reward of following Christ revealed a clear and consistent pattern building up to ch. 19. The cost of holding unwavering allegiance to Christ (that is, becoming a victor or an 'overcomer') would be martyrdom under the beast, and one important aspect of the reward would be participating with Christ at his parousia in his role as conquering witness. Like Christ, the saints would participate in the conflict only as witnesses, both in the active and in the passive senses. They would *bear witness* to the murderous or suicidal nature of the unrepentant human race, and they would *witness* the ultimate proof of it. A complete polarity had thus been developed between those coming from heaven with Christ on the one hand, and those gathered against him on earth on the other. Although this left certain apparently inherent ambiguities (such as whether some of the faithful might in fact survive to meet Christ at his parousia), the overall impression was clear and indelible. In the world-judgment of Christ's parousia, there would be no uninvolved party. According to Revelation 1–19, the parousia would see humanity divided into exactly two groups: the 'overcomers', who would judge the world with Christ, and the 'rest', who would accomplish their own punishment by slaying one another in the process of opposing him.

In the next two chapters these conclusions regarding Revelation 19 were incorporated into a more or less conventional interpretation of the millennial rule of the saints, with the following exceptions suggesting themselves as noteworthy.

First, in harmony with the previous material, Satan's being cast into the abyss (Rev. 20.1-3) was interpreted as his imprisonment in the underworld along with the rest of unrepentant humanity (evoking images both from Isaiah 14 and 24.23-24). The stated justification for his imprisonment, 'that he should deceive the nations no longer', was shown to be entirely consonant with the previous picture of all the (unrepentant) nations being cast into the realm of the dead, as opposed to implying (inconsistently) that some 'nations' were to be conceived of as having been spared at the parousia.

Secondly, consistent both with previous and with subsequent promises in Revelation, the kingdom over which the resurrected 'saints' (20.6) were to reign for the millennium was interpreted as the realm of creation, as at the beginning of the world (cf. Gen. 1.26-28; Rev. 5.10). It had been demonstrated previously that the meaning of promises such as Rev. 2.26-27, which spoke of overcomers expressing shattering power over the 'nations', had already been exhausted in the picture of their participation with Christ in the 'battle of the witnesses' in ch. 19 (see above). In other words, it was shown that nothing in Rev. 20.1-6 required (or even opened up the possibility of) the (inconsistent) idea that ordinary nations might be spared at the parousia.

Thirdly, it was shown that the text intentionally left the reader with hermeneutical puzzles at key places, and with clues which led to paradoxical re-readings.

In the next chapter, all of these findings were brought to bear on a new look at Rev. 20.7-10. Starting from the firmly established assumption that the readers were to have pictured both Satan and all the unrepentant nations incarcerated in the underworld during the millennium, these verses began at once to make clear and vivid sense. Satan's hosts were to be identified as the unrepentant, who, like him, were not to have been freed from the underworld 'until the thousand years were completed' (cf. 20.3, 5). But in their case, release from the underworld indicated nothing less than *resurrection*. In line with this idea (which was confirmed over and over in examining the words and phrases of the section), the attack and defeat of 20.7-10 was interpreted as the result of the final corporate choice of resurrected and unrepentant humanity—a last temptation in the last paradise. As always in Revelation, *judgment* (in this case the *final* judgment) was being presented as the divine act of *revealing* the state of human hearts.

In the following chapter, a new interpretation of Rev. 20.11-15 was developed. First it was demonstrated that the throne, like all the other major visual elements of the heavenly temple/throne-room, was understood by John and presented to his readers as a 'visual metaphor'. In other words, like the bowls full of incense which '*are* the prayers of the saints' (Rev. 5.8), the throne was not presented to the reader as though the seer understood it as an 'object'. Rather, it was presented as a picture revealed to the seer, a picture that conveyed something about the nature of God and his relationship with creation.[1] The throne, the place of God's unhidden presence, could either indicate joyous celebration, or devastation, depending on whether people (or even creation itself) were prepared to meet him (contrast 6.12-17; 7.9-17). It was also shown in detail that the appearance of the divine throne had been linked to the dissolution of the present creation, which was to attend the parousia of Christ. Given this context, the reference to the fleeing of earth and heaven in Rev. 20.11 was interpreted as recalling the parousia, rather than as suggesting something either later or more radical.

Yet, in spite of the clear reference to the parousia in Rev. 20.11, it was possible to show that this connection did not in itself make it easy

---

1. The fact that John could present the same reality under the visually conflicting images of the throne-chair and of 'the ark of the covenant' (Rev. 11.19) demonstrates this.

to 'place' the following scene of judgment (20.12-15) in relationship to the parousia. The dissolution of creation was being referred to; it was not being narrated as part of the scene. A number of puzzling questions suggested themselves. Was the judgment of v. 12 to be understood as another version of that seen in 20.4-5, which had accompanied the parousia? Correspondingly, was vv. 13-15 to be understood as parallel to 20.7-10? If so, how did this relate to the previous verses (20.1-10), which portrayed a thousand year delay in the final resurrection and judgment of the unrepentant? And how were the two versions of their fate in resurrection (war/trial) to be related? It seemed that the reader would have to hold this line of interpretation in abeyance and try another. Was the scene to be read as a single judgment stated twice (20.12 // 20.13) and understood as something that was to happen at the close of the millennium? If so, then (as above) how was this picture of resurrection and judgment as a *courtroom procedure* to be reconciled with the previous picture (20.7-10) of resurrection and judgment as a *battle*? Further, why was there reference to books of deeds (v. 12)? Had not judgment according to past deeds already been accomplished at the inauguration of the millennium?

These apparent oddities began to make sense when it was recognized that John's description of the New Jerusalem invited the reader to interpret it retrospectively as God's (and Christ's) 'Great White Throne'. The scene of Rev. 20.11-15 was finally understood as a composite presentation, in courtroom imagery, of the two-stage judgment of the unrepentant dead, which had been narrated in Rev. 20.4-10. The first stage of judgment (20.11-12) was shown to correspond to 20.4-5 as the negative side of that judgment of the dead which had attended the parousia (cf. 11.18). Verse 12 pictured the unrepentant dead being put to the proof according to their deeds in previous mortal life ('according to the things written in the books'). The unrepentant were being confronted with the full reasons for their exclusion from the rolls of the kingdom ('the book of life'), that is to say, the reasons why they were being refused the gift of resurrection. Verses 13-15 was shown to constitute an alternative viewpoint on the *second stage*, which had been pictured earlier in 20.7-10. In this stage the unrepentant were resurrected, judged according to their deeds (that is to say, they were put to the proof on the basis of their actions), and punished. When read according to the clues tying it to other texts,

Rev. 20.11-15 presented a new, paradoxical and complemenary perspective on the two-step process of judgment which had been narrated in 20.4-10.

Four main points were offered in explanation of this amalgamated presentation of judgment events earlier associated with opposite ends of the millennium (Rev. 20.4-5, 7-10). Two of these points were theological, and two compositional.

The first theological point was that John appeared to be saying that the two judgments formed an essential unity (if not a temporal unity), because they would ultimately reveal the same thing. Those who have chosen estrangement from God in their mortal lives will continue to reject him, even when given the full facts of his and their nature, and when given the chance to start afresh in resurrection. The second theological point was that the millennium-long delay between the two final stages of the judgment (Rev. 20.4-10 // Rev. 20.11-12, 13-15) can be seen from the divine perspective as constituting only a momentary pause, a pause that does nothing to alter the fundamental character of things. In other words, from the human point of view, the passing of time would open the door for a fresh choice, but from the divine point of view, the passing of time would only confirm choices already made. It was argued that these points of view were not designed to undermine the temporal quality of the millennium so much as to relativize the significance of time, particularly as a factor of change in the human heart.

Compositionally, it was first demonstrated that clear parallels stood between Rev. 20.11-15 on the one hand, and Ezekiel 38–39 (an unquestionable background text for the chapter) on the other. The presentation of each of these composite scenes was shown to pave the way for an extended and undistracted description of the good things of the messianic age. Secondly, in terms of Revelation itself, it was observed that John's crafting of the scene in 20.11-15 allowed readers to come away with a coherent and meaningful story of the end, even if (as is obviously possible!) they missed his indications that resurrection and judgment had been narrated in 20.7-10. The main priorities of communication to be gleaned from this compositional strategy were two: to show that the grace of the new age would be extended to, but rejected by, the unrepentant, and to give a positive impression of the joys of the new age that would not be dampened in any way by this.

Results gained in the final exegetical chapter, on Rev. 21.1-8, served to underline this sense of communicative priorities. First it was demonstrated that the phrase 'there is no longer any sea' (21.1c) invited interpretation in terms of the removal of the 'sea of glass' (cf. 4.6; 15.2), the age-old barrier between heaven and earth. Linked with other passages such as 6.12-17, 19.11 and 20.11, and with the following verses (21.2-4), the new creation and the earthing of the New Jerusalem (21.1) could be rightly seen as belonging to the parousia.

There was a persistent puzzle, however. On the one hand, among five possible nuances of the word 'sea',[1] the heavenly 'sea of glass' was the only one being brought clearly to the fore in Rev. 21.1-4. On the other hand, the the same word had just occurred in 20.13, and, given the context of the fleeing of earth and heaven in 20.11, this presented a cosmological paradox. In what sense could it be said *at the parousia* that the sea *of the underworld abyss* (20.13) 'was no more'? It was argued that what John was doing with the image of an underworld of the dead was what he had done with various images of heavenly things: pointing to the limitations of a familiar concept. Viewed from the perspective of God's plans for the judgment of the human race, the parousia would not signal the end of the eschatological story. In that sense the final obsoleteness of the 'underworld' would not come until later, since 'the rest of the dead' were not to be resurrected for the final judgment transaction 'until the thousand years were completed'.

All the same, another fact was more significant from the perspective of the readers' hope for their own future. In the new creation of the parousia, death and the hostile forces associated with it would have no more power whatsoever to threaten the happiness of the redeemed. For the saints, the parousia would mean the end of the 'sea' with its connotation of the potency of death and evil. The paradox, in other words, was demonstrated to be a *cosmological* one aimed at transforming the readers' view of the underworld as a potential threat, as opposed to a *chronological* one aimed at changing the readers' understanding in regard to the sequence of the events previously narrated in ch. 20.

Attention was then given to the description of the descent of the New Jerusalem (Rev. 21.2). The coming to earth of the Holy City was

1. The five meanings are: the heavenly sea of glass, the natural earthly sea or ocean, the turbulant 'sea' of estranged humanity, the sea as an entrance or exit from the abyss or underworld beneath the earth, and the sea as the underworld at large, representing the unresurrected dead.

shown to be completely at home within the growing context of annunciations of Christ's parousia, when he and his chosen ones would appear together from heaven (cf. especially 19.7-9, 11-14). By waiting to describe the new creation and the New Jerusalem until the judgment events of ch. 20 had been narrated to their close, John was neither implying that there would be two New Jerusalems, nor saying that the saints would have to wait a thousand years beyond the parousia to receive their full inheritance. He was instead encouraging his readers to realize that nothing would threaten the condition of perfect wholeness that they would enter upon at the parousia.

The chapter ended with brief replies to some universalistic interpretations of Revelation 21, and to a model positing a deserted earth during the millennium.

Having given a summary of the present study's exegetical results, further reflections on its significance in relation to certain earlier interpretations of the millennium are now offered.

2. *Results of the Present Study in Relation to Previous Interpretations*

First, this study has revived the the earliest interpretative tradition about the millennium in Revelation. Patristic writers such as Barnabas, Justin, Irenaeus, Hippolytus, Methodius and the author of the *Apocalypse of Elijah* all agreed that the millennium would be an age inaugurated by the parousia, enjoyed by the redeemed alone, and set in the context of a renewed (if not always radically re-created) earth.

Secondly, this study has shed a complimentary light on Gry's effort at the beginning of this century to forge a new interpretation of the millennium. The millennium has indeed been described in terms that would have been familiar to a person expecting a limited, earthly, this-age messianic reign. But it has been thoroughly laced with the seeds of a deeper, and radically different, model for the end. Although Gry's attempt to outline the shape of this different model failed, yet his sense that the text was designed to allow two levels of interpretation has been vindicated.

Thirdly, this study has in effect championed an interpretative suggestion made by Wolfgang Metzger. Metzger, convinced that there was something deeply wrong with the idea of a this-worldly millennium, tried to outline a model in which that age had the new creation

(Rev. 21.1-22.5) as its setting. He proposed that in some way 20.7-10 and 20.11-15 might ultimately refer to the same judgment.[1] In a sense, this essay has done for Metzger's interpretative proposal what Fiorenza's thesis did for Schnackenburg's proposal:[2] it has tested its potential strength as fully as possible within the context of the book of Revelation as a whole.

Fourthly, this study has proposed a significant alternative to the a-temporal models of the millennium proposed by such scholars as Wikenhauser, Schnackenburg, Fiorenza and Pohl. It may be repeated here what was stressed at the outset, namely, that this essay would vindicate some of the most significant points made by proponents of the a-temporal view. For example, it has demonstrated that Revelation does not present the millennium as a 'mixed' age belonging essentially to the present creation, but instead as the first instalment of the unending good of the new creation. Viewed in the context of everything that prepares for them, the blessings of Revelation 21 and 22 unmistakably reveal themselves to be inaugurated by the parousia. For example, as Schnackenburg says, the bride (19.7-9) certainly does not have to wait a thousand years beyond the parousia for the consummation of her marriage to her Lord.[3]

The place where the present study has parted company with such views is in its interpretation of the theological significance of the millennium. Revelation does not support the idea of a special class of martyrs worthy of a special reward (Wikenhauser, Schnackenburg, and ambivalently Fiorenza), nor does it support the idea of the church's ages-long hiddenness (Pohl). Instead, it calls all Christians to loyalty and bearing witness even to the point of death during the brief but intense persecution leading up to Christ's parousia (Fiorenza). In the last analysis, Revelation's millennium is simply not presented as a unique period in the life of the redeemed. Rather, it is presented as an age of just recompense expressed in the temporary denial of resurrection to the unrepentant.

I submit that it is this 'judicial' significance of the age that will have to be taken into account if interpreters are to address adequately

---

1. Cf. similarly the view of Smith and Seventh Day Adventist scholars such as Shea. Smith deserves acknowledgment as the first exegete to interpret Rev. 20.7-10 explicitly in terms of resurrection (*Daniel and the Revelation*).

2. Cf. Chapter 3, §5, above.

3. *God's Rule and Kingdom*, p. 346, quoted above.

(from whatever perspective) the question of whether the temporality of the millennium is ultimately disposable. This is obviously not to imply that the matter is more or less settled. For although the present study has put to rest the major arguments previously put forward for uneasiness with a temporal millennium, it has nonetheless served to raise some new questions about the temporality of the millennium that it has not been able to answer definitively.

In particular, this study has discovered that at least two paradoxes have been built into the relationship between the 'judgment' of the unrepentant at the parousia on the one hand, and that which is pictured as their final choice on the other. First, in Rev. 20.11-15, there was the hint that the judgment of the dead at the parousia and the judgment that sees them raised and judged according to deeds *could from some perspective be viewed as a unity*. Secondly, in 21.1 there appeared to be mixed signals as to whether the 'sea' (in the restricted sense of the home of the unrepentant dead) was to be conceived of as having been done away with *in preparation* for the appearance of the new creation and the New Jerusalem. These paradoxes were interpreted not only in harmony with the scheme of last things as narrated in Rev. 20.1-10, but also in harmony with the major theological themes of Revelation, and with the compositional techniques and communicative priorities discussed throughout the essay. But it is to be granted freely that the arguments in this direction have not amounted to proof, in the sense that might be claimed for the cumulative argument in favour of seeing resurrection in Rev. 20.7-10. 'Proof' of the ultimate temporal intent of the millennium has not been possible or even fully relevant within the intended boundaries of this study. Instead, I have put forward those considerations which, to my best understanding, tip the balance with a reasonable degree of confidence in the direction of a model for the millennium that is irreducibly temporal. For others, particularly those whose interpretation is intended for the consumption of a community of faith, such considerations may have to be weighted differently in the context of different assumptions and methods. To such I would offer the following final remarks in a more meditative vein.

3. *Concluding Remarks: Broader Issues and Perspectives*

It is obvious that Revelation never simply takes away with its right hand what it has given with its left. The interpreter may choose to put the maximum degree of weight on the fact that no trace of the millennium is to be found in Revelation before v. 1 and after v. 10 of ch. 20. But this still leaves standing the question of why in the first place John should have given the millennium to his readers as a prophetic picture of the final outcome of things. As we have seen, he was well aware that the things being revealed to him and through him were not easily objectifiable. On the one hand, virtually every image John relates has more than one possible sphere of reference, and on the other, virtually every reality he refers to is accessed by means of more than one set of images. These images purport to be revelations of what God, the world and the future are *like*, not simply literal peeks behind the veil of heaven or into the future. Thus when the images seem to conflict with one another, it is time to ask oneself whether comment is being made on the limitations of the ordinary human perspective.[1] The pictures of Revelation are given to be embraced in the imagination, not to be turned into straight information and pitted against each other. They are to be juxtaposed and viewed stereoscopically (or multi-dimensionally), not truncated or separated out to make pleasing two-dimensional images. Realizing this must make the reader consider carefully before preferring one image or picture entirely at the expense of another.

For let it be supposed (for the sake of argument) that John does offer his readers two fundamentally irreconcilable models for the 'end'. The one pictures (1) a trial at the parousia, (2) a just sentence involving a time of eye-opening self-recognition for the unrepentant, and then (3) a new start, *resurrection*, in which complete grace is given, but refused, and (4) the annihilation of the permanently unrepentant. The other pictures a final trial of all humanity at the parousia, a trial whose immediate outcome is unending torment for the unrepentant. Is the first of these really less compatible than the second with the general eschatological picture gained from other places in the NT?[2]

---

1.   For thoughts along these lines, see, e.g., Prigent, 'Le temps et le royaume dans l'Apocalypse', in J. Lambrecht (ed.) *L'Apocalypse johannique*, pp. 231-45, and 'L'étrange dans l'Apocalypse: Une catégorie théologique', *Lumière et Vie* 31 (1982), pp. 49-60.

2.   At the very least, a model of selective resurrection at the parousia on the basis of one's conduct of life (especially one's relationship to Jesus) can be heard coming from Paul (e.g. Phil. 3.10-11, 20-21; 1 Cor. 15.20-26, 50-55; cf. *Did.* 16.6-8), and

What must remain profoundly disquieting about either of these models, of course, is the idea that God will eventually 'give up' on certain human beings. But this idea, that some people (even the majority of people) might never accept God's grace, is not in the slightest sense peculiar to Revelation among books of the NT. It also coheres uncomfortably well with what can be gleaned from human experience. We humans are a race who have to admit to more than a coincidental relationship with such realities as the Third Reich, Hiroshima and Nagasaki, apartheid, Uganda under Idi Amin, the Khmer Rouge, the so-called 'Falklands War', Tiananmen Square and the war with Iraq. It goes without saying that the list could be expanded indefinitely. It is not just the book of Revelation that urges us to admit that, without God, human beings have a virtually limitless capacity for destructiveness and self-deception. It is also the evidence of the Bible as a whole (particularly the words of Jesus as recorded in the Gospels), the historical Christian tradition, and ineradicable, brutal, empirical fact.

Against all this stands the inner protest, 'Surely they (we, I!) cannot be that *bad*. If a loving God exists, surely all of us will sooner or later choose to love him in return.' We are tempted to imagine that time will cure the problem of human sin in a way that even the preaching of the cross has never promised to do.[1] But time is ultimately nothing but a proof of the human character. What realistic grounds has anyone for the confidence that he or she (or anyone else) will love God in the next life, if they have hated him in this?

This is precisely the mystery of Rev. 20.1-15. According to John, the millennium is the length of the just jail sentence that will be served by those who reject God in this life. And for him the last judgment is a picture of the gracious release granted to those who have served out that sentence. But their release is one whose attendant conditions set the scene for the final test, and the final fall of the rebellious human race:

from Jesus himself as recorded by the third evangelist (Lk. 20.35 // Mk 12.25). I submit that the expression ἐκ νεκρῶν ('from the dead') is prima facie evidence of a selective resurrection model, and I venture to predict that a full study of expressions of the type 'to rise, be raised from the dead (ones)' in the writings of late Judaism and early Christianity would confirm that they always assume 'rise from among the dead, leaving them dead', as opposed to simply 'rise from death'.

1.   E.g. 1 Cor. 1.18.

> The rest of the dead did not come to life until the thousand years were completed. . . And when the thousand years are completed, Satan will be released from his prison, and will come out to deceive the nations which are in the four corners of the earth, Gog and Magog, to gather them together for the war; the number of them is like the sand of the seashore.
>
> And they came up on the broad plain of the earth and surrounded the camp of the saints and the beloved city, and fire came down from heaven and devoured them (Rev. 20.7-10).

> And the sea gave up the dead which were in it, and death and Hades gave up the dead which were in them; and they were judged, every one of them according to their deeds.
>
> And death and Hades were cast into the lake of fire. This is the second death, the lake of fire. And if anyone's name was not found written in the book of life, he was thrown into the lake of fire (Rev. 20.13-15).

There is both a negative and a positive mystery being asserted in this, John's story of the end. The negative mystery is that those who have rejected God's grace in their mortal lives will never allow themselves to be reconciled to him, even though in his mercy they are granted the gift of resurrection itself. The picture of a future 'second chance' has led full circle back to the profound importance of one's response to God in the present. As Jesus says in the letter to Pergamum, 'Repent therefore; or else I am coming to you quickly' (Rev. 2.16).

But the positive mystery is even more profound: that God's patience towards the human race, his grace, and his willingness to give opportunity for repentance never expire, come self-deception, come rebellion, come murder, come suicide. To the very end, and to the very final proof, enter them or not, the doors to his kingdom remain open (Rev. 21.25).

BIBLIOGRAPHY

Allo, E.-B., *L'Apocalypse* (EBib; Paris: Gabalda, 1921).

Apostolic Fathers (trans. K. Lake; 2 vols.; LCL; London: Heinemann, 1977 [1912]).

The Apocalypse of Elijah based on P. Chester Beatty 2018 (ed. and trans. A. Pietersma and S.T. Comstock, with H.W. Attridge; SBLTT, 19, Pseudepigrapha Series, 9; Chico, CA: Scholars Press, 1981).

Auberlen, C.A., *Der Prophet Daniel und die Offenbarung Johannis in ihrem gegenseitigen Verhältniss betrachtet und in ihrem Hauptstellen erklärt* (Basel: Bahnmeier, 1854 [2nd edn, 1857; 3rd edn, 1874]).

Bailey, J.W., 'The Temporary Messianic Reign in the Literature of Early Judaism,' *JBL* 53 (1934), pp. 170-87.

Barclay, W., *The Revelation of John* (Daily Study Bible; 2 vols.; Edinburgh: St Andrew Press, 2nd edn, 1975 [1959]).

Barnard, L.W., 'Justin Martyr's Eschatology', *VC* 19 (1965), pp. 84-98.

Barr, D., 'The Apocalypse as a Symbolic Transformation of the World: A Literary Analysis', *Int* 38 (1984), pp. 39-50.

Bauckham, R., 'The Eschatological Earthquake in the Apocalypse of John', *NovT* 19 (1977), pp. 224-33.

—'The *Figurae* of John of Patmos,' in *Prophecy and Millenarianism: Essays in Honour of Marjorie Reeves* (ed. A. Williams; Harlow, UK: Longman, 1980), pp. 109-25.

Bauer, W., 'Chiliasmus', *RAC* (ed. T. Klausner; Stuttgart: Hiersemann, 1954), II, cols. 1073-78.

—*A Greek–English Lexicon of the New Testament and Other Early Christian Literature* (trans. and adapted by W.F. Arndt and F.W. Gingrich; rev. by F.W. Gingrich and F.W. Danker; Chicago: University of Chicago Press, 5th edn, 1979).

Beale, G.K., 'The Influence of Daniel upon the Structure and Theology of John's Apocalypse', *JETS* 27 (1984), pp. 413-23.

Beardslee, W., *Literary Criticism of the New Testament* (Philadelphia: Fortress Press, 1970).

Beasley-Murray, G.R., *The Book of Revelation* (NCB; London: Oliphants, 1974).

Beckwith, I.T., *The Apocalypse of John* (Twin Brooks; Grand Rapids: Baker, 1979 [1919]).

Behm, J., *Die Offenbarung des Johannes übersetzt und erklärt* (Göttingen: Vandenhoeck & Ruprecht, 3rd edn, 1937).

Bell, A.A., 'The Date of John's Apocalypse: The Evidence of Some Roman Historians Reconsidered', *NTS* 25 (1978–79), pp. 91-102.

Bergmeier, R., 'Jerusalem, du hochgebaute Stadt', *ZNW* 75 (1984), pp. 86-106.

The Biblical Antiquities of Philo (trans. M.R. James; London: SPCK, 1917).

Bietenhard, H., *Die himmlische Welt im Urchristentum und Spätjudentum* (WUNT, 2; Tübingen: Mohr, 1951).

—'The Millennial Hope in the Early Church', *SJT* 6 (1953), pp. 12-30.

—*Das tausendjährige Reich: Eine biblisch-theologische Studie* (Zürich: Zwingli-Verlag, 1955).

Billerbeck, P., and H. Strack, *Kommentar zum Neuen Testament aus Talmud und Midrasch. III. Die Briefe des Neuen Testaments und die Offenbarung Johannis* (Munich: Beck, 1926).

Black, M., 'The "Two Witnesses" of Rev. 11:3f. in Jewish and Christian Apocalyptic Tradition', in *Donum Gentilicium* (Festschrift D. Daube; ed. E. Bammel, C.K. Barrett and W.D. Davies; Oxford: Clarendon Press, 1978), pp. 227-37.

Böcher, O., *Die Johannesapokalypse* (Erträge der Forschung, 41; Darmstadt: Wissenschaftliche Buchgesellschaft, 1976).

—*Kirche in Zeit und Endzeit: Aufsätze zur Offenbarung des Johannes* (Neukirchen: Neukirchener Verlag, 1983).

—'Das Verhältnis der Apokalypse des Johannes zum Evangelium des Johannes', in J. Lambrecht (ed.), *L'Apocalypse johannique*, pp. 289-301.

Boismard, M.-E., 'L'Apocalypse de Jean', in *Introduction à la Bible* (ed. A. George and P. Grelot; Paris: Desclée, 1977), III.4, pp. 13-55.

—'L'Apocalypse ou les Apocalypses de Saint Jean', *RevistB* 56 (1949), pp. 507-41.

Bornkamm, G., 'Die Komposition der apokalyptischen Visionen in der Offenbarung Johannis', *ZNW* 36 (1937), pp. 132-49; reprinted in *idem*, *Studien zu Antike und Urchristentum* (Gesammelte Aufsätze, 2 [BEvT, 28]; Munich: Chr. Kaiser Verlag, 2nd edn, 1962 [1959]), pp. 204-22.

Bousset, W., *Die Offenbarung Johannis* (MeyerK, 16; Göttingen: Vandenhoeck & Ruprecht, 9th edn, 1966 [1906]).

Bovon, F., 'Le Christ de l'Apocalypse', *RTP* 21 (1972), pp. 65-80.

Bowman, J.W., *The Revelation to John: Its Dramatic Structure and Message* (Philadelphia: Westminster Press, 1955).

Bruce, F.F., 'The Earliest Latin Commentary on the Apocalypse', *EvQ* 10 (1938), pp. 352-66.

—'The Spirit in the Apocalypse,' in *Christ and Spirit in the New Testament* (Festschrift C.F.D. Moule; ed. B. Lindars and S.S. Smalley; Cambridge: Cambridge University Press, 1973), pp. 333-44.

Cain, D.W., 'Artistic Contrivance and Religious Communication', *RelS* 8 (1972), pp. 29-43.

Caird, G.B., *A Commentary on the Revelation of St John the Divine* (HNTC; London: A. & C. Black, 1966).

—*The Language and Imagery of the Bible* (Studies in Theology; London: Gerald Duckworth, 1980).

—'On Deciphering the Book of Revelation', *ExpTim* 74 (1962–63), pp. 13-15, 51-53, 82-84, 103-105.

Cambier, J., 'Les images de l'Ancien Testament dans l'Apocalypse de Saint Jean', *NRT* 77 (1955), pp. 113-22.

Charles, R.H. (ed.), *The Apocrypha and Pseudepigrapha of the Old Testament* (2 vols.; Oxford: Clarendon Press, 1913).

—*The Revelation of St John* (ICC; 2 vols.; New York: Charles Scribner's Sons, 1920).

Charlesworth, J. (ed.), *The Old Testament Pseudepigrapha*. I. *Apocalyptic Literature and Testaments* (Garden City, NY: Doubleday, 1983).

Collins, A.Y., *The Combat Myth in the Book of Revelation* (HDR, 9; Missoula, MT: Scholars Press, 1976).

—'The Political Perspective of the Revelation of John', *JBL* 96 (1977), pp. 241-56.

Collins, J.J., 'Pseudonymity, Historical Reviews and the Genre of the Revelation of John', *CBQ* 39 (1977), pp. 329-43.

Corsani, B., 'L'Apocalisse di Giovanni: Scritto apocalittico, o profetico?', *BeO* 17 (1975), pp. 253-68.

Court, J.M., *Myth and History in the Book of Revelation* (London: SPCK, 1979).

Cuviller, E., 'Apocalypse 20: Prédiction ou prédication?', *ETR* 59 (1984), pp. 345-54.

D'Aragon, J., 'The Apocalypse,' in *The Jerome Biblical Commentary* (ed. R.E. Brown, J.A. Fitzmyer and R.E. Murphy; London: Geoffrey Chapman, 1968), pp. 467-93.

de Boer, M.C., 'Paul and Jewish Apocalyptic Eschatology', in *Apocalyptic and the New Testament* (Festschrift J.L. Martyn; ed. J. Marcus and M.L. Soards; JSNTSup, 24; Sheffield: JSOT Press, 1989), pp. 169-90.

Deere, J.S., 'Premillennialism in Revelation 20:4-6', *BSac* 135 (1978), pp. 58-73.

Dehandschutter, B., 'The Meaning of Witness in the Apocalypse', in J. Lambrecht (ed.), *L'Apocalypse johannique*, pp. 283-87.

Deutsch, C., 'Transformation of Symbols: The New Jerusalem in Rv. 21.1–22.5', *ZNW* 78 (1987), pp. 106-26.

Draper, J.A., 'The Heavenly Feast of Tabernacles: Revelation 7.1-17', *JSNT* 19 (1983), pp. 133-37.

Düsterdieck, F., *Kritisch-exegetisches Handbuch über die Offenbarung des Johannis* (MeyerK, 16; Göttingen: Vandenhoeck & Ruprecht, 3rd edn, 1877).

Eichrodt, W., *Ezekiel* (trans. C. Quinn; OTL; Philadelphia: Westminster Press, 1970 [German edn 1965–66]).

Ellul, J., *Apocalypse: The Book of Revelation* (trans. G.W. Schreiner; New York: Seabury Press, 1977).

Ezell, D., *Revelations on Revelation: New Sounds from Old Symbols* (Waco, TX: Word Books, 1977).

Farrer, A., *A Rebirth of Images* (Westminster: Dacre Press, 1949).

—*The Revelation of St John the Divine* (Oxford: Clarendon Press, 1964).

Feuillet, A., 'Les chrétiens prêtres et rois d'apres l'Apocalypse: Contribution à l'étude de la conception chrétienne du sacerdoce', *RevThom* 75 (1975), pp. 40-66.

—'Le festin de noces de l'agneau et ses anticipations', *Esprit et Vie* 97 (1987), pp. 353-62.

—'Jalons pour une meilleure intelligence de l'Apocalypse': 'Vue d'ensemble sur la révélation johannique', *Esprit et Vie* 84 (1974), pp. 481-90; 'Le prologue et la vision inaugurale (chapitre 1)', *Esprit et Vie* 85 (1975), pp. 65-72; 'Les lettres aux églises (chapitres 2 et 3)', *Esprit et Vie* 85 (1975), pp. 209-23; 'Introduction à la partie prophétique', *Esprit et Vie* 85 (1975), pp. 432-43.

—'Les martyrs de l'humanité et l'agneau égorgé: Une interprétation nouvelle de la prière des égorgés en Ap 6, 9-11', *NRT* 99 (1977), pp. 189-207.

—'La moisson et la vendange de l'Apocalypse (14,14-20): La signification chrétienne de la révélation johannique', *NRT* 94 (1972), pp. 113-32, 225-50.

—'Le premier cavalier de l'Apocalypse', *ZNW* 57 (1966), pp. 229-59.

—'Quelques énigmes des chapitres 4 à 7 de l'Apocalypse: Suggestions pour l'interprétaton
    du langage imaginé de la révélation johannique', *Esprit et Vie* 86 (1976), pp. 445-59,
    471-79.
—'The Twenty-Four Elders of the Apocalypse', in *Johannine Studies* (New York: Alba
    House, 1965), pp. 183-214.
Fiorenza, E.S., 'Apocalyptic and Gnosis in the Book of Revelation', *JBL* 92 (1973),
    pp. 565-81.
—'Composition and Structure of the Book of Revelation', *CBQ* 39 (1977), pp. 344-66.
—'The Eschatology and Composition of the Apocalypse', *CBQ* 30 (1968), pp. 537-69.
—'The Followers of the Lamb: Visionary Rhetoric and Socio-Political Situation', *Semeia* 36
    (1986), pp. 123-46.
—*Invitation to the Book of Revelation* (Image Books; Garden City, NY: Doubleday, 1981).
—*Priester für Gott: Studien zum Herrschafts- und Priestermotiv in der Apokalypse* (NTAbh,
    7; Münster: Aschendorf, 1972).
—'The Quest for the Johannine School: The Apocalypse and the Fourth Gospel', *NTS* 23
    (1976–77), pp. 402-27.
—'Redemption as Liberation: Apoc 1,5f and 5,9f', *CBQ* 36 (1974), pp. 220-32.
—'Religion und Politik in der Offenbarung des Johannes', in *Biblische Randbemerkungen*
    (Festschrift R. Schnackenburg; Würzburg: Echter Verlag, 2nd edn, 1974), pp. 261-
    72.
—'Revelation', in *The New Testament and its Modern Interpreters* (ed. E.J. Epp and
    G.W. MacRae; Philadelphia: Fortress Press, 1989).
—*Revelation: Vision of a Just World* (Proclamation Commentaries; Minneapolis: Fortress
    Press, 1991).
—'Die tausendjährige Herrschaft der Auferstandenen (Apk 20, 4-6)', *BibLeb* 13 (1972),
    pp. 107-24.
—'Visionary Rhetoric and Social-Political Situation', in *The Book of Revelation: Justice and
    Judgement* (Philadelphia: Fortress Press, 1985), pp. 181-203.
Foakes-Jackson, F.J., *History of the Christian Church* (Cambridge: J. Hall & Son, 1898).
Ford, J.M., *Revelation* (AB, 38; Garden City, NY: Doubleday, 1975).
—' "For the Testimony of Jesus is the Spirit of Prophecy." (Rev. 19:10)', *ITQ* 42 (1975),
    pp. 284-91.
Gaechter, P., 'The Original Sequence of Apocalypse 20–22', *TS* 10 (1949), pp. 485-521.
Gangemi, A., 'L'albero della vita (Ap. 2, 7)', *RevistB* 23 (1975), pp. 383-97.
—'La morte seconda (Ap 2,11)', *RevistB* 24 (1976), pp. 3-11.
Georgi, D., 'Die Visionen vom himmlischen Jerusalem in Apk 21 und 22', in *Kirche*
    (Festschrift G. Bornkamm; ed. D. Lührmann and G. Strecker; Tübingen: Mohr,
    1980), pp. 351-72.
Giblin, C.H., 'Revelation 11.1-13: Its Form, Function, and Contextual Integration', *NTS*
    30 (1984), pp. 433-59.
—'Structural and Thematic Correlations in the Theology of Revelation 16–22', *Bib* 55
    (1974), pp. 487-504.
Giesen, H., 'Das Buch mit sieben Siegeln: Bilder und Symbole in der Offenbarung des
    Johannes', *BK* 39 (1984), pp. 59-65.
Glasson, T.F., *The Revelation of John* (Commentaries on the NEB; Cambridge: Cambridge
    University Press, 1965).
Goodman, N., 'Twisted Tales', *Critical Inquiry* 7 (1980), pp. 103-19.

Goppelt, L., 'Die Christen in der nachchristlichen Gesellschaft der Endzeit nach der Offenbarung des Johannes', in *Theologie des Neuen Testaments. II. Vielfalt und Einheit des apostolischen Christus-zeugnisses* (Göttingen: Vandenhoeck & Ruprecht, 1976), pp. 509-28.

Gourges, M., 'The Thousand Year Reign (Rev. 20:1-6): Terrestrial or Celestial?', *CBQ* 47 (1985), pp. 676-81.

Gry, L., *Le millénarisme dans ses origines et son développement* (Paris: Picard et Fils, 1904).

Günther, H.W., *Der Nah- und Enderwartungshorizont in der Apokalypse des heiligen Johannes* (Forschung zur Bibel, 41; Würzburg: Echter Verlag, 1980).

Gundry, R.H., 'The New Jerusalem: People as Place, not Place for People', *NovT* 29 (1987), pp. 254-64.

Hadorn, W., *Die Offenbarung des Johannes* (THKNT, 17; Leipzig: A. Deichertsche Verlags-buchhandlung, 1928).

Hahn, F., 'Zum Aufbau der Johannesoffenbarung', in *Kirche und Bibel* (Festschrift E. Schick; Paderborn: Ferdinand Schöningh, 1979), pp. 145-54.

Hartman, L., 'Form and Message: A Preliminary Discussion of "Partial Texts" in Rev 1–3 and 22,6ff', in J. Lambrecht (ed.), *L'Apocalypse johannique*, pp. 129-49.

Hemer, C.J., *The Letters to the Seven Churches of Asia in their Local Setting* (JSNTSup, 11; Sheffield: JSOT Press, 1986).

Hermans, A., 'Le Pseudo-Barnabé: Est-il millénariste?', *ETL* 35 (1959), pp. 849-76.

Hill, D., 'Prophecy and Prophets in the Revelation of St John', *NTS* 18 (1971–72), pp. 401-18.

Hillyer, N., ' "The Lamb" in the Apocalypse', *EvQ* 39 (1967), pp. 228-36.

Hobbs, H.H., *The Cosmic Drama: An Exposition of the Book of Revelation* (Waco, TX: Word Books, 1971).

Holtz, T., *Die Christologie der Apokalypse des Johannes* (TU, 85; Berlin: Akademie Verlag, 2nd edn, 1971 [1962]).

—'Gott in der Apokalypse', in J. Lambrecht (ed.), *L'Apocalypse johannique*, pp. 247-65.

Holtzmann, H.J., and W. Bauer, *Evangelium, Briefe und Offenbarung des Johannes* (HNT, 4; Tübingen: Mohr, 3rd edn, 1908).

Hopkins, M., 'The Historical Perspective of Apocalypse 1–11', *CBQ* 27 (1965), pp. 42-47.

Hughes, J.A., 'Revelation 20, 4-6 and the Question of the Millenium', *WTJ* 35 (1973), pp. 281-302.

Hughes, P.E., 'The First Resurrection: Another Interpretation', *WTJ* 39 (1977), pp. 315-18.

Jeremias, J. 'γέεννα', *TDNT*, I, pp. 657-58.

Jörns, K., *Das hymnische Evangelium: Untersuchungen zu Aufbau, Funktion und Herkunft der hymnischen Stücke in der Johannesoffenbarung* (SNT, 5; Gütersloh: Gerd Mohn, 1971).

Johnston, R.M., 'The Eschatological Sabbath in John's Apocalypse: A Reconsideration', *AUSS* 25 (1987), pp. 39-50.

Jones, W.B., 'More about the Apocalypse as Apocalyptic', *JBL* 87 (1968), pp. 325-27.

Kallas, J., 'The Apocalypse: An Apocalyptic Book?', *JBL* 86 (1967), pp. 69-80.

—*God and Satan in the Apocalypse* (Minneapolis: Augsburg, 1973).

Kiddle, M., with M.K. Ross, *The Revelation of St John* (MNTC; London: Hodder & Stoughton, 1940).

Kline, M.G., 'The First Resurrection', *WTJ* 37 (1975), pp. 366-75.

Kraft, H., *Die Offenbarung des Johannes* (HNT, 16a; Tübingen: Mohr [Paul Siebeck], 1974).

Kretschmar, G., *Die Offenbarung des Johannes: Die Geschichte ihrer Auslegung im 1. Jahrtausend* (Calwer theologische Monographia, Reihe B, 9; Stuttgart: Calwer Verlag, 1985).

Ladd, G.E., *A Commentary on the Revelation of John* (Grand Rapids: Eerdmans, 1972).

—'The Lion is the Lamb (Apoc)', *Eternity* 16 (1965), pp. 20-22.

—'Revelation 20 and the Millennium', *RevExp* 57 (1960), pp. 167-75.

Lambrecht, J. (ed.), *L'Apocalypse johannique et l'apocalyptique dans le NT* (BETL, 43; Leuven: Leuven University Press, 1980).

—'A Structuration of Revelation 4:1–22:5', in *idem* (ed.), *L'Apocalypse johannique*, pp. 77-104.

Lancellotti, A., *Apocalisse* (Rome: Edizione Pauline, 1970).

—*Sintassi ebraica nel greco dell' Apocalisse. I. Uso delle forme verbali* (Coll. Assissiensis, 1; Assisi: Studio Teologico Portiuncola, 1964).

Lattimore, R., *The Four Gospels and Revelation* (New York: Farrar, Straus & Giroux, 1979).

Lesêtre, H., 'Millénarisme', in *Dictionnaire de la Bible* (ed. F. Vigrouroux; Paris: Letouzey & Ané, 1908), IV, pp. 1090-98.

Levoratti, A.J., 'El maná escondido (Apoc. 2,17)', *RevistB* 46 (1984), pp. 257-73.

Lohmeyer, E., *Die Offenbarung des Johannes* (HNT, 16; Tübingen: Mohr, 2nd edn, 1953).

Lohse, E., 'Die alttestamentliche Sprache des Sehers Johannes', *ZNW* 52 (1961), pp. 122-26.

—*Die Offenbarung des Johannes* (NTD, 11; Göttingen: Vandenhoeck & Ruprecht, 2nd edn, 1966).

—'Der Menschensohn in der Johannesapokalypse', in *Jesus und der Menschensohn* (Festschrift A. Vögtle; ed. R. Pesch and R. Schnackenburg; Freiburg: Herder, 1975), pp. 415-20.

Lust, J., 'The Order of the Final Events in Revelation and in Ezekiel', in J. Lambrecht (ed.), *L'Apocalypse johannique*, pp. 179-83.

McGinn, B., 'Revelation', in *The Literary Guide to the Bible* (ed. R. Alter and F. Kermode; London: Collins, 1987), pp. 523-41.

Maier, G., *Die Johannesoffenbarung und die Kirche* (WUNT, 25; Tübingen: Mohr, 1981).

Marshall, I.H., 'Martyrdom and the Parousia in the Revelation of John', in *Studia Evangelica* (TU, 102; Berlin: Akademic Verlag, 1968), IV, pp. 333-39.

Mazzaferri, F.D., *The Genre of the Book of Revelation from a Source-Critical Perspective* (BZNW, 54; Berlin: de Gruyter, 1989).

Mazzucco, C., and E. Pietrella, 'Il rapporto tra la concezione del millennio dei primi autori cristiani e l'Apocalisse di Giovanni', *Augustinianum* 18 (1978), pp. 29-45.

Melton, L.D., 'A Critical Analysis of the Understanding of the Imagery of City in the Book of Revelation' (PhD dissertation, Southern Baptist Theological Seminary, 1978).

Metzger, W., 'Das Zwischenreich', in *Auf dem Grunde der Apostel und Propheten* (Festschrift Bischof T. Wurm; ed. M. Loeser; Stuttgart: Quell-Verlag der Evangelische Gesellschaft, 1948), pp. 110-18.

Michaels, J.R., 'The First Resurrection: A Response', *WTJ* 39 (1976), pp. 100-109.

Minear, P., *And I Saw a New Earth* (Washington: Corpus Books, 1968).

—'The Cosmology of the Apocalypse', in *Current Issues in New Testament Interpretation* (Festschrift O. Piper; ed. W. Klassen and G.F. Snyder; London: SCM Press, 1962), pp. 23-37.

—*New Testament Apocalyptic* (Nashville: Abingdon Press, 1981).

—'Ontology and Ecclesiology in the Apocalypse', *NTS* 12 (1965–66), pp. 89-105.

Moffatt, J., *Revelation of St John* (Expositor's Greek Testament; Grand Rapids: Eerdmans, 1951 [1910]).

Morris, L., *Revelation* (Tyndale New Testament Commentaries; London: Tyndale House, 1969).

Moulton, J.H., and G. Milligan, *The Vocabulary of the Greek New Testament: Illustrated from the Papyri and Other Non-Literary Sources* (Grand Rapids: Eerdmans, 1974 [1930]).

Mounce, R., *The Book of Revelation* (NICNT; Grand Rapids: Eerdmans, 1977).

Müller, U.B., *Messias und Menschensohn in jüdischen Apokalypsen und in der Offenbarung des Johannes* (SNT, 6; Gütersloh: Gerd Mohn, 1972).

—*Die Offenbarung des Johannes* (Gütersloh: Gerd Mohn, 1984).

Mussies, G., *The Morphology of Koine Greek as Used in the Apocalypse of Saint John* (NovTSup; Leiden: Brill, 1971).

Mussner, F., '"Weltherrschaft" als eschatologisches Thema der Johannesapokalypse', in *Glaube und Eschatologie* (Festschrift W.G. Kümmel; ed. E. Grässer and O. Merk; Tübingen: Mohr, 1985), pp. 209-27.

Ostella, R.A., 'The Significance of Deception in Revelation 20:3', *WTJ* 37 (1975), pp. 236-38.

Pesch, R., 'Offenbarung Jesu Christi: Eine Auslegung von Apk 1, 1-3', *BibLeb* 11 (1970), pp. 15-29.

Pohl, A., *Die Offenbarung des Johannes* (Wuppertal Studienbibel; 2 vols.; Wuppertal: Brockhaus, 1983).

Popkes, W., 'Die Funktion der Sendschreiben in der Johannes-Apokalypse', *ZNW* 74 (1983), pp. 90-107.

Preston, R.H., and A.T. Hanson, *The Revelation of Saint John the Divine* (Torch Bible Commentaries; London: SCM Press, 1968 [1949]).

Prigent, P., *L'Apocalypse de Saint Jean* (CNT, Deuxième Série, 14; Paris: Delachaux & Niestlé, 1981).

—'Apocalypse et apocalyptique', *RevScRel* 47 (1973), pp. 280-99.

—'L'étrange dans l'Apocalypse: Une catégorie théologique', *Lumière et Vie* 31 (1982), pp. 49-60.

—'Le millénnium dans l'Apocalypse johannique', in *L'apocalyptique* (ed. F. Raphaël *et al.*; Etudes d'histoire des religions, 3; Paris: Guenther, 1977), pp. 139-56.

—'Le symbole dans le Nouveau Testament', *RevScRel* 49 (1975), pp. 101-15.

—'Le temps et le royaume dans l'Apocalypse', in J. Lambrecht (ed.), *L'Apocalypse johannique*, pp. 231-45.

—'Une trace de liturgie judéo-chrétienne dans le chapitre XXI de l'Apocalypse de Jean', *RevScRel* 60 (1972), pp. 165-72.

Quasten, J., *Patrology* (2 vols.; Westminster, MD: Newman Press, 1950).

Quispel, G., *The Secret Book of Revelation* (New York: McGraw–Hill, 1978).

Reader, W.W., 'Die Stadt Gottes in der Johannes-apokalypse' (doctoral dissertation, Georg-August-Universität, Göttingen, 1971).

Rissi, M., *The Future of the World: An Exegetical Study of Revelation 19:11–22:5* (London: SCM Press, 1972 [ET of *Die Zukunft der Welt: Eine exegetische Studie über Johannesoffenbarung 19.11–22.5* (Basel: Friedrich Reinhart, 1966)]).

—*Time and History: A Study on the Revelation* (trans. G.C. Windsor; Richmond, VA: John Knox, 1966 [ET of *Was ist und was geschehen soll danach* (Zürich: Zwingli-Verlag, 1965)]).

Roberts, J.W., 'The Meaning of the Eschatology in the Book of Revelation', *ResQ* 95 (1972), pp. 95-110.

Robinson, J.A.T., *Redating the New Testament* (Philadelphia: Westminster Press, 1976).

Roller, O., 'Das Buch mit sieben Siegeln', *ZNW* 26 (1937), pp. 98-113.

Roloff, J., *Die Offenbarung des Johannes* (Zürcher Bibelkommentar, NT, 18; Zürich: Theologischer Verlag, 1981).

Rowland, C., *The Open Heaven: A Study of Apocalyptic in Judaism and Early Christianity* (New York: Crossroad, 1982).

—'The Visions of God in Apocalyptic Literature', *JSJ* 10 (1979), pp. 137-54.

Russell, D.S., *The Method and Message of Jewish Apocalyptic* (OTL; Philadelphia: Westminster Press, 1964).

Satake, A., *Die Gemeindeordnung in der Johannes-apokalypse* (ATANT, 21; Neukirchen: Neukirchener Verlag, 1966).

—'Inklusio als ein geliebtes Ausdrucksmittel in der Johannesapokalypse', *Annual of the Japanese Biblical Institute* 6 (1980), pp. 76-113.

—'Kirche und feindliche Welt', in *Kirche* (Festschrift G. Bornkamm; ed. D. Lührmann and G. Strecker; Tübingen: Mohr, 1980), pp. 329-49.

Schaik, A.P. van, 'ἄλλος ἄγγελος in Apk 14', in J. Lambrecht (ed.), *L'Apocalypse johannique*, pp. 217-28.

Schlatter, A., *Das Alte Testament in der Johannesapokalypse* (BFCT, 6; Gütersloh: Bertelsmann, 1912).

—*Die Briefe und die Offenbarung des Johannes* (Schlatters Erläuterungen zum NT, 10; Stuttgart: Calwer Verlag, 1928).

Schlier, H., 'Jesus Christus und die Geschichte nach der Offenbarung', in *Einsichten* (Festschrift G. Krüger; Frankfurt am Main: Klostermann, 1962), pp. 316-33.

Schnackenburg, R., *God's Rule and Kingdom* (trans. J. Murray; London: Nelson, 1963).

Shea, W.H., 'The Parallel Literary Structure of Revelation 12 and 20', *AUSS* 23 (1985), pp. 37-54.

—'The Sabbath in the Epistle of Barnabas', *AUSS* 4 (1966), pp. 149-75.

Shepherd, M.H., *The Paschal Liturgy and the Apocalypse* (London: John Knox, 1960).

Shepherd, N., 'The Resurrection of Revelation 20', *WTJ* 37 (1974), pp. 34-43.

Sickenberger, J., *Erklärung der Johannesapokalypse* (Bonn: Peter Hanstein, 2nd edn, 1942).

—'Das tausendjährige Reich in der Apokalypse', in *Festschrift Sebastian Merkle gewidmet* (ed. J. Hehn, W. Schellberg and F. Tillmann; Düsseldorf: Schwann, 1922), pp. 300-316.

Smith, D.C., 'The Millennial Reign of Jesus Christ: Some Observations on Rev. 20:1-10', *ResQ* 16 (1973), pp. 219-30.

Smith, U., *Daniel and the Revelation* (Nashville: Southern Publishing Association, rev. edn, 1944 [1881]).

—*Thoughts, Critical and Practical, on the Book of Revelation* (Battle Creek, MI: SDA Publishing Association, 1867).

Stadelmann, H., 'Das Zeugnis der Johannesapokalypse vom tausendjährigen Königreich Christi auf Erden', in *Zukunftserwartung in biblischer Sicht* (ed. G. Maier; Wuppertal: Brockhaus, 2nd edn, 1986 [1984]), pp. 144-60.

Sweet, J.P.M., *Revelation* (SCM Pelican Commentaries; London: SCM Press, 1979).

Swete, H.B., *The Apocalypse of St John* (London: Macmillan, 1906).

Taeger, J.-W., 'Einige neuere Veröffentlichungen zur Apokalypse des Johannes', *VF* 29 (1984), pp. 50-75.

Thüsing, W., 'Die theologische Mitte der Weltgerichtsvisionen in der Johannesapokalypse', *TTZ* 77 (1968), pp. 1-16.

—'Die Vision des "Neuen Jerusalem" (Apk 21,1–22,5) als Verheissung und Gottesverkündigung', *TTZ* 77 (1968), pp. 17-34.

Torrey, C.C., *The Apocalypse of John* (New Haven: Yale University Press, 1958).

Trites, A.A., 'μάρτυς and Martyrdom in the Apocalypse: A Semantic Study', *NovT* 15 (1973), pp. 72-80.

Turner, N., 'Revelation', in *Peake's Commentary on the Bible* (ed. M. Black; London: Nelson, 1962), pp. 1043-61.

—'The Style of the Book of Revelation', in J.H. Moulton, *A Grammar of New Testament Greek*. IV. *Style* (by N. Turner; Edinburgh: T. & T. Clark, 1976), pp. 145-59.

Ulfgard, H., *Feast and Future: Revelation 7.9-17 and the Feast of Tabernacles* (ConBNT, 22; Stockholm: Almqvist & Wicksell, 1989).

Unnik, W.C. van, '"Worthy is the Lamb": The Background of Apoc. 5', in *Mélanges bibliques* (Festschrift B. Rigaux; ed. A. Descamps and A. de Halleux; Gembloux: Duculot, 1970), pp. 607-11.

Vanhoye, A., 'L'utilisation du livre d'Ezechiel dans L'Apocalypse', *Bib* 43 (1962), pp. 436-76.

Vanni, U., 'L'Apocalypse johannique: Etat de la question', in J. Lambrecht (ed.), *L'Apocalypse johannique*, pp. 21-46.

—'La decodificazione del "grande segno" in Apocalisse 12,1-6', *Marianum* 40 (1978), pp. 121-52.

—'The Ecclesial Assembly, "Interpreting Subject" of the Apocalypse', *Religious Studies Bulletin* 4 (1984) pp. 79-85.

—'Rassegna bibliografica sull'Apocalisse (1970–1975)', *RevistB* 24 (1976), pp. 277-301.

—*La struttura letteraria dell'Apocalisse* (Aloisiana, 8; Rome: Herder, 1971).

Victorini Episcopi Petavionsensis Opera (ed. J. Haussleiter; CSEL, 49; Vienna: Tempsky, 1916).

Vivian, A., 'Gog e Magog nella tradidizione biblica, ebraica e cristiana', *Revista de Cultura Biblica* 25 (1977), pp. 389-421.

Vögtle, A., *Das Buch mit sieben Siegeln: Die Offenbarung des Johannes in Auswahl gedeutet* (Freiburg: Herder, 2nd edn, 1985 [1981]).

—'Dann sah ich einen neuen Himmel und eine neue Erde', in *Glaube und Eschatologie* (Festschrift W.G. Kümmel; ed. E. Grässer and O. Merk; Tübingen: Mohr, 1985), pp. 303-33.

—'Der Gott der Apokalypse', in *La notion biblique de Dieu: Du Dieu révélé au Dieu des Philosophes* (ed. J. Coppens; BETL, 41; Leuven: Leuven University Press, 1976), pp. 377-98.

Volz, P., *Die Eschatologie der jüdischen Gemeinde im Neutestamentlichen Zeitalter* (Hildesheim: Georg Olms, 1966 [1934]).

Vos, L.A., *The Synoptic Traditions in the Apocalypse* (Kampen: Kok, 1965).

Weiser, A., *The Psalms* (trans. H. Hartwell; OTL; [London]: SCM Press, 1962).

Wellhausen, J., *Analyse der Offenbarung Johannis* (Berlin: Weidmann, 1907).

Wette, W.M.L. de, *Kurze Erklärung der Offenbarung Johannis* (Leipzig: Weidmann, 1848).

Wikenhauser, A., 'Die Herkunft der Idee des tausendjährigen Reiches in der Johannes-Apokalypse', *RQ* 45 (1937), pp. 1-24.

—*Die Offenbarung des Johannes übersetzt und erklärt* (RNT, 9; Regensburg: Pustet, 3rd edn, 1959 [1949]).

—'Das Problem des tausendjährigen Reiches in der Johannes-Apokalypse', *RQ* 40 (1932), pp. 13-25.

—'Weltwoche und tausendjähriges Reich', *Tübinger Theologische Quartalschrift* 127 (1947), pp. 399-417.

Wilcock, M., *I Saw Heaven Opened* (Leicester: Inter-Varsity Press, 2nd edn, 1979 [1975]).

Wilcox, M., 'Tradition and Redaction of Rev. 21,9–22,5', in J. Lambrecht (ed.), *L'Apocalypse johannique*, pp. 205-15.

The Works of Lactantius, I (trans. W. Fletcher; ANCL, 21; Edinburgh: T. & T. Clark, 1886).

The Writings of Commodianus, &c. (trans. R.E. Wallis; ANCL, 18; Edinburgh: T. & T. Clark, 1895).

The Writings of Hippolytus, I (trans. S.D.F. Salmond; ANCL, 6; Edinburgh: T. & T. Clark, 1887).

The Writings of Irenaeus, II (trans. A. Roberts and W.H. Rambaut; ANCL, 9; Edinburgh: T. & T. Clark, 1878).

The Writings of Justin Martyr and Athenagoras (trans. G. Reith; ANCL, 2; Edinburgh: T. & T. Clark, 1892).

The Writings of Methodius, &c. (trans. W. Clark; ANCL, 14; Edinburgh: T. & T. Clark, 1906).

The Writings of Tertullian, II (trans. P. Holmes; ANCL, 15; Edinburgh: T. & T. Clark, 1884).

Zahn, T., *Die Offenbarung des Johannes* (Kommentar zum Neuen Testament, 17 ; 2 vols.; Leipzig: A. Deichertsche Verlags-buchhandlung, 1924, 1926).

Zerwick, M., *Biblical Greek* (trans. J. Smith; Rome: Pontifical Biblical Institute, 1963).

INDEXES

INDEX OF REFERENCES

OLD TESTAMENT AND APOCRYPHA

CHRISTIAN AUTHORS

OTHER WRITINGS

INDEX OF AUTHORS

JOURNAL FOR THE STUDY OF THE NEW TESTAMENT

Supplement Series